THE MORNING AFTER

A FRENCH JOURNALIST'S IMPRESSIONS
OF CUBA UNDER CASTRO

THE MORNING AFTER

VICTOR FRANCO

Translated by
IVAN KATS and PHILIP PENDERED

FREDERICK A. PRAEGER, *Publisher*
New York · London

FREDERICK A. PRAEGER, PUBLISHER
64 UNIVERSITY PLACE, NEW YORK 3, N.Y., U.S.A.
49 GREAT ORMOND STREET, LONDON W.C. 1, ENGLAND

Published in the United States of America in 1963
by Frederick A. Praeger, Inc., Publisher

First published in France in 1962 under the title of
LA RÉVOLUTION SENSUELLE
by Éditions Bernard Grasset

© 1962, Éditions Bernard Grasset
English translation © 1963, Frederick A. Praeger, Inc.

Library of Congress Catalog Card Number: 63-18531

Printed in the United States of America

THE MORNING AFTER

CHAPTER 1

There is no stewardess aboard the Miami-Havana flight. And there's no candy, either. What we did get was a glass of rum, like convicts before execution. I looked around for a chaplain but couldn't find one.

There were some sixty of us aboard, all keeping quiet.

"No smoking. Fasten your seat belts."

The steward was kind and considerate. He brought each one of us the tall glass of sweetened rum. He seemed to pity us, convinced that we were heading for certain death. This may have been why he was more kind and thoughtful than other airplane stewards. Everyone is friendly and patient with those who are about to die.

He handed me the glass and said, "What the hell are you going to that place for? They're all crazy down there. Believe me, you'll all get killed. They kill everyone. They even kill Americans. Last week they arrested someone who had come over in that same seat, and they shot him. He was an American."

Of course, this was not very reassuring. Those last two weeks in

Miami, I continually heard people repeat the news which had filled the New World with astonishment. "They shot Americans!"

A former American diplomat in Havana, now recalled to Miami after the breaking-off of diplomatic relations, told me in just the same voice as the steward, "They even kill Americans. No government before had even dared so much as touch an American citizen. All over the world, people know it just isn't done. At the end of the last century the same held true for the British. A subject of the Queen was sacred everywhere. Do you know the story of the Bolivian dictator and the British chargé d'affaires?

"A certain Melgarejo, a stupid and violent man, was the boss in La Paz. One day he had a quarrel with the representative of Great Britain. He had him undressed by his soldiers, put on a donkey, and paraded around town. Do you know what happened then?"

"Queen Victoria broke off relations with La Paz."

"Better than that, she ordered the name of Bolivia struck off all the maps printed in her kingdom and colonies. Overnight, Bolivia ceased to exist for the 500 million subjects of the British Empire. When a Bolivian landed in Liverpool, the immigration officials would say, 'A Bolivian passport? What's that? Bolivia doesn't exist.' London was then the center of the world's business, and when a British bank was asked for a transaction involving La Paz, the letter was returned to the sender, marked 'Unknown.'

"Nowadays," the diplomat went on, "the nineteenth century is over, and the Russians have come into their own. If we get mad when Castro shoots an American, we are told, 'Watch out for Khrushchev's missiles.'"

I reminded the diplomat that I was not an American.

"Who says Castro won't start shooting Frenchmen? The only ones he won't harm are the British. And not because of the Bolivian precedent. Castro wouldn't care if Cuba were struck off the map. He doesn't give a damn about anyone except the British— and the Russians, of course. Along with Franco's subjects, the British are the only Westerners who have kept up regular trade relations with Cuba. Believe me, if I were you, I wouldn't go there. I just wouldn't take the chance."

I think I shall take chances all my life. It's part of my trade. Nothing gets on my nerves more than advice, warnings, and the stereotyped portraits that are handed out all over the world. In Europe, I had heard and read only Fidel Castro's praise. He was the disciple of Montesquieu, the knight-errant, the defender of the weak, the reincarnation of Don Quixote; he was bearded and wise and kind like God the Father himself. In Miami, this stereotyped image had given way to that of a cruel and bloodthirsty ogre that knows no law of any sort and follows only its basest and most bestial instincts.

When I left Paris, out of romanticism, perhaps, I leaned more toward the image of the hero—though the hero may have had his faults, he was essentially good and generous.

It did not take me long to conclude that no ideas can be quite so false as those formed *a priori*.

I arrived an hour early at Miami airport, superb with its marble tiles and its richly decorated shop windows. I took my place in one of the three lines of passengers leaving for Cuba. Most of them were men, the majority Cuban. They had the meek look of cattle being led to the slaughterhouse. There were five or six women, no longer very young and quite plump. In front of me, a woman who pushed her suitcase forward whenever we moved up a step, was crying. I sympathized and asked her why she was crying.

"Because of the way things are over there. Who knows what's going to happen to us."

"Then why are you going back?"

"I have to. I left Cuba twenty-nine days ago. According to the law, anyone who stays away over thirty days is a traitor. He loses all his property. I don't want them to take my house away!"

Checking in was exasperatingly slow. The official in charge took forever to fill in a form in duplicate for each traveler. Name, first name, address, profession, reason for travel. The travelers were well-behaved. Like good students, they replied nicely to the official's questions. Sometimes they went further than was necessary and talked about their own lives.

My turn came. The official thumbed through my passport. "Where is your Cuban visa?"

"I haven't got one."

"To go to Cuba, you need a Cuban visa."

"Not for the French."

"Why not?" he asked, surprised. "Why shouldn't the French need a visa to go to Cuba, when the Americans do?"

"How do I know? The point is that I don't need a visa."

"OK," muttered the official, "you settle it with them. If they don't shoot you first."

Then on to the immigration services. A man in uniform asked me why I was going to Cuba. "I am a journalist."

Handing back my passport, he asked, "Are you sure you'll get out alive?"

An endless and sinister cement tunnel led to the departure hall. At the line marked "passengers only," two characters were trying to sell Cuban pesos. They made their offer in Spanish. "Four pesos to a dollar. Over there they'll give you only one." Nobody seemed to pay any attention to them. But the last passenger slowed down. He stopped, looked around, and bought a bundle of notes.

At the end of the hallway we were herded into a windowless room with bare cement walls and no seats. A lightbulb threw its dim glow on the scene. "This is the antechamber of death for many of these people," said a French businessman with whom I had just struck up an acquaintance.

In silence we watched the metal door blocked by a huge, passive policeman with a crew cut. Standing next to him, an airline official held a stenciled sheet, the passenger list. Both policeman and official were silent.

The telephone on the wall rang, and the official answered it. "OK, I'll take them aboard." He called off our names, one by one. The policeman checked the passports. Like the immigration official earlier, he asked, "Are you sure you'll come out alive?" I could have replied that no one is ever sure of anything, but I merely shrugged my shoulders. "Well, good luck anyway, and take it easy," he added.

A customs officer was waiting outside. He took my briefcase, opened it, looked inside, foraged among my papers, took out my pipe. "No weapons?" he asked.

The plane was waiting under a clear blue sky. The weather was warm and pleasant. At the foot of the stairs, another official checked my ticket. "First class? There is no such thing on the Havana flight. You'll get the difference back in Paris."

And there I was in the plane, about to take off—an hour and a half behind schedule.

Usually, once on board an airplane, I get settled comfortably, untie my shoelaces, and order a whiskey and soda. The take-off is the moment I enjoy most; it is the time to relax. But on this Miami-Havana flight, there was no whiskey. "I'm going to give everyone a glass of rum," the steward said. "It's more convenient." Why it was more convenient remained a mystery.

The DC-6 was old and dirty. It reminded me of those crates which the French Army puts at the disposal of journalists for certain official trips. The woodwork was scratched up, the curtains greasy. My neighbor's seat suddenly collapsed. The steward came running. "Take it easy," he said. "Relax and have another rum."

"Why is this plane such a filthy mess?" the passenger asked.

"It's done on purpose," said the steward, chuckling. "This aircraft is the dirtiest and the oldest we've got. We use it on purpose. From time to time those bastards swipe one, so to cut the losses the company sends its worst planes. It's only normal, isn't it?"

A little later, bringing me my rum, he asked, "What the hell are you going there for?"

"I'm a journalist."

He opened his eyes big as chewing gum balls. "What the hell are you going to that place for? They're all nuts. They'll kill you. They kill everyone. Even Americans."

CHAPTER 2

Three guitarists, wearing wide-brimmed sombreros and looking like the Mexican singers who perform in Paris cabarets, were on hand to greet us when the plane landed. I said to the French businessman, "It isn't today that they're going to shoot us."

"Don't be too sure. In this country, it is common for musicians to escort men sentenced to death to the place where they're going to be executed. They play a farewell serenade before the final volley. We are being greeted with music. Why shouldn't a volley follow?"

We went down the stairs, carrying our parcels and suitcases. A huge streamer was spread across the front of Rancho Boyeros Airport, welcoming us to "*Cuba, territorio libre de America.*" On either side of this welcome were the two slogans which I was to hear and read everywhere throughout my stay: "*Venceremos*" ("We will win"), "*Patria o muerte*" ("Fatherland or death").

We proceeded toward a glass door, just opened for us by a

soldier. Not far from us and to the left, toward the hangars, was a strange cemetery of derelict airplanes. Constellations, DC-3's, and DC-4's were lying about, some without motors, others without noses or propellers. Others had their wheels on blocks. My French traveling companion explained: "The Cubans have been short of dollars ever since the United States stopped buying their sugar. They can no longer get the spare parts needed to keep their airplanes operating. Most Cuban airplanes are grounded, at least those made in the States. Fidel Castro has succeeded in keeping one or two Constellations and three or four DC-3's in the air, thanks to a kind of smuggling."

He gave me his calling card before leaving, and said, "Call me if you need anything. I'll try and help you. Please don't mention my name, it wouldn't be prudent under present circumstances."

"I'll call you Dupont. Mr. Dupont. How do you like it?"

We all then went into a room lined with dark wooden benches. An official told us to sit down. But we remained standing, in silence. As when leaving Miami, we kept looking at the door that would have to open for us to go out. A sound of voices reached us from the other side. I noticed that the Cubans always sound angry when they talk. They hammer the stressed syllables with the brutality of a woodsman hacking away with his axe. To make myself heard I felt I would have to raise my voice, and to tell a woman that I loved her I would have to display the wildest fury.

Two hours went by with typical Latin American slowness. We were still waiting, riveted to the same spot, not saying a word. The passengers who had chatted in the airplane now acted as if they had never met. Mr. Dupont pretended not to know me. He deliberately turned his back on me. A vague sort of uneasiness was growing among us, each one wondering, "What are they going to ask me?" "If they ask such a question, should I give this or that answer?"

A door opened suddenly, and we were led into a second glass-walled room. A soldier was placidly watching us from behind a counter. We obediently formed a line. But the soldier said, "Sit down. We have to wait for the *jefe*, the boss."

I was the only one to follow that piece of advice. The other passengers remained standing stiffly. As in a movie when the film is suddenly stopped, they remained motionless, some in ridiculous postures, continuing to hang on to their suitcases.

Another hour of waiting. The *jefe* still failed to show up. A young *barbudo*, through the glass pane, spotted a girl friend among the passengers. He whispered a few words to the soldier on guard, who said "V*a bién*" without even checking her papers! In other places such blatant favoritism would have led to a storm of protests. But in Cuba, under the equalitarian regime of the Revolution, no one says a word.

Finally, the *jefe* arrived. He crossed behind the counter, glanced at the passenger list, and disappeared. The soldier told us to step forward. He looked at each passport, asked two or three questions, checked a list lying beside him, stamped the passport and said, "Next."

When my turn came, he asked me whether I was related to the "Tyrant of Spain." "No."

"Nevertheless," he pointed out, "your name is Franco."

"Yes, but I am not related to the dictator."

"*Que bueno!* [So much the better!], *que bueno!*" He leafed through the stamped and worn pages of my passport and observed, "You travel a great deal."

"That's my job."

"*Que bueno! Que bueno!* Now, if you don't mind—I'm just asking out of curiosity. Franco, is that a popular name in France, like Garcia in Cuba?"

"No, it is of Spanish origin."

"*Entonces*, you may be a relative of the dictator."

"No, I am not related to him."

"Do you know him?"

"No."

"*Entonces*, why are you called Franco?"

"Because my father was called Franco."

"Perhaps your father was related to him?"

"No, he wasn't."

"*Que bueno! Que bueno!*"

And he went back to studying my passport, which seemed to fascinate him. He tried to decipher the French, English, Hebrew, Arabic, and Italian stamps, and pointed to one, "That! What's that?"

"Israel."

"You've been to Israel?"

"Yes, I have."

"*Bueno*. And that?"

"England."

"You've been to England?"

"Yes."

"*Bueno*. Now tell me where the Soviet stamp is."

"I haven't got one."

"Why not?"

"Because I have never been to Russia."

"Why not?"

"I've never had a chance to go."

"And Czechoslovakia? Have you been to Czechoslovakia? It's not far from Paris. Our planes go there twice a week."

"No, I've never been to Czechoslovakia. But I might go, some day, if anything happened there."

The official looked perplexed. "I don't mind letting you in. I've got nothing against you. But your name is funny. I have to talk about it to the *jefe*. Just wait a moment."

I turned toward my traveling companions to show them that I was sorry to make them waste time. I faced a row of expressionless faces, and said, "I'm sorry."

A sharp reply came. "Who's asking you? We're in no hurry."

The official came back with the *jefe*, a heavy-set soldier wearing on his shoulders the five-pointed star which marks the rank of Cuban lieutenant.

"Come here," he ordered, addressing me in the familiar "*tú*." I looked at my watch. We had taken less than an hour to come from Miami to Havana. We had already wasted five hours at Rancho Boyeros Airport!

The *jefe* brought me to an office where two soldiers were sleeping on a bench, with their automatic rifles next to them. "Sit down," he said, showing me a chair. "Your name is Franco?"

"Yes, it is."

"Why?"

I told my story again, but this time worked down starting from my great-grandfather.

"Are you related to the other one?"

"No."
"And your father?"
"No."
"And your grandfather?"
"He isn't either."
"Que bueno! Que bueno!"
He then asked me why I had come to Cuba.
"I have come to write articles and a book."
He told me to write down the name of my paper, *Parisien Libéré*. "Pa-ri-sien Li-bé-ré," he read out. " '*Parisien*' is from Paris. But what does '*libéré*' mean?"
"Liberated."
His youthful face lit up. He rose, walked around the table, embraced me. "*Parisien libre!*" he exclaimed. "Just like *Cuba libre! Libre de los Yanquis.* You must be a friend of Jean-Paul Sartre. *Viva Cuba libre! Viva Parisien libre! Viva Jean-Paul Sartre!*" He handed me by passport, warmly shook my hand, and escorted me back to customs. He introduced me to the two officials. "This gentleman is a French journalist on the staff of the *Parisien libre*. Like *Cuba libre.* Our friend Jean-Paul Sartre is his friend also." The two officials shook my hand. They told me I could go, without even checking my luggage. "*Viva Jean-Paul Sartre! Viva Parisien libre!*"

Night had fallen. It hit me with a blow when I walked out of the airport. It looked like a Hollywood stage set. Palm trees glistened under the moon.

There were no busses to take the passengers to Havana, but shiny black Cadillacs. Eight passengers had to squeeze into each car. I got in front, on the right of the driver's seat. Between us, I recognized the passenger who had bought pesos on the black market in Miami.

The Cadillac, in starting, sounded like a jalopy. Two, three explosions, a few shakes, and finally a purring or rather puffing, that sounded like a motorboat. The driver tried to comfort us. "Don't worry. Everything is O.K. It's just the ignition. The spark plugs are worn, and we can't replace them. We'd have to buy them in the States, and the Yankees want to be paid in dollars. We haven't got any. So we have to make do with the old spark plugs. *No tenemos dollares.*"

"How about the puffing? Don't you hear the puffing under the car?"

"*No es nada.* It's nothing at all. There is no exhaust pipe. I lost it last month. I've looked for one everywhere. There isn't a single one to be had, even in the stores specializing in secondhand spare parts. As a matter of fact, I am among the luckier ones. The other drivers are in even worse trouble. One has no more headlights, the other no taillights. Driving in the country at night has become hazardous. We manage as long as we can. Juanito made himself taillights out of plastic and paint. It's all right so long as the motor holds out. It's all the Yankees' fault," he added. "Why don't they accept pesos? Pesos are money, too, *verdad?*"

"*Claro,*" said my neighbor, "it's all the Yankees' fault. Why do they refuse to buy our sugar? Revolutionary sugar is just as sweet as Batista's sugar, *verdad?*"

"Why did the Yankees cut out the quota?"

"It doesn't matter. No quota, but no master. No flour, but free. I've had very little work since the tourists stopped coming over. The other day I needed tires, so I went to see the authorities. They told me, 'There aren't any tires because of the Yankees. They think that by keeping us from having tires they will destroy the Revolution.' Then the man added, 'But just wait! The brother nations are going to help us produce our own tires, free Cuban tires.' I asked, 'How long will I have to wait?' They answered, 'Have patience. *Venceremos! Patria o muerte!*' I replied, 'No importa. No tires, never mind. *Patria o muerte! Venceremos!*' "

The man sitting next to me said, "You want to know how I feel about it? *Los Yanquis son todos hijos de putas.* The Americans are all sons of bitches. *Todos hijos de putas.* Take my word for it. I know what I'm talking about."

"I believe you. You're perfectly right. The Yankees are all sons of bitches. *Hijos de putas! Todos!*"

"Me, I've just come back from there. I can tell you I didn't stay long. I just went to New York to settle some urgent family business. I came back as fast as I could. I didn't want to stay among those sons of bitches, not me. It disgusted me just to speak their language. They wouldn't even let me speak my own.

They kept on saying, 'Speak English.' Our language is just as good as theirs, *verdad?*"

"*Claro,*" said the driver.

I was getting the feeling that the two men were showing off their pro-Castro feelings. The traveler insisted on his patriotism, his civic sense. Not a word about those pesos he bought in Miami. He spoke loudly, making sure that the people in the back could hear all he was saying.

"*Los Yanquis,*" he began again, "*son todos hijos de putas. Asesinos! Criminales!* When they heard that I really meant to go back to Cuba, they wanted to send me to the electric chair."

"*Claro!*" said the driver. "They want to send all patriots to the chair. That's what they did with the Rosenbergs. They were patriots. They weren't doing any harm. They both died in the chair. The chair. It's disgusting. Shooting is much cleaner."

The road to Havana is beautiful. On that Sunday evening, cars returning to the capital were as numerous as on George Washington Bridge. Strong lights set off advertising for Coca-Cola, and for brands of cigarettes and beer.

We passed a small building decorated with a red lantern. "*El Bamboo Club,*" said the driver. He pronounced it "clew."

"The Yankees used to come here a lot. For the girls. They were the best-looking in the West Indies. Now these girls are no longer for the Americans only. *Nada para los imperialistas! Todo para el pueblo!* Nothing for the imperialists! Everything for the people!"

"*Claro,*" was my neighbor's comment.

The driver turned to me. "You aren't Czech because the Czechs don't come via Miami. They don't take American planes, but Dutch ones."

"I'm French," I replied.

"Well, well." He laughed. "The French are like the Cubans. They like the girls. You'll feel at home. Cuban girls are the prettiest in the world. If you want, some evening I'll show you the good spots. The Blue Moon, the Bamboo. . . ."

CHAPTER 3

The Habana Libre Hotel, formerly the Havana Hilton, where the Cadillac dropped me off, is the biggest, the most handsome, and the richest hotel in the West Indies. It was built less than ten years ago. The twenty-five towering stories cost some $25 million. After his triumph, Fidel promptly nationalized the establishment and changed its name. Yet in spite of the Cuban name, it retains a typically American palatial look. The glass doors have English signs: PUSH and PULL. The elevator buttons are also labeled in English. The bellboys and porters have "Bellboy," "Bell Captain" embroidered in silver thread on their lapels. There are signs for CAFETERIA, BOOKSHOP, BARBER and SWIMMING POOL.

At the reception desk, the receptionist speaks English. He gave me a suite on the twenty-first floor. "It will cost you $12 a day," he said. "Before the Revolution, it cost 30. You can thank Fidel for the saving. It was he who decided to cut the hotel rates."

"I'll thank him as soon as I see him."

"I am warning you: because of the black market, we can only accept payment in dollars."

I took a few steps into the lobby and a crowd of bearded young men burst into the hotel, some in uniform, others wearing untidy civilian clothing; many were armed. I asked an employee, "What's going on?"

"That's the way it is every evening. Today a delegation from the Rebel Youth of the province of Oriente has come to express its solidarity with Fidel."

"The Rebel Youth? Why 'rebel'?"

"All revolutionaries are called rebels. Ever since Fidel rebelled against Batista's tyranny, his partisans have been called rebels. His army is the Rebel Army, his youth movement is the Rebel Youth. There are also Rebel Students, Rebel Actors, Rebel Union Members."

"And you?"

"I'm the porter."

"Rebel porter, of course."

As I was about to be swallowed up by the elevator, a voice whispered into my ear, "*Señor Franco.*" I turned around. A tall, thin colored man, wearing an old felt hat, slipped something into my hand.

"It's for you. Don't read it right away. Wait till you are alone." And he disappeared just as mysteriously as he had come. I went across, locked myself in the toilet, and unfolded the message. It was in good French, and typewritten: "The Cuban patriots welcome you. They hope that the Communists will allow you to carry out your mission of information. You will soon be hearing from them, and you will understand their motto, '*Cuba sí, Rusia no.*'"

My "suite" was splendid: it had a mahogany door. There was a bathroom to the right of the entrance. A little further, a room no bigger than my Paris apartment opened onto an enormous terrace.

The bellboy who accompanied me turned on the radio. A raucous voice filled the room. "It's Fidel," said the boy. "He is giving a big speech."

When the bellboy had left, I tried to turn the radio off; I

turned the two knobs but it wasn't any use. I called the chamber-maid. She showed me a knob hidden underneath the radio. Progress is a beautiful thing!

I tipped her. She said *"Gracias,"* and switched the radio on again.

"No," I said.

"Yes, yes," she answered. *"Este es Fidel!* He is making an important speech. You must listen to him!"

There was a fantastic view from the terrace. Down below, lights were shining like so many stars on a black carpet. The dark shiny mass of the sea was clearly distinguishable. Far beyond, on the other side of Havana Bay, between two flickering advertising signs, the blunt outline of the *Castillo del Morro* was vaguely visible. A travel guide, which I found on the bedside table, gave me the following details: "The walls of the fortress rise to 120 feet above the Gulf of Mexico. Once upon a time, the bodies of criminals were tossed into the sea from this height after execution. Several generations later, sharks continue to haunt the waters at the bottom of the cliffs, hoping for a feast like the one that used to delight their ancestors."

I looked in vain to the right of the *Morro* for the sinister *Cabaña*, where the Spaniards once tortured Cuban patriots, and where the Castro people now shoot their enemies. The prison was not to be seen. The pamphlet stated that one part of the *Cabaña* has been converted into a museum where a torture room is presented with all the proper equipment. There is even a dummy, stretched out on the rack with a grimace of pain on its face.

At the foot of the Habana Libre Hotel lies the *Vedado* neighborhood. *"Vedado,"* in Spanish, means "guarded, forbidden." In the past, it was forbidden to build here; the *Vedado* had to remain an open space where pirates could not land without being sighted by the watchmen of the *Castillo del Morro*.

The following morning, on awakening, I picked up the white telephone from my bedside table. *"Patria o muerte. Venceremos!"* said the switchboard girl.

"I'd like my breakfast."

"Impossible at this time. The comrade waiters are at training."

"What training?"

"Military training. They are training in the streets surrounding the hotel. We can't disturb them."

I did not want to miss this sight.

The hotel personnel, carrying rifles, were marching round the building in double columns. The valets, the headwaiters, the bartenders were wearing their uniforms of white vests, striped waistcoats, and black evening suits. Over this they had put on American cartridge belts, and topped this with the black army berets. While parading, they all shouted out a marching song.

Having thought the question over, I decided to move. Not because the personnel preferred to serve the nation rather than the customers, but because I was suspicious of the Habana Libre, as it was too crowded. Also, I discovered that whenever I left the hotel I was trailed by a civilian or a soldier.

So I went to the far more modest Presidente. Its old-fashioned ten-story tower overlooks the nearly empty Avenue of the Presidents. Its lobby was not so crowded, and it was possible when leaving to see whether I was being followed or not. I knew that I would be relatively freer there than at the Habana Libre.

I ate my first lunch at one o'clock at the Presidente. The dining room was empty. I was the only customer. Three waiters with white jackets and black trousers busied themselves around my table. There was a choice of three luncheons, priced at $1.50, $1.75, and $2.00. I chose the second. First there were some *frijoles negroes*, black beans hardly bigger than peas, served with white rice. It was an unexpected but not unpleasant hors d'oeuvre. After that, there was grilled steak with chopped onions. For vegetables, potatoes and fried *plátanos* (green bananas).

I was about to start on my dessert—guava jelly—when two young women and the head elevator boy, Fernando, came over to me. They took chairs and sat down at my table without further formalities.

"*Compañero*," said Fernando, "we must talk to you." He then turned to one of the women and said, "Go ahead."

She talked to me in French. Like the head elevator boy, she used the familiar second-person form. "Comrade, we welcome you to Cuba, the first free territory of the Continent!"

"Thank you very much."

"I believe you are a journalist."

"Yes, I am."

"I'm a journalist too. My name is Lina. I'm not Cuban, but Chilean. My friend Luisa is Argentinian. She is also a journalist. We're both reporters for *Bohemia*.* After Fidel ran out Batista and began the Revolution, we joined him immediately. We're going to set up socialism with him, not only in this country, but in all of South America. Bolivia, Argentina, Chile, everywhere."

Fernando, who didn't understand French, seemed ill at ease. He was shuffling around, resting his elbows on the table and taking them off again, crossing and uncrossing his arms. Finally, he could stand it no longer, and told Lina, in Spanish, "Ask him for his card number."

I quickly replied, "What card? My press card?"

"No, your party card."

"Which party? I don't belong to any party."

"The Communist Party," the Chilean woman explained. "Why haven't you taken out your card? I registered in 1948, in Santiago de Chile when I was seventeen years old!"

The elevator boy asked me, "Who invited you to Cuba? The ICAP?"†

"Nobody. I'm a journalist. I don't need an invitation."

He rested his elbows on the table, looked me straight in the face and asked, "What do you think of Cuba?"

"I don't know. I've just arrived."

"*Bueno.* But, tell me, *Compañero*, why do your countrymen murder Algerian patriots? Tell me, what do you do in France, to help the cause of these victims of imperialism?" I shrugged my shoulders. He went on, "All right, we won't talk about it any more. But I hope that you will serve the Revolution loyally. You must come and cut sugar cane with us next Sunday. We are leaving at four A.M. We'll come back in the evening. We'll be among patriots. A patriot must help cut sugar cane. Else he is not a patriot, but a counterrevolutionary who sold out to the interests of capitalism and Yankee imperialism!"

"I am not a Cuban."

"But you're a patriot."

---

* A Havana weekly.

† The Cuban Institute for Friendship Among Peoples, set up by Fidel Castro to welcome friends of the regime.

"Yes, but I'm a French patriot, not a Cuban one. I haven't come here to bring in the harvest, and no one will make me do it."

"OK," Lina said. "Don't get angry. We hope that you'll write honest things. We read all the newspapers in Cuba. We'll know right away if you tell lies."

Fernando interrupted her. "Tell him about the Committee."

"Comrade Fernando," Lina continued, "wants you to know everything about our Committee. Following the instructions of our supreme guide, Dr. Fidel Castro, we have set up a Committee of Revolutionary Vigilance at the Hotel Presidente. Similar committees have been set up in each of the country's houses, apartment buildings, stores, universities, and workshops. Comrade Fernando is our leader. From now on, you will go to him for orders."

"I take orders from no one!"

Without paying any attention to me, Lina went on, "Don't forget that every morning you are to read the instructions posted on the blackboard in the hall, in front of the elevators. Which reminds me that tonight the opening of the Popular Library is to take place where the souvenir shop used to be. You absolutely must come. It is compulsory. And it will be very interesting, you will see. There will be a representative from the FEU* and Che Guevara has promised to send someone."

"Why did you get rid of the souvenir shop? Tourists like to buy presents, post cards, cigarettes."

"Tourists shouldn't waste their money on trifles. There will be educational books and magazines for them, free of charge. Come, I'll show you. Follow me."

The new library was located at the end of the covered terrace—a table, six chairs, and shelves with books and magazines. Some of the titles taken at random: Sartre's book on Cuba, the complete works of Mao Tse-tung, Thorez's *Son of the People*, *Guerrilla Warfare* by Che Guevara. Among the periodicals, there were publications in Spanish issued by the Chinese and Soviet embassies, there were magazines published by the psychological warfare services of the National Institute of Agrarian Reform (INRA) and "*Verde Olivo*." Olive green is the color of the Castro army.

Fernando apologized for having to leave us. He had to get back

* Federation of University Students.

to his elevator. I invited the two women to have coffee with me. We returned to the dining room.

Lina talked about her job on *Bohemia*. She does stories on co-operatives, youth centers, the "literacy brigades." "*Bohemia*," she said, "is a terrific paper!"

I told her that before coming to Cuba, I had a talk with journalists of *Bohemia Libre*, in New York. These are former reporters and editors on *Bohemia* whom Castro forced into exile.

"These people from the so-called *Bohemia Libre*," said Lina, "are a bunch of traitors and crooks. What a pity that they were allowed to leave Cuba. They should have been shot!"

This was not how I felt about it. Miguel Angel Quevedo, the director of *Bohemia Libre*, and Francisco Pares, its editor-in-chief, were for a long time on the staff of *Bohemia*. I told Lina, "Quevedo and Pares used to be sincere partisans of Fidel Castro. I saw a photograph, published in *Bohemia*, of Fidel embracing Quevedo. Everything went very smoothly until the day the regime decided that Quevedo and his team of journalists were acting too independently."

"You are wrong," Lina replied. "We threw them out the day we understood they were betraying the Revolution. They sold out to the Yankees."

"If they had sold out, they wouldn't be in such straits now. I went to *Bohemia Libre* in New York. It's a small office across from Grand Central Station. The paper survives from hand to mouth, on an absurdly small budget. Pares and Quevedo are never certain they will be able to go to press the following week. As to salaries, they only get paid after the returns come in. Say what you want about them, but don't tell me that they've sold out."

"You don't understand," Lina said. "All those who are not unconditionally with Fidel are traitors and have sold out. Have you been to Miami? Have you seen the Cubans there? Didn't you understand that they are all scum and mercenaries? Didn't you feel like spitting in their faces and killing them?"

"I spent two weeks in Miami. I'll gladly admit that many exiles are former profiteers of the Batista regime. But the others, the vast mass of refugees, no. I don't agree with you. They are neither scum nor mercenaries. I have talked with them at length. I've seen how they live, and I've observed them sufficiently to conclude that they're honest and unhappy people, and most certainly sincere."

I remembered one of the exiles in Miami, called Henrique: twenty-four, medium height, strong, with a round open face. A friend in New York had given me his name and a telephone number where I could contact him.

He came to see me at my hotel one evening. We talked, and he told me about his life as a student in Havana. His father had died at the hands of Batista's killers.

"When I was at the University," he said, "I used to run a pro-Fidel organization." His face lit up at the memory of his student days. "We used to print leaflets, distribute arms, handle funds, plant bombs. After Batista's fall, the other guys in the organization and I put ourselves at the service of the Revolution. We wanted the Cubans to be free, happy, independent of the United States as well as of Russia. But gradually things went wrong. Like Batista, Fidel tried to organize the students and get them under his control. If you disagreed, it meant prison. If you argued, prison. If you got out of step, prison."

At nightfall, Henrique and I went out. I had hired a car. We used the familiar *tú*, as Cubans always do among friends.

"Where shall we go, Henrique?" I said. I was aware of something restrained in his attitude, a kind of shyness. He had his right hand in his trouser pocket, and was counting over what coins he had left. He didn't want to go anywhere expensive, for his *dignidad*, that Cuban dignity which strikes every foreigner and forces his respect, wouldn't allow him to accept charity. He intended to pay his way, and to set his mind at rest I felt bound to say, "Don't worry about that. It all goes down on my expense account."

So he relaxed. "OK, let's go to Miami Beach. I haven't been there yet."

There's a narrow strip of sea between Miami and Miami Beach, but it's no trouble to get across. I asked Henrique, "How long have you been here?"

"Six months."

"And you've never been to Miami Beach?"

He shrugged his shoulders disdainfully. "I don't like playing the bum."

"What do you live on?"

"I work."

"Well, what?"

"I've got a job. The pay's nothing great. At least I'm working and making an honest living."

"It's all right, you can tell me. I've promised not to mention your name in my book."

He blushed as he told me, and I can't say I'd ever have guessed the answer: shrimp stripper. "I'm in a cannery near Coral Gables. It's not exactly out of this world. I have a little gadget, a kind of shaft with notches on it. I peel the shrimp one by one. It's piece work, so you get a little better each day with the practice. Of course you don't need to spend five years at a university to become a shrimp stripper. I wanted to be an architect, build bridges, skyscrapers, and dams. I guess you don't always do what you want in life. Mind you, I'm very happy. *No hay problema* for me."

No hay problema, there is no problem, was an expression Henrique used many times that evening. I soon realized that each time it was a device to conceal the distress he refused to betray. He pretended to laugh about his job. "Shrimp stripper! A good joke, don't you think?"

I felt that if he had been five or ten years younger, he would have burst into tears. Again and again that evening he made me promise, "Whatever you do, don't tell anyone I'm a shrimp stripper. It's a bit too much like strip-teaser, and that doesn't sound too great."

Later on I succeeded in getting him to talk about his mother, who had stayed behind in Havana. "She lives in a little apartment behind the university. She keeps a stationery store. When you go over there, don't forget to go and see her. She'd be glad to see you."

Like most of the exiles, Henrique always referred to Havana as "over there," either out of shyness or superstition. I never discovered which.

"Yes," he said, "when you're over there, go and see my mother. She lives on the fourth floor. There's no elevator. You can't miss it, it's on the right of the stairway. Tell her you've seen me, that I'm in good shape, that I'm happy, well, that, *no hay problema*."

I was driving and watching the red taillights of the cars that passed mine and the speed limit signs that came up every 500 yards. I couldn't see Henrique, and I remember feeling glad that I couldn't. There must have been tears in his eyes. His voice was trembling. It had changed very much since the start of our conversation.

We had a drink in a bar near the port. Then we walked back up Collins Avenue as far as Lincoln Road. In this district, away from the bright lights of the city center, Miami is like some gigantic old people's home, a kind of rest home in scale with the American continent. The little hotels you come to here and there along the avenue are peaceful places. In front of the entrance there is usually a porch, one step up from the pavement. Wicker chairs are lined up side by side. In the cool of the evening the people come out and sit there. I never saw one who looked less than fifty years old. Most of them were very old. Facing the street, they watched the passers-by and talked in low voices.

Henrique and I stopped for a moment in front of one of these hotels. Through the open window we could see a group of old folk sitting around in a lounge with ugly, nondescript furniture, while in the center a large female, with a twanging voice, sang songs in Yiddish, the audience solemnly taking up the chorus. The whole scene was utterly sad and depressing.

"Over there," said Henrique, "you'll have a better time. They're younger there than at Miami Beach, and the girls are prettier. You're bound to like it. Mind you, it may have changed since I left. Before, you didn't need to know Spanish to make friends. You just said, *mucho gusto*, it's a pleasure, and everybody smiled. When you had a drink you said, *salud, pesetas y amor, y tiempo para gozarlos*, health, wealth and love, and a long life in which to enjoy them. Besides, Batista had just been kicked out. That was enough to make life worth living. Now. . . ."

"Now?"

"You'll see for yourself. Police, soldiers, and no freedom to write or say what you really think. You'll see."

Later on we went back to Miami. Henrique wanted to show me the office of one of the associations of Cuban refugees. It was a wooden bungalow with screened windows, on 27th Street, away from the noisy districts. We went in without knocking, pushing open a wooden door that closed behind us on a spring, and found ourselves in a square room, the walls plastered with posters denouncing Castro. Near the door stood a plain wooden table and chair. On the table was a telephone, constantly in use, and next to it a money-box to which a note had been stuck: "We're not rich, neither are you, but if you can afford it, put ten cents in the box every time you make a call."

Henrique said with pride, "This is our headquarters." The room was filled with men and women. Some of them carried suitcases or baskets. "New arrivals," explained my friend.

I was feeling hungry, so I suggested to Henrique that we go for dinner. "On one condition," he replied, "that I pay the bill."

"But why? I can put it on my expense account."

"Never mind; you paid at Miami Beach. Now it's my turn. *Es mejor.*"

I didn't understand why it was better that way, but I didn't insist for fear of offending his *dignidad*. We went to a Cuban restaurant situated down a few steps in a noisy room full of smoke. Every table was occupied, but there were few people actually eating. Most of them had nothing but coffee, which they drank from little white cups.

"What's it all about?" I asked Henrique.

"They're refugees. They've nowhere to sleep. The restaurant is open all night long and the owner is a Cuban and doesn't object, so they all come down here. They order a coffee and wait for dawn."

"And then where do they go?"

"Then, it's not so easy."

There are fifty thousand Cuban refugees in Miami, fifty thousand exiles rich in *dignidad*. They arrived with nothing but the clothes they walked in. Some of them were able to take along a few belongings squeezed into a suitcase. The luckiest were able to come by air. It's not every Cuban who can afford a flight from Havana to Miami or to Kingston or to New York. To fly, you've got to be rich or to have rich relatives, since you have to send the price of a return ticket in dollars back from abroad. Those who were not so lucky got away like the French who crossed over to England during the last war. The rector of the University of Las Villas escaped in a boat without a motor. He had to row 130 miles.

Hardly a day goes by without the American Coast Guard picking up passengers half dead with exhaustion in some flimsy craft that has been adrift on the Atlantic Ocean or in the Gulf of Mexico, sometimes for as much as eight or ten days.

And now, as I sat listening to Lina in the hotel at Havana, while she lashed out at the Cuban exiles, I was reminded of how impossible it is to remain objective over this Cuban affair. It didn't take long to realize that. I had promised myself, when I landed, to remain cool, to look and listen, to keep an open mind and make as few judgments as possible.

But 50,000 refugees from a country of less than 7 million inhabitants is a large proportion. If the United States had the same proportion of exiles they would number more than 1.2 million. That so many men and women should have chosen to go, leaving behind all their belongings, giving up their security and their settled way of life for the uncertainty of a new life, seemed a sign, if not proof, that there was something wrong with the regime, at least so far as freedom was concerned.

CHAPTER 4

"Just you wait till you see the cooperatives."

I had been hearing this remark ever since I arrived. Nothing in fact would have pleased me more. Unfortunately, though, a visit to one of these temples of the Revolution was not within the realm of possibility for just any journalist. You needed the proper permit made out in the correct manner and issued by the right *autoridad*.

A French colleague told me that these permits were issued by the Ministry of Foreign Affairs. You had to apply to the chief press officer, Merino.

"Are they easy to get?"

"You never can tell with the Cubans. It's a complete toss-up. They're either crazy about you, take you everywhere, can't do enough for you, or else they consider you an enemy and ignore you entirely. In which case you're left in peace and can go where you

like. But you'll get nothing from them. Sometimes you may even
run into trouble."

The Ministry of Foreign Affairs was only a step or two from my
hotel, on the other side of the Avenue of Presidents, a white building, neither handsome nor ugly. I hesitated in front of the wrought-
iron railings which surrounded it and adjusted my tie before
passing through the gateway. Although it was still comparatively
early in the morning, the sun beat down on the back of my neck
like a leaden weight and made me feel like doing anything rather
than work. I approached with measured steps, and the gravel
seemed to crackle under my feet.

A flight of marble steps led up to the main entrance, and at the
top was a desk on which a telephone and a machine gun were
displayed. From behind it a girl in olive green trousers and RAF
blue blouse smiled at me. She was nice looking, with well-formed
breasts, a long face, aquiline nose, and curly hair. I said to her,
"I've an appointment with His Excellency Mr. Merino."

The smile hardened into a frown. "There are no Excellencies
here. We're in a socialist country. There are only *Compañeros*."

I tried again. "Excuse me. I'm sorry, excuse me. I've an appointment with *Compañero* Merino."

"Very well, *Compañero*, I'll tell him you're here." She picked
up the receiver, dialed a three-figure number and said, "There's a
man wants to see you. Says you gave him an appointment. What's
his name? Wait a second, I'll ask him."

I gave the necessary information.

"OK," she said, "I'll send him up."

Like so many Cubans, she said "OK," in American. The seventy-
five years of American influence have left their mark on popular
speech. One evening, as I passed him in the hall of the Habana
Libre, I heard Castro say "OK" and "all right" several times.

The press office was hidden away at the end of a long, dark cor-
ridor. I had to ask my way several times. It was a cold room despite
the glare of the lighting. There was a rattling of teleprinters. A
man in shirt sleeves was tearing off the dispatches as they came
in and sorting them into baskets marked AP, UP, PL. He pointed
to a yellow plastic chair.

"Sit down, Comrade. Comrade Merino will see you in a moment."

The moment lasted three hours. At midday, I began to show signs of impatience. I fidgeted, I looked at my watch every five minutes. He finally took the hint. "I'll go and find out if Comrade Merino can see you." He disappeared through a frosted glass door. Five minutes later he came back. "Comrade Merino asks you to excuse him. He's very busy right now, and suggests you contact Robert Taber. He's our public relations man, with the special job of looking after foreign journalists."

"I'd like to visit a cooperative," I said. "I don't care which one."

"Look, Comrade, Bob Taber will take care of that for you. You'll see. He's very nice. He understands journalists' problems. He's a journalist himself. Comrade Merino has called him, and he's expecting you this afternoon at 6 o'clock."

Taber's apartment was in a new air-conditioned skyscraper in the center of the Vedado, not far from the Habana Libre. The government had requisitioned it to accommodate foreign technicians. As with every building in town, the entrance was guarded by a soldier who sat at a table.

"Bob Taber?"

"Do you have an appointment?"

"He's expecting me."

"Twenty-fifth floor, apartment seven. I'll give you a pass. Don't forget to get it stamped by Taber, or you won't be allowed to leave. Name? Profession?"

Physically, Bob was a typical American. Very tall, strong, well-built, with reddish blond hair in a crew cut. He told me he was from the States, New York in fact. He had worked for some time for CBS. He first came to Cuba in 1957.

"I interviewed and filmed Fidel in the jungle, in the Sierra Maestra. I visited the battlefield twice, in the spring and during the summer of 1958. I spent several months with the guerrillas and their leaders. Afterwards, I was there at the *barbudos'* triumphant entry into Havana in January, 1959. I shall never forget that. If you had seen how the crowd mobbed them, Fidel Castro, his brother Raúl, Che Guevara. They went wild. The women embraced the men, just as they were, covered with dust from the mountains. They gave themselves to them, shamelessly, as if they were their lovers or husbands."

I looked round the room. As in so many Cuban homes, no

attempt had been made at tasteful furnishing. Two 1930-style armchairs, a television set with a V-shaped aerial on top, a low brass table, and the sofa on which I was sitting between a Rollei-flex and a machine-gun.

I looked out of the window at the white roofs and terraces, with a patch of brown or orange here and there, sloping away to the hard blue of the sea. The sun was getting ready to sink into the Gulf of Mexico, and its rays created a wonderful ballet of colors, like the finale to some magnificent show, as they tinged the water with every shade of green.

Down below, the palm trees of the Hotel Nacional seemed to be caught motionless in their swaying. The cars looked Lilliputian, and the passers-by reminded me of those pins with large heads that I used to stick into maps when I was in my teens, dreaming of being an explorer and of sailing round the world.

Bob Taber brought me back to reality with a cough, and began to lecture me on the "mistakes" and "crimes" of the U.S.A. "The Americans behaved like Chicago gangsters," he said. "It's a disgrace that such a great nation should be so dead set against such a small country. The Americans should never have stopped their imports of Cuban sugar. It was a negligible item of expenditure for them, whereas for Cuba it was a vital source of income. Let me give you an example to demonstrate the disproportion between the two countries' resources. The amount of money spent each year on cosmetics by Americans is a good deal larger than the entire Cuban budget."

Then he told me about his present work with the newspapers *El Mundo* and *Revolución*. He had just finished writing up the situation in Escambray, where anti-Castroists were holding out in the jungle. He showed me a picture of himself in military uniform with a machine gun across his chest. "I spent a fantastic couple of weeks. The men I fought with were wonderful guys, courageous, honest, direct, good revolutionaries, unlike the men on the other side, who are mercenaries in the pay of the Americans. We gave them a fine licking."

I had been longing to ask him one question. "How is it that you, a citizen of the U.S., became a Castro propagandist against your own country?"

"Well," he admitted, "that may seem strange to you. But I

know Fidel so well that I have sworn to do everything I can for the success of his revolution. His cause is a just one. It's the cause of men in love with liberty. I look upon Cuba as my own country now. I've pushed the U.S. out of my life. In my place, what would you have done? The same thing, wouldn't you?"

Bob Taber drew his armchair up to the sofa and lowered his voice. "Why did you leave the Habana Libre?"

Coming point blank like that, his question knocked me sideways. I had to invent something on the spur of the moment. "It was too expensive, twelve dollars a day."

"Yes, I thought that was it. Now—Merino has already agreed to this—I don't want you to have any financial worries. There's a suite at the Habana Libre reserved for you. Go back there tonight, or tomorrow morning at the latest. It won't cost you a cent. The Foreign Affairs Ministry will look after that.

"Now don't be offended. Everybody knows a young writer has difficulty in making ends meet. If you'll let me, I want to help you a little during your stay in Cuba. Here are a few hundred pesos for daily expenses. Come on, don't refuse. You must accept. From tomorrow morning on, a limousine and chauffeur will be at your disposal. You'll be able to see all the cooperatives you want."

How I hate this kind of proposal! I must have turned visibly pale. I stood up at once and swore.

"Don't get nasty," he replied. "It's just a question of helping you in your work and looking after your worries."

"I didn't come to ask you for money. I want to visit a cooperative. That's all. Tell me once and for all. Can I visit one, or can't I? If not, too bad."

"Come on, don't get excited. In Cuba we always help honest writers, especially when they're young and deserving. I've got some good ideas for you: an exclusive interview with Fidel Castro and Che. That would be a good deal, wouldn't it? You can watch an execution, too. Tomorrow morning in fact. It so happens they're going to shoot a couple of guys. Would you like me to arrange things for you? You could even take some photos. They'd sell pretty well."

It took my breath away. I didn't know whether to be indignant, scornful, or just burst out laughing. In the end I chose a fourth solution. "You can keep that sort of stuff for others. It's not for me."

He caught up with me on the stairs. "Let's forget about that conversation. I've got to call in at *Revolución*. If you've nothing better to do, I'll take you along there."

Revolución is the official organ of the 26th of July Movement, which gave birth to Castroism. A 10- or 12-page paper comes out every morning. Its offices are in a large building on the Civic Square, not far from INRA and the monument to the memory of José Marti, poet, patriot, and hero of the Cuban War of Independence. Strips of bunting are stretched across the façade and on them is written in letters one yard high, "We shall defend this building floor by floor. And if there is nothing left but rubble, we will go on defending it."

On the ground floor, guards surrounded the elevator cage, their fingers on the triggers of their machine guns. Others, similarly armed, were carefully marking down visitors' identities. We took the elevator to the editorial office on the fourth floor. More soldiers, and, as always, more machine guns.

Mr. Arcocha, the managing editor, received us in his office. A young man, about thirty, who seemed pretty nice. He spoke good French and asked me if I was a friend of J., a Parisian journalist. "We've some friends in common," I replied, "but we've never met."

"J. is a remarkable man," explained Arcocha. "He met Castro when he was in hiding and helped him a lot by making him known to the French. He's just published an excellent book on the Cuban Revolution."

I was sitting in front of a table piled high with papers and newspapers. The smell in that office ought to have been familiar to me, not so very different from the smell in a Parisian editorial office, where there's always the odor of printing ink; but here I detected another smell which I remembered from somewhere else. Arcocha's office smelled like a barracks. Resting on a dictionary was a pot of gun grease. Beside it lay a formidable-looking Luger automatic.

"Coffee?" suggested Arcocha.

We touched on several topics, the Algerian war, the sugar problem, the French Revolution. Finally Arcocha asked me for my

opinion on Cuba. "It's still a little early for that. What can I say?
I can only give a few impressions."

"Let's hear them all the same. Be quite frank."

"All these weapons," I said, "all these soldiers with their machine guns, rifles, pistols, bandoleers, and all that, they make me
wonder, especially in an editorial office."

"We've got to guard the newspaper against the enemies of the
Revolution."

"You guard bridges, tunnels, ministries, politicians with weapons,
but not newspapers. Before entering this office I saw four soldiers
go into the next room. On the door I read the words 'Editorial
Staff.' When soldiers or policemen, whatever their reasons, think
they've a right to occupy an editorial office, in my opinion it's time
for journalists to leave it."

Merino had a telephone message passed on to me: "We have
made inquires at our Embassy in Paris, and find that the publications with which you are associated do not appear on our list of
friendly magazines. It therefore seems unprofitable to us to help
you in your work in Cuba."

CHAPTER 5

In the old days, when the American tourists came in the thousands, every evening was a date with Havana. As soon as darkness fell, the city transformed itself into a beautiful woman swathed from head to toe in an immense and mysterious checkered robe of black velvet. Beneath this disguise throbbed a life of hot passion, and the jewels with which she was adorned sparkled with fire.

But Havana only showed her face to those who knew how to love her. She became herself only when complete darkness fell. How could it be otherwise for a tête-à-tête? I too waited for darkness. Then I took a taxi toward the Prado.

The Chevrolet moved along without hurry, turned onto the *Malecón* and went past the American Embassy, where the doors and windows were hermetically sealed. The pavement shone. On the other side of the bay, to the right of *La Cabaña*, two neon signs perched up on the hillside spelled out against the darkness

BACARDI and COCA-COLA in scarlet letters winking in a ring of white light.

I asked the driver, "Do they still have Coca-Cola in Cuba?"

"Of course, but it's not the same Coca-Cola. We nationalized the factory that produced it in Cuba." Coca-Cola, in fact, was "liberated" along with everything else.

The *Malecón* goes down toward the port, and we kept it on our left. I had some difficulty in finding my bearings again in Havana. Street names are enough to give a foreigner a headache. Every street has several names. There is the official one that appears on the maps. But the inhabitants have different names for them. If you plan to meet someone on G Street, you have to ask for Avenue of the Presidents. *La Calzada*, which I spent one desperate morning searching for, is easier to find if you ask for Seventh Street. *La Linea* is known as both Ninth Street and Wilson Avenue.

We arrived at the Prado, a wide avenue in the Spanish style with marble arcades, divided down the middle by a terrace and lined with oleanders. I met Havana at the very end of it, on the corner of the Street of Virtues. What could be a more suitable place for a pretty girl to meet her lover?

I got out of the taxi and stood in the middle of the street, filled my pipe and struck a match. I looked up the narrow street with its dim lighting. An exuberant crowd overflowed the sidewalks and spilled into the street, scarcely leaving room for cars to pass. Men and women were sauntering up and down, talking in loud voices and gesticulating.

The men seemed in high spirits. At every step I heard a shout of laughter. Anything was an excuse for a joke. A girl went by in close-fitting slacks and an off-the-shoulder blouse. A passerby in canvas trousers and *guayabera** shouted after her, "You're like poetry, the way you sway your hips like a tigress. Those slacks moulded to your curves and your bare shoulders will give me a sleepless night tonight." And he laughed.

You'll dream about them, these *Habaneras*. The most virtuous man will become a Don Juan on meeting them. Graham Greene couldn't help writing, "Living in Havana is like living in a factory that mass-produces beautiful women."

---

* A plain shirt with four pockets and mother-of-pearl buttons, worn outside the trousers.

They're to be found everywhere, these goddesses, in the streets, in bars, in offices. Whether secretive or provocative, sentimental or cynical, serious or easy-going, they are forever sinuously moving with that same African rhythm that you find in aphrodisiac dances like the *maracas* and the *bongo*. Throughout the world I have seldom come across women who dress as suggestively as the *Habaneras*. They are especially fond of slacks as close-fitting as a pair of tights. Their dresses reveal the curves of their bodies just as faithfully.

The wife of a European diplomat once told me about her misadventure in Cuba. She had ordered a suit from a fashionable tailor. "I knew I'd never dare to wear it. The skirt was so tight I might just as well walk around in a bathing-suit. I told the tailor that an ambassadress couldn't think of wearing such an outrageous garment. 'Why not?' he replied. 'You're a woman first, aren't you?' "

I had hardly gone a few steps, when first one, two, and then half a dozen children surrounded me. "*Checo, Señor? Ruso?*" (Czech, sir? Russian?)

"No."

"American Mister? Come on! Nice girls! Mister, come on. Girls, girls. Fourteen years old. Any color. Little boys, cheap. Cheap! Yes, sir! Cheap, cheap!"

They spoke English with that vulgar accent you can always spot where G.I.'s or Tommies have been.

"Mister, come on. Nice girls, little boys. Come on! Cheap!"

I explained that I wasn't American. "*Francés.* I'm French, from France."

But they pretended not to understand my Spanish. They hung on to my arms and caught hold of the flaps of my jacket. "Mister."

"Nothing doing. Get away."

They were insistent. "Mister, come on. Pretty girls, fourteen years old! Any color, white, black, Chinese. Very pretty, fourteen years old. Clean. Only five pesos. Mister, come on!"

Three *barbudos* elbowed their way through the crowd and came to my rescue. They chased the kids away, clouting them over the head and swearing at them. "*Vaya! Vaya!* You crowd of scamps! Where do you come from, you little skunks? What kind of impression of our Revolution do you think *you* give foreigners? V*aya!* V*aya! Seminaristas!*"

I thanked the three soldiers. They replied, "You're welcome. You mustn't form a bad opinion of Cuba because of those lazy slugs. Their parents ought to be jailed. Soliciting's been forbidden by Fidel."

I suggested going for a drink. But the *barbudos* were on duty. They patrolled the district to prevent street urchins and prostitutes from pestering tourists. "Just one drink, it won't take a moment," I said. "I won't keep you from your duty."

"That's true," agreed one of the *barbudos*. "One drink doesn't take long. It's not against orders. We're on duty all right, but we're free."

"Cuba," added the second soldier, "is a free country now, and Cubans are all free. If we want a glass of rum, nobody's going to stop us."

"Of course not," agreed the third. "We're all free."

We went through a swinging door. Inside, the bar was in almost total darkness. You couldn't make out people's faces. "It's as dark as a tunnel," I said.

The soldiers laughed. "It's specially planned for lovers. If you find a *muchacha*, take her into a bar like this. You'll be allowed to do what you like. No one can see you. Look, the waiters have flashlights to see their way around. They shine them on the ground so as not to disturb the couples."

The *barbudos* ordered *Cuba libres*. This is not, as you might expect, a recently invented cocktail. Nothing to do with the Revolution and the present anti-Americanism. It dates back to the beginning of the century. In a desire to express their gratitude to the U.S., which had just liberated them from Spanish rule, they mixed their native rum with American Coca-Cola, and called it *Cuba libre*.

One of the *barbudos* said to me, "Thanks to Fidel, prostitution is on the way out."

"What about those fourteen year olds they were offering me just now?"

"Of course, it hasn't been completely suppressed. There are still whores, but less than before. Fidel has had most of the brothels shut. The girls have been rehabilitated. They were taught sewing and cooking and have become honest women. There are still a few brothels going. You can't get rid of them all. There'll always be whores. It's like bars. You can't close them all down. You always have to have a few bars. Not many, a few's enough. It's the same with whores. You have to have a few."

"In Batista's time," said the second *barbudo*, "there were whores everywhere. In this street you couldn't go a yard without being accosted. They fought for their clients. Now it's forbidden. If a tourist wants a girl, he has to ask her himself. The whores have to keep their mouths shut and just wait."

I looked at my watch: eleven o'clock.

"We've got to go," said the third.

"Where are you going now?" I asked.

"To inspect the Shanghai. Come with us. It's worth seeing. The Shanghai's something left over from Batista's days. It's been kept on as a kind of museum of depravity. When they're grown up, our kids must know what things were like once."

The Shanghai is on Zanja Street, not far from the Street of Virtues. In old days they showed obscene films there. People paid high prices to see the world's dirtiest movies. If you were afraid of being recognized there, you could cover your face and head with a hood.

On the outside it now looks like an ordinary neighborhood movie. The name of the place is encircled with colored lights. It doesn't cost much to get in: one peso. "In the old days," explained one of the *barbudos*, "it cost from five to ten pesos. Fidel has ordered prices to be lowered. He's done the same at the Bamboo Club and the other brothels that are still going."

There weren't many people in the audience. We saw the end of a film about nudism. Then the lights came on and the screen disappeared. "The strip tease will now begin," announced a loudspeaker.

A woman appeared on the stage. She was fat and old. Her hair was dyed red. Her act was poor and vulgar. She undressed completely, to the coarse jeers of the audience. She had huge legs and withered breasts.

After her came a couple whose miming didn't leave much to the imagination. Feeling disgusted, I didn't wait for the end, and went back to the Street of Virtues.

I finally chose a place that looked respectable, almost luxurious, and sitting down in a corner not far from the tiny stage, I ordered a daiquiri. The four-man colored band began to play a cha-cha-cha, and a dancer came running onto the stage. She was beautiful, with blond hair, a slender figure, and high breasts. Her spangled dress had a long train, and a slit up the side revealed her well-proportioned leg from the thigh downwards.

At the next table, a man in his fifties had just finished his rum and soda, and was looking at me out of the corner of his eye. As though the question had been bothering him for some time, he asked me abruptly, "You Cuban?"

"No, French."

"Do you mind if I join you? I'm bored all alone." I offered him a drink, which he accepted. "When did you arrive in Cuba?" he asked.

"Eight or ten days ago, I can't remember."

I watched the blond dancer. She was twisting her hips in jerks, posing suggestively. She began to undress. My guest interrupted my rapt attention. He proffered his right hand. "My name's Carlito." Then he asked, "You like that girl, don't you?"

"Yes, I do. She's very beautiful."

Carlito was delighted with my opinion. He again gave me his hand to shake. "You've got good taste in girls," he exclaimed. "That's obvious. That girl is beautiful, isn't she?" Then he added, "She's called Angelita. She's my daughter. All the men like her. She's the star of the club."

The dancer had taken off her black gloves, and was now pretending to be struggling with the zip-fastener of her dress. "If you like," went on Carlito, "I'll introduce you to my daughter. Yes, yes. Don't refuse. I'll introduce you. She'll be proud to know a Frenchman. You're from Paris? Yes, when Angelita hears that, she'll go wild. She's a nice girl. She's no whore. No, no, she's no whore. You'll see. I don't want to influence you. You'll see for yourself. Mind you, I'm not saying that because she's my daughter. It's the truth. You can tell a whore right away, the *muchachas* who sit by themselves. Look over there. She's a whore. And there's another one at the next table. A *muchacha* on her own in a club is a whore, otherwise she'd be accompanied by a chaperon. Normally, Angelita's mother would be here to chaperon her. But she finds it tiring to sit up late at night. She can't take it these days. Besides, a man is stronger, tougher."

Carlito never stopped talking. From time to time, to attract my attention which kept wandering to the strip teaser, he caught me by the arm and shook me. "Hey listen! I'll introduce you to Angelita later on, when she's finished. You'll see. She's a great kid. But don't treat her like a whore. She's not a whore. You mustn't expect to take her to bed straight away, just like that. Even for money. She'd be offended. In Cuba a pretty girl always says yes. Only you have to know how to ask her. If Angelita likes you, there'll be no problem. She'll let you know. I won't say anything. It's only her happiness I care about."

I looked at him in amazement. It was the first time a man had ever thrust his daughter into my arms quite so openly. Carlito noticed my astonishment, but didn't understand its cause. "You're wondering what to do," he said. "Nothing. Of course, a *muchacha* loves a man to give her something. She thinks that's what a man's for. That's what all *muchachas* think, everywhere. I'm sure it's the same in France. Offer her what you like, a rum, a lighter. No, I know what she'd like: a carton of American cigarettes. I bet you have some in your hotel. You can't get them in Havana any more. Sometimes you can get them from a guy who's just visiting. But they cost a lot, one and a half to two pesos a pack."

He grinned and dug me in the ribs. "With a carton of American cigarettes you can have any girl you like. Angelita prefers Chester-fields. Got any at your place? If not, any brand will do. It doesn't matter much."

The heavy velvet dress, with its train, slipped down to Angelita's feet. She now had nothing on but her underwear. The dance became slower and more lascivious, each movement with erotic eloquence evoking every phase in the act of love-making. The men in the room began to grow restless.

"Hurry up! Take it off. Take off your bra."

"Hurry!"

Angelita answered each time, "*Calla te*, Be quiet." She stretched out her hand towards a man. "If you're a man, come and unfasten me."

He hesitated, looked around him like a shy and pimply ado-lescent. Angelita offered him her back. There was a hook to unfasten. He took a long time over it, fumbling. Finally he succeeded in getting off the little scrap of clothing, and was emboldened to try to caress her. "Hands off," she ordered. Carlito laughed.

She hadn't yet revealed her breasts, but kept them covered with her hands. She began to dance to a blues rhythm. "Angelita's nineteen," went on Carlito. "She's beginning to get old. You know. She'll soon have no future. She must hurry up and marry or she'll never find anybody."

He became nostalgic. "In the old days, everything was fine. Three years ago, Angelita's future seemed a sure thing. She had an influential friend who worked for Batista. He was a nice guy, not a swine like the rest of Batista's friends. He didn't hurt anybody. On the contrary, he found me a good job, and the same for my sons and brothers-in-law. But it all collapsed with the Revolution. It's a pity. We weren't unhappy in those days. Angelita had no worries about her future. And then, thanks to her there was always plenty of money in the house. Now. . . ."

Angelita began to writhe about more wildly than before, though still carefully covering her breasts with her hands, lashing out with her legs, twisting her belly, shaking her head. The music stopped. With a quick movement she uncovered her breasts, blew us a couple of kisses, and ran out.

Day is about to break. The dawn smells of oranges and rum. It is a smell of drunkenness. But dawn has a sense of decency. She doesn't lay bare the town at one go. She knows that, like all women, Havana dislikes being surprised in her early-morning slovenliness. Dawn waits for the sun to clothe the houses in warm colors.

I went back on foot. The capital was awaking calmly, almost noiselessly. There was only the lapping of the sea against the rocks of the *Malecón* and the throb of the cars that whirled past.

When I reached the monument to the victims of the explosion of the battleship *Maine*, I found a car parked by the sidewalk in which two lovers had fallen asleep in one another's arms.

The sun was now high enough to rouse the town. Two policemen came out of police headquarters, yawning. Some housewives were lining up in front of a grocery store which still had its blinds down.

CHAPTER 6

She is called Anita, age twenty-two, large almond eyes, milky skin, and a slender waist. Her face shows a slight trace of African ancestry. She has, in fact, a rather broad nose and thick sensuous lips.

I made her acquaintance in a ministry where she worked as a secretary. I have seen her several times since then, but this is the first time we have dined together. Up till now, every time I invited her she eagerly accepted, but at the last moment she would phone to say, "I'm sorry, I can't come. I'm on guard duty tonight." She was an enthusiastic Castrist and had joined the army. The first time we met she told me proudly, "I have the rank of *jefe*. I'm in command of a whole platoon, twenty-four girls."

By some miracle she phoned me this evening. "I'm free tonight."

She came to fetch me at my hotel, only an hour-and-a-half late, which for a Cuban is evidence of extreme punctuality. Usually you can expect to wait at least three hours, and if you don't want to die of hunger, it's wise to have some sort of a snack ready at hand.

We went to the Centro-Vasco, a Basque restaurant where they serve some fifty different kinds of fish and good Spanish wine that doesn't burn out the stomach.

I complimented Anita on her light summer frock. She smiled. "I'm not often out of uniform." She looked at me and added, "Let's use the familiar *tú*. I can't stand formality. Everybody in Cuba uses the familiar form." She told me gravely about her day's work. She got to the INRA at eight o'clock in the morning and left at six.

I asked her, "What do you do after work?" I expected her to reply, "I go home like a good little girl, Mom and Pop are waiting to have dinner with me." Or she might have said, "My fiancé comes and picks me up."

But Anita is not like other girls. She replied, "I attend the meeting. There's a meeting every evening at the ministry. I take an active part in them. You have to explain the aims of the Revolution to those who haven't yet understood it properly. There are discussions, votes on different motions. Meetings last an hour and a half."

"But afterwards?"

"Sometimes I go home afterwards, but as I am a *jefe*, I have to spend the night at the ministry three or four times a week. There are guard duties, weapon-cleaning."

"Don't you ever get to sleep?"

"Yes, we're on guard for only two hours. We take turns. There are mattresses laid out for us on the ground floor."

"Don't you ever go out in the evenings?" I asked her in astonishment. "A pretty girl like you could be engaged at your age, or at least have a boy friend. What does your *novio*, your fiancé, think of the way you spend your time?"

Anita bit her lip. "I don't have a *novio*. One day, if things go well in Cuba, I'll look for one. Right now I haven't the time. I have to think of the Revolution first. But don't think I'm abnormal or anything. I want to marry one day like everybody else, have a house and kids. I wouldn't consider myself a human being if I didn't."

"What's to prevent you leading a normal life now?"

"You've seen for yourself. Every time I have a date I have to call it off. No man would stand for that."

"Are the other girls in the platoon the same way?"

"We're all crazy about the army. We're proud to serve under Fidel. He's a real leader, a genius, a hero, a fine, noble-hearted man. And besides. . . ." Anita lowered her voice. "Besides, it's very useful for a girl to be in the army. It means she can go out without a chaperon. If I wasn't in the army, I wouldn't be here dining alone with a man. My sister would have accompanied me."

She was gazing at me dreamily. I laughed. "What are you thinking about? Your platoon? The ministry?"

"Nothing," she replied abruptly. The next moment she said, quite unexpectedly, "You're a real white. Cuban girls like me, with mixed blood, dream of going out with a man like you. The Revolution has done away with color prejudice, but to marry a white man, one hundred per cent white, that would be great.

"*That's* a wonderful thing the Revolution could do. It ought to step up the process of making Cuba white. It wouldn't be difficult. You'd only have to invite white men and women to come and settle here. There's room for plenty of people. In that way the coloreds would soon become absorbed, and there'd be no more negroes, no more prejudices, no more anything. Isn't that a good idea? If you see Fidel you should suggest it to him."

Anita then told me that she didn't read much. She hardly had time for it. She'd like to go to the movies more often. "I only go once or twice a month, when I'm not on duty." She became thoughtful again, half closing her eyes. "You must find me strange," she said. "I'm trying to imagine your life in France. For example, I'd like to know what you'd be doing right now if you were back there. And then . . . I can see myself walking arm in arm with a white man. Tell me, are you married?"

"Yes."

"To a white woman?"

"Yes."

I thought that Anita's voice had begun to tremble. She bit her lip again, grew pale, fidgeted, opened her bag looking for a cigarette. "And if you weren't married, could you be interested in a girl like me, a half-caste, with a colored skin?"

"Why not? Colored skin doesn't bother me. If I love a girl those kind of things don't enter into it."

"You're not saying that just to please me?"

"No, honestly."

After dinner, I suggested going somewhere for a drink. "I know a good club near here," said Anita. "There's dancing, and their *Cuba libres* are excellent."

We got up from the table, and were just making for the exit when a waiter called us back with a shout.

"Fidel's going to speak on television."

"You must listen to Fidel," said Anita.

"We can read his speech in the newspapers tomorrow."

"You have to *listen* to Fidel."

"Sometimes he goes on speaking till dawn."

"I know, but you *have* to listen to Fidel."

So it was good-by to my evening and the club. It was the second time Cuban television had done me a bad turn. One evening shortly after I had settled in at the Presidente Hotel, the head elevator boy came to my room. "*Compañero*," he said, without further ceremony, "why aren't you downstairs with the others? Fidel's going to speak on television."

"I'm tired and sleepy."

"You should go down. The television's in the little room in back. There'll be free drinks."

"I'm sleepy. I want to sleep."

"Comrade! You must be out of your mind! *Fidel is going to speak on television.*"

There was nothing to be done about it. I had to get dressed again, go down eight floors to the ground floor, and sit in the little room. In addition to the guests, every member of the hotel staff was there: the manager, the night telephone operator, the Chilean, the Argentinian, the bartender, the three waiters, the cooks.

As a kind of curtain raiser there was a newsreel of Escambray. We were shown soldiers advancing with machine guns, throwing themselves flat on the ground, and taking up firing positions, but nothing of the actual fighting.

When it was over, a vast photograph of Jean-Paul Sartre took up the whole of the screen for a moment, and then shrank to the size of a passport photograph, part of the cover design of a book entitled "Sartre in Cuba," while a thundering voice announced, "Read and make others read the great philosopher Jean-Paul Sartre's magnificent testimony."

After an hour there was still no sign of Fidel. I asked Lina, who was sitting close by, "When is the speech due to begin?"

"Wait, Comrade. Fidel is a very busy man. He is sometimes delayed."

"Oh, I see. Excuse me."

After the advertisement for Sartre came an animated cartoon, American of course. I waited till Mickcy Mouse had finally disappeared from the screen and then asked once again for news of the *lider máximo*. Lina replied, "Well, you're certainly no progressive."

That was enough. I got up. "If that's how it is, I'm going up to bed." I found both elevator doors locked, and since I didn't want to climb up eight flights of stairs I went to fetch the operator.

Fernando looked amazed. "What do you want, *Compañero?* Why do you come and disturb me just at the very moment when Fidel is about to speak, *Fidel, nostro lider máximo?*"

"Fidel is not about to speak. I'm sleepy. I want to go up to bed. There's nobody to run the elevator."

"Wait till the end of the revolutionary manifestation like everyone else."

"No."

Fernando raised his voice, began to make a scene. "*Compañero,*" he shouted, "your attitude is extremely suspicious. I wouldn't be surprised if you weren't a counterrevolutionary. I refuse to serve a lackey of foreign imperialism."

That made me lose my temper. "Nonsense! Revolutionary or counterrevolutionary has nothing to do with it. I'm a hotel guest paying eight dollars a day. Get into your elevator at once and take me up to my floor, or else."

"Or else?" he grinned.

"Or else I'll go to the INIT* tomorrow morning and tell them that Fernando, head of the Revolutionary Committee in the Presidente Hotel, is undermining the Revolution's tourist policy."

"You'll tell them that?"

* National Institute of the Tourist Trade.

"I shall also tell them that after dinner, when you took me to my floor, you asked me not to forget to give you a tip, and when I gave you ten centavos you almost bowed to the ground to thank me."

Fernando lowered his head and walked past me. In the elevator he said, "Would you really have gone to the INIT?"

"No. I just said it for something to say."

"You shouldn't have treated me like that in front of everybody. Now what will they think of the head of the Committee?"

"You shouldn't try to mix politics with your job."

Sitting there in front of the television set in the *Centro Vasco,* Anita had eyes and ears for nobody but Fidel. She had forgotten all about the color of my skin and her pleasure at going out with a white man. Fidel's beard was there on the screen before her, and nothing else mattered.

I was forced to admit that Anita was in love with Fidel Castro. She was perfectly aware, of course, of the many adventures with which the leader of the *barbudos* is so generously credited. We had even talked about it at the beginning of the meal. "It's normal for a man," she had replied.

With a leader like Fidel, the Revolution has taken on an unexpected aspect. It has become sensual. Jean-Paul Sartre is supposed to have confided his disillusionment to a European ambassador in the following remark, "The Castro regime is childish and sensual. It has all the elements of a bad tragedy." For proof of the accuracy of this judgment you have only to watch Fidel on television. His speech is addressed entirely to the women, and he speaks to them in a language which only they are capable of understanding.

This evening, for example, the *líder máximo* was taking part in a round-table discussion with trade-unionists, delegates from youth organizations, representatives from women's associations. These others gave their views in little speeches full of learned but abstract arguments, making use of such expressions as "the struggle of the proletariat," "the ruling class," "the victory of the working class," "historical materialism."

Fidel Castro used more direct and more sentimental expressions. His genius lies in his ability to appeal to a woman's heart. The camera showed him making a little sketch on the table in front of him. You couldn't see what he was drawing, but it was easy to imagine that he was sketching out on paper what he was describing over the microphone. He said: "We're going to fit up some beaches for the people. Look, there'll be a beach here." He drew a line across the paper. "You see that line? That's the sea. And this line over here? Beach huts. I can already see these beach huts. They'll be white with sloping green roofs, like the rich have." He sketched a few vertical lines and then some slanting ones. "Close by, here, in fact, we'll build a miniature golf course. Everybody will be able to play minigolf. It's a good game to play. We'll have trees all around, lots of trees. There'll be trees everywhere." He drew some circles and shaded them in. "Fruit trees, of course, so that the kids can go and pick all the fruit they want. Fruit's good for children. It's full of vitamins."

On television, Fidel plays the role of a young lover planning the future with his fiancée. A lot of what he tells her is mere dream talk. The girl is not taken in, but she needs the dream. She enters into it, she imagines as real the lavish descriptions of her fiancé, and ends up with the vine-covered cottage coming to life before her wondering eyes. There's nothing missing, bathroom, spare bedroom, kitchen, nursery, everything.

A professor at Havana University once said to me, "Castro understands the importance of the Cuban woman better than anyone else. He realizes that she plays a crucial role, that her influence in daily life is decisive, and that her power is almost dictatorial. When he makes an appearance on television he gives every woman in Cuba the deliciously guilty feeling that she is spending the evening with her lover, with impunity."

I crept away on tiptoe, leaving Anita, the *muchacha* who never went out without a chaperon, in a tête-à-tête with her *novio*.

CHAPTER 7

The boy who sells lottery tickets in front of the hotel and calls me *"Señor Francés,"* Mister Frenchman, came running up to me with his series of "hundredths" pinned to a large rectangular board. *"Señor Francés,* buy a hundredth. I've got number 25,314. It's bound to win."

"Not just now. I've got to go to Cojimar."

"You going to Mr. Way's* place? Take me with you, I'll show you the road."

"Get in, then."

He climbed into my hired *Aronde,* and lay back with his board jammed between his dangling legs. He kept his eyes on the road with a serious look on his face.

"Put your board in back."

"Don't worry, *Señor,* I'm fine."

* Ernest Hemingway.

"You'll be more comfortable."

"*Muchas gracias.*"

The boy looked a little like those alert urchins you find in the Arab quarters of Algiers. He was small, with a round face and a crop of curly hair. "Don't you go to school?" I asked him.

"I'm on vacation."

"What, already?"

"Of course," he replied, "it's the *Año de la Educación.*" Paradoxical "education year": all the schools have been closed since April 15.

We entered the tunnel, built by a French company in Batista's time, which passes under Havana Bay. At the far end of it starts the highway that leads to the elegant east-coast beaches. I stopped at the toll gate. In exchange for ten centavos a soldier gave me a ticket with a quotation from Fidel Castro printed on the back: "These people are really fine men, the engineers, doctors, and technicians who have not run away, nor betrayed their country, nor sold themselves for the exploiter's gold."

We passed the slopes of *La Cabaña* fortress. Seen from the road it looked ridiculous, a great open space marked off here and there by miles of barbed wire and blockhouses which looked like country railroad stations. "This is where they shoot people," exclaimed my passenger.

A little further on we passed a group of apartment buildings under construction. This "great development project" is Castro's pride. No foreign journalist or visitor is allowed to miss it. He is told right away, "Look what the Revolution is achieving. Decent houses for the workers." All day long, cargoes of awestruck visitors are unloaded from black Cadillacs, guests of the ICAR,* with all expenses paid.

"What's your name?" I asked the boy.

"*Jesus, Señor Francés.*"

"Jesus? like Jesus Christ?"

"*Si, Señor Francés.* I'm called Jesus."

"How old are you?"

"Twelve, *Señor Francés.*"

"What does your father do?"

* Cuban Institute for the Friendship of Peoples.

"He works in a café, *Señor Francés.*" It was his turn to ask questions. "Are there cars in your country, like here?"

"Yes."

"And tunnels?"

"Yes."

"Do the children go to school in your country?"

"Yes."

"All of them?"

"All of them."

"Then you have the Revolution, too."

"No, we don't have the Revolution."

Jesus was surprised. "But if you don't have the Revolution, how come that all the children go to school? If there's no Revolution, there can't be an education year."

"It's not quite the same in France," I said. *"Te gusta Batista?"* I asked him, "Do you like Batista?"

He made a scornful face. "Batista is a shit-eater."

"And Fidel? *Te gusta Fidel?"*

"No me importa."

I was insistent. *"Fidel, te gusta o no?"*

"No me importa!"

We arrived at Cojimar, the village made famous by Hemingway's novel, "The Old Man and the Sea." Pirates used to hide in this part of the coast, which stretches round in a crescent below the mountains. Today the men fish for sharks, which they cut up on the beach only a few steps away from the huts where they live, built of driftwood and old packing cases. The shark's liver is treated on the spot; it's as valuable as cod liver, apparently. The skin ends up in second-hand shops, while the fins are sold to Chinese soup vendors in Havana. The meat is served in cheap restaurants as cod.

I drew up in front of a café. You get a good view of the harbor, like a picture postcard: water, jetty, gently rocking boats, and the old Spanish fort the color of Breton granite.

"You been here before?"

"Si, Señor Francés."

"Has it changed much?"

"Si, Señor Francés. Before, there were a lot of yachts. Mister Way had a beautiful one called *Pilar.* It was big and white. Mister

Way used to moor it here. Sometimes he went out fishing. He would go as far as Jaïamanitas. Did you know Mister Way?"

"No, did you?"

"Yes, I knew him. He was very tall. He had a beard, like Fidel. Only, his beard was white, and Fidel's is black. And then Mister Way had a funny way of speaking Spanish."

There was an old man with a beard sitting on the quay, quietly fishing, holding his line in his hand. Without taking his eyes off the sea, he volunteered the information that Hemingway had lived there and written "The Old Man and the Sea" there. He gave me an accurate resume of the story and ended up by adding modestly, "I'm the old man." Then he shouted out indignantly, "Mister Way never even asked my permission, and yet he made a lot of money out of his story. Naturally. He's like all Americans. He exploited us." As I was about to move off, the old fisherman said, "Give me a *kilo* [peso]. I told you the story."

Ten yards further along, there was another old man with his legs dangling over the quay, fishing in the same manner, who also stopped me to tell the same story. He too assured me in the same tone of voice that he was Mister Way's old man. That cost me another peso. There were at least ten more of them on the quay, all pretending to be Hemingway's hero.

"When there were tourists," explained the boy, "there were many more of them, and they used to make plenty of money. Today they hardly get enough to buy a handful of *frijoles negros.*"

"Why do they have a grudge against Mister Way? After all, they make their living off him, don't they?"

"Yes, but since the Revolution, they can see through the Americans. These fishermen now know that Mister Way exploited them."

"How did they find out?"

"Thanks to the Revolution. I know that too, I learnt it at school."

We started back for Havana. We passed the tollgate and entered the tunnel at 40 m.p.h. All of a sudden, a red light came on, so I braked and stopped. A soldier on guard on the service road came running toward me with a machine gun in his hand. "*Vaya!*"

"I can't," I said. "It's red." I pointed to the traffic lights.

The sentry aimed his weapon at the car. I heard the click of a safety catch, and drove away without more ado.

It's safer not to argue with a soldier in the Havana tunnel. I had learnt that quite recently. A few Sundays earlier, one of them had sprayed seventeen bullets into a French engineer's car. He said afterwards, as an excuse for his nervousness, "The car was backfiring. I thought it was terrorists shooting."

When we got back to the hotel, I said good-bye to Jesus and gave him two pesos, which he politely refused. "You took me out for a ride. That wasn't work."

"Sell me four lottery tickets, then, and keep them for yourself; if you get a winner, you'll be rich."

"If I do, *Señor Francés*, I'll get some gold teeth. I've got an uncle who has two, and he's quite somebody in his neighborhood."

I've seldom met such dandies as the Cubans. They're even keener on jewelry than Eastern peoples. Everybody, whether rich or poor, has a ring, sometimes with huge stones, diamonds, emeralds, and rubies. I should have said "had," for last spring the government started to requisition metals and precious stones. To keep gold is a counterrevolutionary crime. So it is better to have it in your month than on your fingers or wrist. Dentists have never been so busy, and an incredible number of people have gold fillings.

CHAPTER 8

There was a line of housewives stretching along the sidewalk as far as the corner. The women had hard expressions, resigned and pathetic, like Parisian women in the black days of the German occupation.

They were lining up outside a closed store. There was a small opening in the shutter, hardly more than one foot by two. The storekeeper's arm kept on reaching out with a little package which the housewife at the head of the line would take in exchange for a few bills. "Next," said the storekeeper's voice. "Have the right change ready."

I asked one of the women what they were selling.

"Butter."

"Why are you lining up? There's as much butter as you want in Cuba."

"As much as you want? Where's that? Give me the address. It

sounds interesting. I don't have as much as I want. I have to get up at five and be one of the first in line, just to get a quarter of a pound." I didn't dare to admit that in my hotel I left butter on my plate every morning at breakfast.

I wanted to get a picture of the scene, and was just aiming my camera at the housewives when a policeman caught a hold of me. "Your papers?"

"I'm a journalist."

"Follow me," he said.

We went to the nearest café. There was a telephone on the wall by the door. "Do you have a five centavo piece?" he asked me. I gave him one.

He put the coin into the slot, dialed the number, and said, "There's a guy here taking photographs of a line. He's alone, no officials with him. What should I do? You're coming to get him? OK. I'll keep him here."

He hung up. Meanwhile I had ordered a coffee at the counter. The cop pointed his finger at me. "Come here." I paid and went over to him. He pulled out the revolver that was dangling against his thigh. He cocked it with his thumb. "Don't move. Otherwise. . . . Here, give me that camera."

I obeyed. He called the café owner and the clients as witnesses. "You're obviously a spy. Why were you taking photos?" I didn't lose my head, and quietly went on filling my pipe without answering. "Give me that. Spies aren't allowed to smoke."

The waitress began to shout, "*Al paredón el espia*, send the spy to the firing-squad."

"Let's wait outside," I said to the policeman.

"No, you might try to get away. Here I've got people to help me guard you."

"*Al paredón el espia!*" shouted the waitress.

"I wouldn't have left her the change if I'd known she was like that," I said.

The cop came over and poked the barrel of his revolver into my face, then moved it from one side of my head to the other. "Shut up."

"I shall complain."

"No you won't. You'll be shot," he replied.

"*Al paredón el espia!*" shouted the waitress.

An Oldsmobile with a tall aerial skidded to a stop outside the café. Two policemen got out, caught me each by an arm, lifted me off the ground and threw me into the back of the car. The Oldsmobile shot away with a roar. Five minutes later it stopped abruptly on the *Malecón* outside police headquarters. Three years ago Batista's men used to torture Fidelists in this building. Now Fidelists torture the ex-cops.

The two policemen carried me into an office where there was a crowd of people in uniform, all armed to the teeth. They put me on a chair and handcuffed me. Then they gave me a punch in the stomach, two slaps, and another punch in the stomach. "Speak up. Why were you taking photographs?"

"I'm a journalist."

"How long have you been working for the Americans?"

"I don't work for the Americans. I'm French, a French journalist."

"Shut up." Another punch in the stomach. "Come on. How much do the Americans pay you for taking photos?"

"I don't sell photos. I write articles. The photos are to illustrate them."

A couple more slaps and a punch. "Shut up."

Even if I had wanted to speak, I was quite unable to by now. Winded, doubled up, I just tried to dodge the blows. At first I had imagined that things wouldn't go too far, but I was beginning to get uneasy. If the cops went on beating me they'd do me some real damage, and then they'd have to invent a valid reason to justify themselves.

On the wall over the desk there was a clock which showed twenty to eleven. "You'd better be careful," I said. "I've an arrangement with some friends, foreign correspondents. I ring them up every morning at eleven-thirty. If they don't get my call they'll alert the Embassy right away. Be careful. If you keep me here, there'll be all hell to pay."

"Shut up," they all answered. I collected a volley of punches and slaps. I put up a fight, lashed out with my feet. By this time, I thought I would really be finished off.

All of a sudden a miracle happened. The door opened, and in walked a thin skinny man with a gipsy moustache and goatee. I recognized *Comandante* Almejeiras, head of the Havana police.

I had met him three or four days before. A French girl had introduced us in the bar of the Vedado Hotel.

I shouted out to him, "You've got an odd way of treating journalists."

He immediately ordered his policemen to take off the handcuffs. He began to rail at them, calling them idiots and provocateurs. "That's great, what you've done. This journalist will now have plenty to say against the Revolution, and it'll be all your fault."

Almejeiras gave me back my camera and brought me a double whisky. He made what excuses he could. "Mustn't get mad at them. They thought you were working for the Americans." He showed me a copy of *Revolución*. On the front page there was a story about a professional photographer who had been arrested for taking photos of an anti-Castro demonstration. "This traitor intended to sell his pictures to the American United Press agency to be used against Cuba. Yesterday evening he was charged with high treason. He will soon answer for his criminal actions before the judges of the revolutionary tribunal."

As far as I can make out, I was lucky to get off as lightly as I did.

If I hadn't got up early I wouldn't have seen the line of Cuban housewives, nor of course, would I have made the acquaintance of Castro's police.

Cuba suffers badly from shortages. The Cubans used to be the sort of people who stocked up hoards of every conceivable commodity. They stored away everything they could, from gold coins to food. After two and a half years of revolution, their supplies are exhausted. Different articles are beginning to run out completely, one after the other, like a store that has received no deliveries. In the electrical appliances shops, for example, the display windows are gradually being completely cleared out. In some of them there is nothing but empty shelves.

It took me some time to realize the scarcity. It was in the hotel that I first began to wonder. For some days, every time I asked for a beer the barman would reply, "There isn't any beer."

The first time I put it down to the heat. I said to myself, there's been a sudden run on beer. But after a week, I asked the barman for an explanation. "An announcement appeared in the newspapers," he replied. "There's no more beer because the breweries have run out of cork for bottle tops."*

When I left police headquarters, a little shaken, I went to see a doctor. "Who fixed you up like this?" he asked.

"The police." And I told him about my mishap.

"I'm not at all surprised," he burst out. "Castroism is a little shy and tries to conceal its weak spots. While housewives are getting up at dawn to be first in line for a small bar of bad soap, the bathrooms in the luxury hotels are glutted with the finest scented soap. If you have a girl friend you want to give something nice, collect a dozen bars of soap from the soap dishes in your hotel.

"Every evening, my wife, like all Cuban women, wonders what will be unobtainable next? Last week it was razor blades. There is a shortage of milk, eggs, fish, chocolate, beans, cheese, butter, rice, salt, oil. Meat is practically rationed; you can only eat it three times a week."

The shortage of meat is all the more surprising when you consider that before the Revolution Cuba was extremely well supplied with livestock. As for fish, there are 2,500 different species swimming around the island. "Why can't you find any on the market?" I asked.

"Since they have been forced to form cooperatives, the fishermen consider themselves grossly underpaid," said the doctor. "They refuse to work for ridiculously low salaries, far below their former incomes."

"I don't understand," I said. "Wherever I go, in restaurants, hotels, and elsewhere, I eat all I want and as much as I want."

"Of course. You're a foreigner. You pay your hotel bill in dollars. With dollars you are entitled to all kinds of privileges. You're the king of the castle, even in a socialist country."

* A few months later, food rationing was imposed.

CHAPTER 9

Only one table in the Floridita's huge and luxurious dining room was occupied: ours. Each of us was served by a headwaiter, a wine steward, and an army of ordinary waiters.

The proprietor had received us at the entrance and said with a low bow, "Thank you for coming. You're the first guests this week."

Three years ago, before the Revolution, the Floridita was one of the most famous restaurants in the New World. It was something like Maxim's in Paris. Hemingway had made it his headquarters. He used to get there at seven o'clock in the evening, each time with a different crowd of friends. "Behold the daiquiri sanctuary," he would say, gesturing toward the bar with its mahogany bar stools, the row of rum bottles of every brand, the heavy velvet curtains hiding the tall, narrow windows, and the fine panelling, in style and richness reminiscent of Europe at the turn of the century.

The Floridita became a place of pilgrimage for American tourists. They went there in the hope of meeting the author of "A Farewell to Arms." If their idol wasn't there, they had the consolation of admiring his bronze bust enthroned on the bar and of reading the dedications on the photographs hanging on the walls.

"You should have seen the place in those days," said one of my friends. "There was always a crowd spending money like water. Two hundred diners an evening! You had to reserve your table twenty-four hours in advance."

One of the men I was dining with was well acquainted with the problem, being a restaurateur himself, and a friend of the owner of the Floridita. "Please don't interview him," he said. "It would get out sooner or later. Besides, he wouldn't tell you anything. I can describe the situation to you. In the old days, the bar alone would take in as much as 2,500 pesos an evening."

One of the headwaiters was following our conversation with great interest. He was standing beside the table, very upright, with his feet together. After a few moments of hesitation, he said to us, "Phew! Now I can talk. The waiters are in the kitchen. I mistrust one of them. He's in the army." Suddenly becoming aware of the strangeness of his behavior in interrupting us, he began to make excuses. "I am sorry. I gathered that this gentleman was a journalist, and I thought that I could give him some useful information."

"Thank you very much," I said. "You needn't feel embarrassed about interrupting. On the contrary."

"Do you realize that thanks to you, a party of four, we have beaten our record for the month? Last week we had only two, the week before that, two, the week before, none. The first Sunday of the month, there were three.

"The end of tourism has finished off business for us. Perhaps it's in line with government policy, but everybody profited by the dollars the tourists brought in. The really scandalous thing, though, is that nobody is willing to recognize how bad the situation is. We are told to keep going as if business were humming. As a result, every morning we have to throw out all kinds of spoiled food. It would be better to give it away before it got spoiled."

A waiter came out of the door at the back. I warned the head-waiter, "Look out."

"Don't worry. It's only Tony. I've known him for twenty years. I'll get him to come over and talk to you himself. Tony!" The waiter came up with a napkin folded over his right arm. "How much did you make in tips in the old days?" the headwaiter asked him.

"It varied. Clients were more generous on Sundays than on other days."

"How much did you average?"

"Oh, anything from six to fifteen pesos an evening. Sometimes I made as much as twenty or even thirty, but I never went below four."

"And now?"

"I consider myself very lucky if I make twenty-five pesos in a whole month. Things certainly have changed since the tourists left."

"In that case, why does the Floridita keep going? Wouldn't it be wiser to close down and wait for better days?"

"It's not possible," explained one of my friends. "The Floridita is by no means the only one in this position. The Miami has the same difficulties. Their proprietors would have closed down long ago if they hadn't been ordered by the state to remain open. With a full staff, too: headwaiters, waiters, bartenders, cooks, lavatory attendants. They were absolutely forbidden to dismiss a single employee. A waiter left the Floridita the other day. Next morning the Ministry of Labor sent over a replacement to take over his job."

He wiped his hand across his forehead, and looked all round him. The headwaiter reassured him. "The soldier's not there. You can go on."

"We are being forced by the regime to ruin ourselves. When we've got down to the very end of our funds and don't have an-other centavo left, when our savings are completely gone, the State will come to our aid. There is a euphemism which is used in Cuba to describe the action of the Revolutionary authorities in those cases. They 'intervene' for a moribund concern. They don't con-fiscate. Oh no, they are quite content with sequestration; then they don't have to pay indemnities."

No more dollar-producing tourists. For evidence, you don't have to go to the Floridita. A glance around the hotel restaurants, night clubs and gambling rooms is enough. Not a single tourist left. The only foreigners you meet are journalists, experts from Communist bloc countries, and admirers of the Castro regime invited by the government.

There always used to be twenty thousand tourists in Havana at any one time. These twenty thousand men and women, mostly from the United States, brought in an average of sixty million dollars. They arrived by the plane load from Florida, New York, and all the East Coast. Havana was served by forty different airlines. At present, all that is left is a daily service to Miami, and two planes a week to New York.

The government is making vain attempts to revive this source of income. The National Institute of the Tourist Trade (INIT) has come into existence, with its offices in a glass skyscraper on La Linea. Various measures have been taken, some of them extremely clever. For example, there has been a reduction in air fares and hotel room charges. There has even been a decree controlling the composition of restaurant menus. Every restaurant, whatever its category, must offer its clients at least one *comida criolla*, a typical Cuban dish.

In contrast to the intelligence of these measures, there is also indescribable disorder. I spent a fortnight desperately looking for a map of the island. Before the nationalization of the foreign oil companies, Esso and Texaco printed and handed out free colored maps which were very practical. I asked for one at some of the filling stations of the new Cuban oil company, but I always received the same answer, "The authorities came and took them away."

"What authorities?"

"INIT."

I went to INIT, where I was politely received by a young press representative who first kept me waiting the whole morning. "I'm very sorry," she told me. "We have no maps."

"What happened to the Esso and Texaco ones?"

"We burned them in order to remove all trace of American imperialism. But you may rest assured, we are expecting to have some new ones printed."

The day after our dinner at the Floridita, I undertook a little opinion research of my own on the question: "What is the use of INIT if tourists no longer come to Cuba?" I asked the manager of my hotel. He wisely sent me to the head of the Revolutionary Watch Committee. "Ask Lina. She'll know the right answer."

I asked the taxi drivers parked outside the hotel. "*No sé*," they all said.

I called the young press representative at INIT. She seemed surprised. "INIT? Well, INIT is carrying on the Revolution."

On 23rd Street, I asked the representative of an airline. "I don't know what the point of INIT is. I can only say that it has invented a kind of 'negative' tourism. Suppose I'm a storekeeper and my business is going downhill, but for the sake of appearances I want to make a display of prosperity. What do I do? I imitate INIT. I invent a clientele. I invite my relatives and friends, my relatives' friends and friends' relatives all to come to my shop. I give them everything free, charging them nothing, not even reduced prices. My neighbors are immediately impressed by all this activity. They don't realize that I'm eating into my stock and rapidly heading for ruin.

"That is precisely the method INIT has adopted. The hotels in Havana and Santiago de Cuba are empty? Never mind. We'll soon fill them. So all foreign sympathisers are invited. Look at the Havana Libre, the Vedado, the Saint James. Whole busloads of this new type of nonpaying tourists arrive there. Most of them are sympathisers, but there are plenty of spongers who pretend to be Castroists in order to get two weeks of free vacation under the tropical sun."

10

A prosperous-looking villa in Marianao, the good residential quarter of Havana. On the door, a brass plate inscribed DR. PEREZ, ATTORNEY. To one side, a rocking chair. Seated in it, a tall lanky Negro with his tommy gun across his knees, sucking Coca-Cola through a straw.

"Doctor Perez doesn't live here now," he shouted at me, aggressively. "What do you want with him? He was a traitor. He ran away to Miami to escape being shot."

"I was just passing by. It's a nice house. I stopped to admire it."

"You're right, *hijo* [son]. It's a very fine villa. Take a good look at it. It doesn't belong to capitalists any more. It's the property of the people. There's a *comandante* who lives in it. He's a man of the people, like me. Mind, I live here too. Look up there, the window on the left. That's my room. I sleep in it. Yes, sir, in this house built by white men, for white men. And I'm a Negro.

What's more, they feed me, do my washing, and give me sixty pesos a month."

"What's your job?"

"I'm a guard. You can see for yourself. I'm the sentry, keep out all traitors. If I see one I let him have it in the stomach." He took two cigars out of the pocket of his grey blouse. "Take one." He bit off the end of his cigar, spat on the ground, and struck a match. "Sit down," he said, pointing to the step. "We'll have a talk if you've got nothing better to do. Don't go yet."

"Do you like it here?"

"Sure I do. I haven't told about half of everything yet. Besides my room up there on the left, and my washing, my food, and my sixty pesos, I've got a country club card. You got a country club card?"

"No."

"I've got one. INIT gave it to me."

I pretended not to know about INIT. "INIT? What's that?"

"You don't know about INIT? It's an institution working with Fidel to make things better for the people. Thanks to INIT, Negroes don't feel like Negroes any more. They have become white men. See what I mean? Let me explain. I didn't know what it was like to be hungry before. Of course I was hungry, morning, noon, and night. But I was so hungry I didn't realize it. Sometimes I couldn't have told you if I had eaten the day before or not. It was always the same, I was hungry all the time. Hunger, that was something the rich felt. Negroes knew nothing about being hungry and sleepy. Only the rich did. When they felt hungry, they had a meal. When they were sleepy, they just went to bed.

"Since Fidel came along, I've discovered hunger. If I haven't swallowed anything all day, by three o'clock I get that twisting feeling in my stomach. I know I'm hungry because I didn't eat at lunch time. I'm like the rich. I get hungry."

He drew in deeply on his cigar and blew out the smoke in a thin jet. "That's nothing. I don't give a damn if I know about being hungry or not. There's something else much more important. I wasn't a man before. I was a nigger, only the whites were men.

"Before Fidel, I was a shoeshine boy at the Miami. I used to see heaps of marvellous foods every day. Fish in some transparent kind of stuff. I didn't know what it was. Hams like I'd never seen in all my life. The white people took at least an hour over their meals. Sometimes they stayed there for two hours, just eating and drinking. I didn't even give them a glance. I didn't think anything about it. I didn't even wonder if all that stuff was good to eat. I didn't try to imagine how it tasted, that ham sliced off so pretty. I just thought, 'Well, it's not for niggers.' It might have been good or bad. Didn't concern me. I wasn't white.

"I didn't have my pockets stuffed with dollars, or cars as big as houses or beautiful women smelling sweet. I didn't have cameras and new suits pressed fresh and boys to shine my shoes while I ate and drank. I had nothing like that. How could I? I was a nigger. And to prove it, the white folk didn't even look at me. While I was shining their shoes, they took no notice. Sometimes they gave me a coin, without looking. Sometimes they didn't.

"I couldn't say anything about it. How could a Goddamn nigger say anything? If the rich man didn't give me anything, it was best just to say, 'OK, so he didn't want to.' If I did push it, a guy in uniform threw me out, saying, 'Get away, dirty nigger.'

"Then Fidel came along. He said: 'Negroes and white folk are all the same, all of us just men.' I'd already heard the preacher in my neighborhood say the same: 'White folk and Negroes are all the same, all of them just men.' I happened to go into that church by accident. The preacher was giving a sermon. But I didn't believe him. How could I believe him? He said: 'White folk and Negroes are all the same, all of them just men.' But the seats in the church were reserved for the white folk. Negroes were only allowed to stand, near the door, so as not to disturb the white folk.

"When Fidel said: 'Negroes and white folk are all the same, all of us just men,' I believed him. Every Negro believed him. We've got good reason to believe Fidel. The *commandante* comes up to me the other day and says: 'Come on, I'll take you to the Nacional, there's a banquet with Fidel.' You know, I'd never been inside the Hotel Nacional. Negroes weren't even allowed in. I didn't even know what it was like. When we got there, there were other Negroes. All of them said Fidel had invited them because they were good revolutionaries. They stayed in the rich men's rooms. Why, they even had those guys in black tail coats and white ties bringing them their breakfast in bed. They hadn't ever seen that before. They didn't know you could have breakfast in bed. I didn't know that either. Seems it's quite the regular thing for the rich.

"Of course, the guys working at the Nacional, they kicked up quite a fuss. They said that niggers were low-down dirty bums because they didn't give tips. They said that niggers were disgusting because they spat on the floor. That's not true either. I never once spat on the floor in the Nacional. I took care not to, so did the other Negroes. I never even saw one person spit on the floor. Wait, though. I mustn't exaggerate. I saw one, a country hick, spit on the floor. I bawled him out. I said, 'You're a disgrace to Fidel! Behave like the rich do. Don't spit on that floor. Do the rich spit on the floor? They've special places for spitting. You better act like them. Go somewhere else to spit.'"

I thought to myself how clever Fidel Castro was to understand what these sons of slavery wanted, what embittered them. He didn't promise them the earth. He simply said, "You're no longer pariahs. You're men." Such language had never been heard in the West Indies before.

"You know," the sentry went on, "Fidel thought about the women too. He said to the Negro women, 'That's all finished, your old life. You're going to live like the white women.' I've got a sister, Rita. Before Fidel, there were two things she could do, become a maid for white folk, or become a whore. A whore makes as much in one night as five maids in a month, so my mother, she says to my sister, 'You become a whore. That'll mean something to eat for the whole family.'

"You tell me. You're not stupid. What is a whore? Just a girl who gets two or three pesos for saying 'I want you' to a white, even when it's not true. And the white who gives the two or three pesos, and a pack of Camels too, maybe, what does he think? He thinks, 'For two or three pesos any Negro woman will go to bed with you.'"

"Couldn't your sister have found some other sort of work?" I said.

"That's what they all say. But it wasn't easy. Before Fidel, you had to do something if you didn't want the family to starve to death. My sister would've done anything to bring a few pesos into the house. If a white sailor said to her, 'Kiss my ass, you slut, I'll give you five dollars,' she kissed his ass. Why, five dollars was enough to live on for a week. Rita thought it was worth it. Besides, before Fidel, Negroes didn't argue. That's what they were made for, kissing white men's asses.

"Now that's all finished. They gave my sister a job, sweeping up in an office. She's quite happy now."

He gave me his machine gun. "Hold that a moment. I'm going to show you something." He searched through his pockets and pulled out a cardboard folder with papers carefully arranged in it.

"There you are," he said, taking back the gun. "Look at this. It's my country club membership card. I told you INIT gave me one."

"What is the country club?"

"I don't know. I don't give a damn, either. The thing is I've got a card and can go there if I want to. Negroes in the United States, they can't go to a country club. That's reserved for the whites. They couldn't here either, before Fidel. They'd get thrown out. It was reserved for the whitest of the whites, the whites who had more money than the other whites."

"You been to the country club? I've heard there's a fine golf course and a swimming pool."

"Yes, I've been there once. But I didn't go in."

"Why not?"

He hesitated, lowered his voice. "I didn't dare. I thought everyone would stare at me if I went in. It's hard to say to myself: 'Pablito, all that's finished. You're not a nigger any more.' Pablito's my name. Ever since Fidel said, 'Negroes and white folk are all the same, all just men,' I look at myself in the mirror every morning. 'Pablito,' I say, 'Pablito, you're not a nigger any more. You've become a white man. Fidel said so, and Fidel's always right.'

"But as I told you, at the country club I didn't dare. I waited for a long time. I looked at the door and repeated over and over: 'Pablito, you're not a nigger any more. You've become a white man. Fidel said so, and Fidel's always right.'

"I still didn't dare go in. There was a guy at the door who stood watching me with a strange expression. I'm sure he was saying, 'What's that dirty nigger want!'

"Finally I got up the courage. I went to the entrance and I said to the guy there, 'Fidel said that Negroes and white folks are all the same, all of us just men, and Fidel's always right.' 'Fidel's Fidel, and he's always right,' he replied. That reassured me a bit. So I said, 'INIT gave me a membership card.' But the guy never answered. He'd gone to attend to a Captain, a white man who had come in with a blonde.

"So I waited."

"What did you wait for?"

"For the guy at the door and the others to tell me to go in."

"What others?"

"The others. The whites who didn't yet know that I was like them, that I wasn't a nigger any longer."

The sentry finished his cigar, threw it down and crushed it with his foot. "You like Negroes?" he asked.

"When I was at college, I had some friends who were Negroes."

"Tell me why the Americans don't like Negroes. Why do they treat them so bad. I've seen it in the movies. There were American policemen beating Negro women and their little girls and undressing them. One of these days Fidel will go to the States. You know, he's strong, Fidel. Got the Russians and Chinese behind him. The Russians, they're stronger than the Americans. They send guys up to the moon. The Americans can't send guys up to the moon. One of these days Fidel's going to the States. He'll send the war criminals to the *paredón* and he'll say to the Negroes over there, 'You're not Negroes any more. You're white folk.' "

CHAPTER 11

The Gomez family lived on Maloja Street, almost at the corner of Placencia Street, in a district on the outskirts of Havana reminiscent of the back streets you find in some European capitals, with sad dark buildings above which you glimpsed strips of sky that looked poor, dreary, and dirty. It no longer had the same rich blue, the same pure brilliance that it had in the good residential quarters. Their apartment was on the fourth floor of one of these buildings, and consisted of one room and a cupboard used as a kitchen.

I was with *Compañera* Lina. *Bohemia* had sent her to interview the Gomez family who were shortly to be rehoused in one of the new buildings put up by INAV, an organization in charge of slum clearance.

Mrs. Gomez must have been between forty-five and fifty. She was fat, with light coffee-colored skin. She was happily excited

and said to Lina, "You the journalist comrade? Come right in. I'm
going to tell you about the house our beloved Fidel has given us
poor honest workers. Come on in."

She excused herself for receiving us so badly. "In the morning,
you see," she said, "the house is always in a mess. You wait till
we've settled in *there*. Coffee? Yes, come on. What a pity Eulogio's
not here. He'd have loved to talk to you."

Eulogio was her husband. He worked from seven in the morning till six at night in Sears, Roebuck, one of the big American
stores Castro nationalized. As far as I could make out from Mrs.
Gomez's descriptions, Eulogio must have been a porter. She said
vaguely, "He helps, you know. He carries up parcels from the
basement. They send for him when they have to move any furniture. It's a good job; 110 pesos a month."

Suddenly her face hardened. Her conversation stopped short,
and her expression became serious and mistrustful. She nodded her
head in my direction.

"Who's that? The Sears Watch Committee [she pronounced
Sears 'Sayarays'] didn't warn me about his visit."

"He's a Frenchman. I brought him along so that he could see
that the Revolution takes care of the people."

"You were right," agreed Mrs. Gomez. "The Revolution does
take care of the people." She came up to me and looked me
straight in the face. "Would you like me to tell you something?"

"Yes."

"Fidel is my god, my soul, the light of my life. And that's the
truth. When we heard the news about our new house, I said to
Eulogio, 'You know, Eulogio, that I've always been a good wife
to you, and never deceived you. I've always remained faithful. But
if Fidel asked me to go to bed with him, I must admit it to you,
I wouldn't hesitate. Don't be angry. That's how it is.'"

"And what did Eulogio say?"

"Eulogio is like all men. He can't help contradicting. He replied, 'Fidel won't ask you to go to bed with him. He doesn't need
you. He's got all the young girls he wants.'"

Mrs. Gomez passed from her husband to her children. She had
five: a girl of sixteen and four boys between the ages of fifteen
and ten. "What a shame they're not here," said Mrs. Gomez.
"The *chicos* would have loved to see you. But they're a long way

away. They joined the Conrado Benitez Education Brigade, all
except the youngest, that is. They've gone to the Oriente to teach
the peasants to read and write."

I looked around. Everything was small, poor, and old. But everything was clean and well-kept. The white calico curtains with a
red flower pattern had been washed and ironed recently. On the
floor, black and white tiles formed a checkerboard design and
shone brightly. The sofa, which was covered with a tartan rug and
some yellow cushions, must have been used as a bed at night.
There wasn't any running water, and Mrs. Gomez explained how
she had to go out into the courtyard to fetch it.

"In the new house," she said, "there'll be a bathroom. A real
bathroom with a shower and chromium taps. There won't be a
bathtub, though. Eulogio says that bathtubs weren't meant for
workers. They're for the capitalists' wives. Eulogio says that capitalists' wives don't have baths in water but only in milk. I wonder
what they do to smell so nice. Milk doesn't have a very nice smell.
Anyway, we'll show you the bathroom when we've settled in, and
the three rooms, and the cupboards. There are going to be cupboards everywhere, in all the rooms and in the kitchen.

"We won't have a garden. Eulogio is very disappointed about
that. He wanted to plant a mango tree, one or two banana trees, an
avocado tree, and flowers. He wanted lots of flowers. But the head
of the Watch Committee told him, 'Your apartment will be on
the fifth floor. A garden with a mango tree, banana trees, and an
avocado tree on the fifth floor? Quite impossible.' It's a shame.
You can't have everything in life, a fine house *and* a garden, can
you?"

Mrs. Gomez sat opposite Lina and me, on the other side of
the square, slightly rickety table. She joined her hands together
and looking upwards said:

"*Fidel, Fidel! Que Hombre! Que Hombre!* But for Fidel we
would still be living like pigs, without hope. We've lived here ever
since our marriage seventeen years ago. Before the Revolution, we
paid thirty-five pesos a month. Fidel ordered the rents to be
halved. Now we only pay seventeen-and-a-half pesos. I said to
Eulogio, 'It's like a pay raise.' "

Lina interrupted her to remind me that one of the regime's
first measures was to slash the rents by 50 per cent for all under

100 pesos a month. "The price of electricity, water, and gas was also considerably reduced. These measures were all taken as part of the urban reform plan. The INAV sequestered all apartment houses. The tenants will become owners within ten or twenty years."

"With full ownership?"

"Of course."

"Will they be able to transfer their apartments, sell them, or rent them out."

"No."

"Then it won't be full ownership."

"Fidel has promised to solve the housing problem in less than two years. Soon 150,000 houses and apartments will be under construction."

"I've looked at the official statistics," I said. "Only 6,000 new homes were built last year. That's a long way from the promised 150,000. It's also far short of the pre-Revolutionary figure of 40,000 per year."

"You can say what you like. The urban reform is a wonderful achievement. It finds decent homes for the workers. To have a home, you need only be Cuban and over twenty-one. You've also got to work of course, in order to have the necessary funds to pay the contribution."

"Contribution?"

"Yes, that's what we call rent in a socialist country. And in order to apply for a home, you have to present a health certificate to prove that you're not infected with any contagious disease, and also a certificate of good conduct."

"Where can you get one of those?"

"From the head of the Revolutionary Watch Committee."

Mrs. Gomez still didn't know when she would be moving. The new building was not yet under construction. The head of the Watch Committee at Sears, Roebuck had merely told her husband, "Comrade Eulogio, I have to inform you that you will receive an apartment on the fifth floor of a building which is going to be built by Fidel in the Eastern suburbs, on the other side of the bay. Your name appears in a list to that effect published this morning in *Revolución*."

Mrs. Gomez declared that she was in no hurry. She didn't

mind waiting now. Of course, she would have been terribly pleased if the move was to have taken place next day or next week. At any rate, she knew she would have her house. It said so in *Revolución*.

"*Revolución*," she said, "is Fidel's paper, and Fidel is always right."

Lina agreed. "The proof that you will have your house is that we're here interviewing you."

"That's right," said Mrs. Gomez, "I will have my house. It said so in *Revolución*. It wouldn't have been in the paper if it weren't true. Three rooms, a bathroom, and a toilet. Yes, there'll even be a toilet, like the rich people have in Marianao. Please excuse my talking about that sort of thing. But toilets are perfectly natural, aren't they? And there's no need to be ashamed about mentioning them in a modern country like Cuba. All the same, please excuse me."

Mrs. Gomez referred to the toilet as the *excusado*, so her excuses were slightly comic.

I asked Mrs. Gomez to tell me about her family life before the Revolution. "Things were very bad."

"Did your husband earn less than at present?"

"No, but he spent more. First of all, the rent. Thirty-five pesos is a lot of money. And then there was the *bolita*. Eulogio used to gamble. Every evening when he got off work with his friends, he would buy whole books of lottery tickets. He never won. He used to lose at other games too. He would lose one, two, or even five pesos. I remember one Saturday when he lost twenty-five pesos. Twenty-five, can you imagine?

"There was nothing to be done about it. It was no good lecturing him. Every evening, when he went to bed he would say, 'I didn't have any luck. But don't worry, I'll end up by winning. I have a fool-proof system, it's only a question of mathematics. I'll win. You wait, I'll come back one day with a whole bagful of thousand peso bills. We'll buy a house at Marianao, and a car, and television, and fine new clothes.' He even said that he would go to the best dentist in the *Vedado* to get some gold teeth. Luckily, Fidel came along and kicked out that swine Batista. He put an end to gambling. He was right to forbid the people to gamble. That *bolita*, you know, it's worse than a man who's always drunk."

"That swine Batista." Everybody in Cuba, whether great or small, rich or poor, everybody says that. I did not meet a single person who said anything different, "That saint Batista," for instance.

"That swine Batista" has become part of the Revolutionary liturgy. Pious Arabs, when they speak of the dead, say, "Peace be unto his soul." When Cubans speak of their ex-dictator, they piously say, "That swine Batista." "We have to," a storekeeper on Galiano Street told me the other day. "If we just said 'Batista,' we would risk being taken for sympathizers of the old regime."

It's easy to heap abuse on someone who has been defeated. So I will not pass judgment upon the former sergeant who became dictator, but stick to material facts, both tangible and irrefutable. Batista had transformed Havana into a *rue Pigalle* on an American scale. All vice records were surpassed: fifty thousand women gave themselves over to prostitution, thirty thousand men drew their incomes from gambling. Havana, in fact, was a gambling den and a brothel. To these figures should be added the thousands of pimps and dope peddlers, the Chicago gangsters wanted in the United States, but well established on Batista's island. They carried on their racketeering quite openly, and in broad daylight, practised all kinds of crooked activities considered illegal in other countries.

The dictator and his large family found these racketeers extremely useful on more than one occasion. It was they who organized gambling, of which Batista's relatives held the monopoly. His brother-in-law, Roberto Fernando Miranda, lived off slot machines. These machines, which worked like bottomless coffers, became an integral part of the Havana decor. They occupied a prominent place in all public buildings. Ministries, hotels, railroad stations, public toilets, and post offices had to have at least one of these machines against their walls.

Mrs. Batista merely appropriated the lottery profits to pay off her monthly accounts. There were several *bolitas*: the "national," which had a draw every day, and the so-called clandestine ones, put out by the Chicago gangsters who gave Mrs. Batista a cut.

Corruption under the old regime reached a pitch which the most corrupt Arabian Sheikh would never dare imagine. The construction of the tunnel under Havana Bay cost the Cuban budget twice the real price. The difference found its way into Batista's secret strongboxes. When the Dominican Republic borrowed a million dollars from Cuba, the negotiator, Batista himself, pocketed a hundred thousand dollars commission. Considering, no doubt, that his country owed him something by way of reward, he also had the interest on the loan paid into his personal account.

12

Fidel Castro has a large number of relatives in Havana. In the telephone directory a whole column is devoted to his family. You can find Fidel's brother, Raúl, commander in chief of the Revolutionary Army, Emma, one of his sisters, Ramón, one of his brothers—all complete with addresses and telephone numbers. But if you try to call them up, there is either a busy signal or no answer.

With a little luck, however, an obstinate journalist ends up by meeting a lawyer, teacher, or doctor who will put on a conspiratorial air and whisper in his ear, "If you want to speak to a close relative of Fidel's, I can quite easily arrange it." In this way, I interviewed crowds of cousins, uncles, and aunts, all of them authentic. Each time I demanded proof, and each time I was shown incontestable documents, after which only a few discreet enquiries were necessary for verification. From this enquiry emerged a remarkable portrait of Fidel.

I had always believed that the leader of the Revolution was the son of a good family who rebelled against the bourgeoisie. This is far from the truth, and it explains his attitude of revolt.

Fidel Castro was born on August 13, 1926, on his father's *finca* at Mayarí, a small town in Oriente Province. Up to the age of twelve or thirteen, he was "the bastard," the illegitimate son whom everybody despised. His father, Angel Castro, did not marry Fidel's mother, Lina Ruz, until after the death of his first wife. Lina was his mulatto servant and could not refuse to share her master's bed.

Angel was a Spaniard from Galicia, who had come to the island in 1898 to fight against the Cuban rebels. After his country's defeat he left the army to avoid going back to Europe. He joined the Nipe Bay Company (affiliated with the United Fruit Company) as a manual laborer. At this point, there are two different versions. One cousin of Fidel's told me, "Angel worked for the Nipe Bay Company for seven years. He was dismissed for stealing sugar." Another said, "Angel was certainly accused of theft, but it was a mistake. The real thief was another Spaniard."

At any rate, after seven years of work Angel found himself a rich man. He bought an estate, and shortly afterwards profited from the troubles that broke out in Oriente Province. Two rival clans joined open hostilities. Angel gathered some men together and offered his services to one of the factions. During the campaign, he seized the possessions of his side's enemies. He also made use of circumstances to enlarge his estate, to the loss of the American planters, by shifting the boundaries.

Angel's first wife, a schoolteacher, bore him two children, Lidia and Pedro, who, as frequently occurs in such cases, hated Ramón, Fidel, Raúl, Emma, and Juana, the offspring of an affair between their father and a servant. One of Fidel's sisters confided to me, "Our half brother and sister treated us as intruders. They called us 'bastards.' Fidel and Raúl have harbored a deep resentment against them. It is one of the reasons why they expropriated a large part of the family fortunes. They have had their revenge.

"From his earliest days, Fidel has regarded himself as a pariah, a proletarian. He hated our father, and never ceased plotting against him among the workers on the *finca*. He used to repeat to them: 'You are being odiously exploited by that *latifundista*

Angel Castro. I am ashamed of being his son. Rebel against him. Once, he even succeeded in fomenting a strike.

"Our father was afraid of him. He expected to be murdered any day. He used to say, 'If it's not my son who kills me, it will be one of his friends.' He never went out without slipping a revolver into his belt."

After attending the parish school at Mayarí, and later the Jesuit College at Santiago, the capital of the province, Fidel was sent to Havana, to the Jesuit Fathers of Belén (Bethlehem). Belén College was situated in a fine park in the Vedado district, and before the Revolution was one of the smartest establishments in Cuba, a kind of West Indian Eton. All the aristocratic families sent their sons there.

The Fathers were difficult to get hold of for an interview. "We are at the mercy of the government's anger," their director told me. "The soldiers on guard at the door have only to mention your visit to cause great trouble." A friend to whom I explained my difficulty solved the problem by inviting Father Z., one of Fidel's teachers, to have lunch with him.

To avoid attracting attention, he came dressed as a layman. I should like to describe him, for he was a splendid man, but one of the conditions of the interview was that I respect his anonymity. "Fidel has already had me put in prison several times," he explained bitterly.

My own father was a teacher and I know that he often considered his pupils as his children. Their behavior toward him delighted or pained him almost as much as that of his own children. The same was true of Father Z. He was no longer a young man, and he spoke wearily, sighing between sentences. In spite of his bitterness, it seemed to me that in his heart of hearts he still felt indulgent toward Fidel. "He was my pupil," he murmured. I may have been mistaken, but when the old man uttered those four words, I thought he betrayed a mixture of pride and shame.

When my father said, "He was my pupil," I know that he experienced either great joy or infinite sorrow. He felt himself responsible for his students' successes and failures. In the first case the phrase meant, "This boy is a great credit to me." In the second, it covered up a kind of self-accusation, "No doubt I didn't do all I should have for him. *Mea culpa.*"

Father Z. seemed divided between these two apparently con-
tradictory feelings. "He was my pupil," he repeated, "a very good
pupil. He was first in his class in everything, history, literature,
mathematics, science, even in sports. Unfortunately he had some
serious failings, but I don't think he can be entirely blamed for
them. I've seldom known a personality so riddled with complexes.
He had, at all costs, to be head of every prize list, and when,
through some mischance, he was placed second it made him sick.
When he first arrived, and wasn't yet getting top marks, he would
do anything to draw attention to himself. For example, in the
middle of a lesson he suddenly began tearing up his books. He
tore out the pages one by one, cut them into little pieces, dropped
them in a heap on the floor and set fire to them. It's all very well
being lenient, but there are some things you cannot tolerate in
a class. But nobody dared to remonstrate with him, because his
tantrums inspired the whole college with terror.

"One day he all but killed a monitor who had the nerve to
forbid him to smoke. On another occasion a teacher went so far as
to send him out of class, and Fidel shouted, 'I'm going to get my
revolver and finish off that lousy priest.' It was not an empty
threat. Half an hour later he came back brandishing a weapon,
and if his school friends hadn't practically knocked him out, the
Father would certainly have been murdered.

"On several occasions we thought about sending him home, but
we felt so sorry for him. He had fits of depression which changed
him into a shy, unhappy little boy. He can't have been quite right
in the head. There were certain words which it was inadvisable to
use in his presence. 'Bastard,' for example, sent him off the deep
end. Once he said to his friends, 'I'll show you what a bastard can
do.' He grabbed a motorcycle belonging to one of the college employees and rode it full throttle against the courtyard wall, a stone
wall two feet thick. The poor boy was in a coma for five days."

On leaving Father Z. I went to see Doctor T., an old friend of
Fidel's who had fought with him in the Sierra Maestra. At the
beginning of the regime Fidel had given him a high appointment
in the new administration. I had first met him at a friend's house,
and had then asked him why he had quarrelled with Castro and
left the government to go back to his patients. "Don't ask me
that," had been his reply. "One day you will understand it all

without my having to explain." I had the feeling that now was the moment T. would give me the explanations I wanted.

I found the doctor in his clinic. "I have been talking to Father Z. He's told me some fantastic things, and I'm expecting you to tell me the rest."

"Let's go back to my place for a drink. We'll be able to talk there."

T. lives alone in a modern apartment in Havana. "I thought it better to send my wife and children away," he said. "You can never tell what may happen these days."

While getting the bacardi-and-sodas, T. asked me, "Did Father Z. tell you the story of the motorcycle and the wall?"

"Yes."

"Then you know everything. Fidel Castro is not normal, medically speaking, I mean. He suffers from logorrhea, a syndrome characterized by a disordered flow of words. This complaint is the result of the shock he sustained at Belén College. Don't forget that he remained in a coma for five days.

"To that must be added his heredity of alcoholism. His father, Angel, was a brutish soak. When he first started as a planter at Mayari, his favorite pastime was shooting at Negroes as if they were so many rabbits. He terrorized the whole area. He was drunk from morning to night and would draw his revolver at the least provocation. Having such a father marks a child."

I asked the doctor, "Why did you leave Fidel?"

"I didn't want to remain with a man capable of declaring war on the United States at any moment. Why do you think the Russians refused to supply him with Migs? They realize that Fidel might suddenly, in a fit of temper, set off a world war by bombing Miami.

"I was there, behind the scenes, at Fidel's televised broadcasts. At the beginning he behaved normally. But after seven or eight hours of speaking he was no longer in control; his reactions became quite automatic. He stammered and made such incoherent remarks that they could easily have caused a catastrophe.

"Raúl Castro and Guevara always ended up by intervening. They had the broadcast stopped without asking his opinion, and literally dragged him away from the camera. He would let himself be carried out without resisting, reacting, in fact, just like an epileptic. Now, logorrhea is a form of epilepsy."

At the age of nineteen Fidel enrolled at Havana University. His mother urged him to become a lawyer. "We need to be able to protect our fortunes against the covetousness of our neighbors," she would say. In fact, the planters who had been dispossessed by Angel during the troubles of 1917 brought several suits against the Castro family.

Doctor T. knew Fidel during this period; I let him continue his reminiscences. "By tradition, the students at Havana have always meddled in politics. They are forever talking politics and from time to time they stage demonstrations, but for all their noisiness they do little damage. The arrival of Fidel had the effect of transforming this turbulent tendency into violence and rioting.

"From the very first Fidel asserted himself by his great height—over 6 feet—his great strength, and his eloquence. He used to speak for several hours on end."

Doctor T. began to laugh. "It's funny," he said. "It all suddenly comes back to me. Fidel had a curious method of attracting attention: he was filthy. He never washed, wore stained and tattered old clothes, never went to the barber, and only shaved now and then. During lectures he used to take his shoes off and proudly display the dirtiest feet you could possibly imagine. He used to put them up on his neighbors' desks and say, 'Have a sniff, you sons of bitches.' We used to call him 'mud pie.'"

"Why didn't he take care of himself?" I asked. "Didn't he have enough money to buy decent clothes and get a haircut?"

"Yes, his mother sent him 200 pesos every month. The other students weren't as rich as that, but it didn't prevent them from taking a weekly bath."

T. looked at his watch. It was after nine o'clock. "Let's have dinner together," he suggested. "I have an idea. I'll call up my friend Doctor B. He knows Fidel better than I do. They were in politics together at the university."

We met at the Centro Vasco. "It's a good place to go to for the sake of one's reputation," said T. drily. "Rolando Cubela, Che Guevara, and other notables of the regime often come here for a daiquiri at the bar."

The two doctors and I sat down in a corner of the room. "B.," said Doctor T., "you must tell us about Fidel's exploits at the university."

"Fidel," he began, "was possessed by boundless ambition. He was always saying that he would become president of Cuba one day. He also used to say that he had no time to lose, that to succeed in politics you had to start as early as possible."

Doctor B. spoke in a low voice, in French, as did Doctor T. No one could hear us. On sitting down, my friends had casually passed their hands under the table to make sure there were no hidden microphones. "They are in fashion just now," said T. "For the last few days government employees have been turning up at all the embassies, ostensibly to check up on the telephone wires, but actually to install microphones."

Doctor B. told me that he had studied medicine while Fidel Castro was doing law. "We went out together on several occasions," he said, "we carried on an intrigue for control of the Federation of University Students [FEU]. Fidel's ambition in 1947 was to become president of FEU. But he had a rival, Léonel Gomez, an intimate friend of the President of the Republic, Ramón Grau San Martín. Do you know what he did?"

"No."

"Well, Fidel did away with Gomez. He shot him with a revolver in Ronda Street, just around the corner from the university."

"I knew that Fidel had had one or two people killed. But I thought they were political assassinations of Batista's partisans."

B. and T. grinned. "The murder of Gomez took place four years before Batista's entry into politics." B. went on with his story, speaking emphatically, underlining his words. "And Manolo Castro? He wasn't a Batista man. Why did Fidel bump *him* off, do you think?"

"Who was that, a relative of Fidel's?"

"No, he was president of FEU. He hated Fidel. He said that you couldn't be sufficiently on guard against him. For several weeks Fidel, and this was the true Fidel, openly declared his intention to kill Manolo. He ended up by doing so—once again out in the street."

The next morning I was awakened by the ringing of my room telephone. It was Doctor T. "Can I see you right away?"

"Sure. What's up?"

"Nothing. Get dressed quickly. Go downstairs and leave the hotel. Start walking up the Avenue of the Presidents. I'll pick you up on my way by. Hurry."

There was certainly the smack of the thriller about it. After last night's disclosures I couldn't help feeling just a little bit uneasy. At any rate, I had no time to ask questions.

Ten minutes later, as I was walking along the avenue, a car came up from behind me close to the sidewalk. The front right-hand door opened. A hand reached out, seized me by the arm and drew me inside. T. was driving. Behind him sat a young girl. "I hope no one was following you," said T., stepping on the accelerator.

I reassured him. "I came out without an escort, as if I were going to buy a paper." But I was beginning to grow uneasy. "What's happening? Where are we going?"

"You'll see." We turned off to the right, went down 17th Street as far as the Paseo, then to the right again. At 7th Street we turned off to the left and went straight on, crossed the river Almendares and drove along a double highway. T. said nothing, neither did the girl.

She was quite a pretty blonde. She wore a tiny black cross on her breast.

"What's that?"

"The badge of the members of *Acción Católica*."

We passed through the residential quarter of Miramar and went round a traffic circle. To the right was the entrance of the Yacht Club. To the left, a large building with two huge signs, one above the other. The top one said, CINODROMO, the other, PATRIA O MUERTE! VENCEREMOS! A little further on, we turned off to the left. Doctor T. asked me to forget where he took me after that.

We stopped in front of a tall narrow villa, two stories high, with a flat roof. A white-haired man opened the door. It was D., head of one of the anti-Castro organizations in Havana. T. had spoken to me about him the evening before. He had said, "Castro would pay a lot to get his hands on him."

There was no beating about the bush. D. showed me a long typescript, the résumé of a document 269 pages long that was extremely compromising to Fidel Castro. The information it contained had been compiled by S. Diaz Versón, editor of the newspaper *Información*.

On January 11, 1959, the son of one of the men associated with Versón met Castro in the Havana Hilton. He disclosed to him the existence of this ultra-secret document, which, if published, would have proved beyond doubt the collusion between Castro and the Communists. One hour later, Fidel summoned Carlos Rafael Rodríguez,* Luis Más Martín, Luis Fajardo, the Escalona brothers, and Jorge Quintana. He briefly told them what he had just learned. They decided to raid *Información*. The raid took place on January 24, 1959, at dawn. All the records of the newspaper were seized and destroyed. But the 269 pages marked A-943 had somehow been spirited away.

I knew of their existence. But I did not think I would ever get the chance to read them. Here are some extracts:

> On April 17, 1943, Mr. Maxim Litvinov, the new Soviet Ambassador, arrived in Havana. A few months later, he was replaced by Mr. Andrei Gromyko. With him came one hundred and fifty Soviet officials.
>
> Among them was a certain Mr. Gumer W. Bachirow, who spoke Spanish perfectly and had spent some time in Spain during the Civil War. Mr. Bachirow did not take up residence at the Soviet Embassy, but in a small isolated house in Miramar, a district some way out from the center of Havana, at No. 6, 2nd Street.
>
> Very soon, his house became the meeting place for a number of young Cubans; among them were Fidel Castro, Manuel Corrales, Luis Más Martín, Baudillo Castellanos, Eduardo Corona, Antonio Carneado, Jaime Garbalosa, Juan Bradman, Jorge Quintana, Flario Ortega, Arquimides Poveda, Augustín Clavijo, Raúl Valdes Vivo, Antonio Núñez Jiménez, Alicia Alonso, Oscar Camps, Walterio Carbonell, Alfredo Guevara, Abelardo Adams, and René Baldomero Alvárez Rios.

I ask the reader to forgive this long list of names. Some of these people—not to speak of Castro himself—now hold important posts at the very core of the Revolutionary regime. Antonio Núñez Jiménez, for example, is director of INRA; Alfredo Guevara (not

---

* Member of the Central Committee of the Cuban Communist Party, editor of the Communist daily paper, and in 1962, appointed President of the National Institute for Agrarian Reform.

to be confused with Che) runs the Cuban Institute for Friendship among Peoples.

The document goes on:

> In the middle of 1944, Bachirow left for Moscow. He came back to Cuba a few weeks later with fresh instructions to have his young friends worm their way into the bourgeois political movements.
>
> On February 2, 1948, Mrs. Frances Mackinnon Damon, an American from Honolulu, treasurer of the World Federation of Democratic Youth Movements in Moscow, landed in Havana with $50,000. Bachirow introduced his friends to her. The next few days were devoted to discussions.
>
> On February 25, the Miramar group was reinforced by a truly international delegation: Vassili Bogarew (President of the Soviet Youth Movements), Jaroslav Boucet (Czech), Luis Fernández Juan (a young Spanish Communist), Eugène Carboul (French), Ivan Mischine (another Russian), and Milorad Pesic (a Yugoslav, member of the Cominform, holding a French passport).

This gathering was motivated by the forthcoming conference of the Organization of American States (OAS), which was to take place on April 9, 1948, at Bogotá, Colombia. Its central theme was to be "the denunciation of Communist activities in Latin America." Bachirow and his friends were given the task of preventing this conference from taking place by provoking riots in Bogotá. They appointed three men as a commando force for organizing sabotage.

> A short time later, this force, consisting of Fidel, Alfredo Guevara, and the trade-unionist Lázaro Peña, landed at Bogotá airport. They went to the Claridge Hotel where they signed in as "students." They immediately made contact with the local Communist Party activists, and gave them some leaflets that had been printed in Havana, and also some weapons.
>
> On April 3, the President of Colombia, Doctor Ospina Pérez, and his wife were present at a performance in the Colón Theater. At about ten o'clock, shortly after the beginning of the third act, the audience was showered with leaflets. Castro and Peña were arrested by the police and taken to the police station. When the head of police asked them their reasons for demonstrating, they replied, "We want to unite Latin America." The head of police told them, "Foreigners are forbidden to meddle in the internal affairs of

Colombia." Castro and Peña promised not to do this again, and were then released.

On April 9, at midday, a former leader of the Colombian Communist Party, Jorge Eliecer Gaitán, who had been accused of deviationism, was assassinated right in Bogotá's busy commercial center. The murderer was a pale young man. Witnesses had seen him in conversation with Fidel Castro and Lázaro Peña a few hours earlier.

The crowd went wild with anger, and seized and lynched the pale young man. At that moment some agitators accused the government of having perpetrated the crime. The inhabitants of Bogotá rushed off to storm the presidential palace. The rioting lasted for several days and spread to the whole of Colombia. Dozens of buildings were burnt and churches were sacked. More than a thousand people died, including several Catholic priests. Castro, Peña, and Guevara took refuge in the Cuban Legation, from which they made their escape to Havana.

The document notes the following facts:

On their return, Fidel Castro and Lázaro Peña boasted of having actively taken part in the rioting and shooting. Castro even claimed that he had personally dispatched two priests.

Bachirow congratulated them. They then asked to be sent to Czechoslovakia, but only Guevara's request was granted. Shortly afterwards, Fidel Castro sent a post card to Abelardo Adams saying, "Our friend has told me that I am being kept here for more important tasks. So there is no question of my going abroad for the moment."

At the end of 1951, the electoral campaign was at its height. The document goes on as follows: "Fidel Castro and Eduardo Corono, who had joined the Orthodox Party at the instigation of Bachirow, put themselves up as candidates. They held their meetings in a hall at No. 109, Prado."

Doctor T. clarified a historical point that I knew already. Everybody in Havana, in fact, is aware that Castro and Batista knew each other before the beginning of the Revolution. They had all but collaborated together. In 1951, they met in order to coordinate their respective projects. Batista was running in the presidential elections. Castro, undisputed leader of the student organizations, hoped to become a deputy. The elections were to take place on June 1, 1952.

T. told me, "The Batista-Castro interview took place in the country, on the Premier's *finca*. My family acted as go-between. Fidel was then twenty-five, and hadn't started wearing his famous beard. Batista was fifty-one. A tough, squat little man, with his swarthy skin, sharp eyes, wide nostrils, prominent lips, strong jaw, and wide forehead, he looked like a boxer."

The two men had a cordial interview. Fidel agreed to support Batista, who, in return, promised to give the young man an important post in his administration. Fidel wanted to become Minister of Education. But all these projects of his came to nothing. Batista was running against Doctor Carlos Heira, a Havana engineer, the nominee of the Authentic Party, which was then in power. The Orthodox Party had nominated Doctor Roberto Agramonte, Professor of Sociology. In spite of all his efforts, Batista realized that he would be beaten. The public opinion polls agreed that Agramonte would win so he decided to take action.

On March 10, 1952, at 2:43 P.M., Batista, accompanied by sixteen men, made his way to the Columbia military camp on the outskirts of Havana. He gathered together a number of young officers and noncoms, and there and then promoted them to colonels and captains. With their help, he captured staff headquarters. A few hours later he had Havana under his control, while President Carlos Prío Socarrás fled to Miami. Batista announced that Congress was dissolved and proclaimed himself Head of State.

A short while later, on April 3, the new dictator broke off diplomatic relations with the USSR. The 150 officials at the Soviet Embassy immediately left Havana, but Bachirow waited until July 14. He went to Mexico, where, according to D.'s document, "He was joined by Fidel Castro. Fidel travelled with a false passport under the name of Castillo Ramírez. He stayed in Mexico for one month, and then went back to Havana."

Hardly had he returned before Fidel told his friends, "Batista is a traitor. He cheated me, but I shall make him pay for it." He brought an indictment before the Court of Injunctions in Havana, accusing Batista and his accomplices of having violated six articles of the Civil and Penal Code. He demanded the application of the law which required heavy prison sentences. Naturally, the indictment was rejected.

"Since I cannot get satisfaction through legal channels," Fidel Castro announced, "I shall use other means."

He organized a band of two hundred young men. Nobody knows where the necessary funds came from for the purchase of arms and ammunition. One thing is certain, as D.'s document makes clear. Bachirow refused to finance the affair. It seems that the Soviet agent was afraid of the young lawyer's reckless bravado. Castro wrote to his brother Raúl, who was at that time studying in Prague, "B[achirow] advises us to procure the necessary arms and funds ourselves. He says that the U.S.S.R. does not want to become involved in the events about to take place in Cuba." Now, this letter was intercepted by Western secret service agents, who were already beginning to take an interest in the activities of the Castro brothers.

On July 26, 1953, after having assembled men, equipment, and money, Fidel launched an insane attack on Moncada fortress, situated at the entry to Santiago de Cuba. One hundred and sixty men attempted to take the island's second largest fortress by storm and overpower the thousand soldiers defending it. Part of the plan was that if they succeeded they would seize the armored vehicles there and make straight for the radio station from which Fidel would call the people to rise in revolt against Batista's dictatorship.

The inexperience of the attackers and the tactical blunders of Fidel and his brother led to a lamentable failure. A lot of young people died even before being able to fight, others fell into the hands of the Batista forces, who tortured and then summarily executed them. The others were captured within the next few days.

Fidel and Raúl escaped into the mountains nearby, where the two brothers were tracked for several days by the police, the army, and the air force before finally separating. Fidel was captured by a patrol one evening while he was sleeping. Lieutenant Sarria, the patrol commander, recognized him. While searching him he whispered in his ear, "Don't tell me your name. I've got orders to kill you." A short while later Raúl gave himself up.

In the normal course of events, the two brothers would have been shot. It was what Batista wanted. However, Monsignor Péres Serantés interceded for them.

On September 21, 1953, Fidel, Raúl and 120 of their comrades appeared before the Oriente Tribunal. Fidel was sentenced to fifteen years of hard labor, Raúl to thirteen, and the others got lighter sentences.

They were sent to the penitentiary on Pine Island, where at first they were put in solitary confinement. Gradually, however, their conditions were eased. On May 15, 1955, Batista reprieved them all. Fidel went back to Havana and remained there for several months. That same July, he went into exile, flying to Mexico, where his brother was awaiting him.

13

"There's only one person who can tell you the rest of Castro's story," said D., "and that's Bayo. He's one of the VIP's of the Revolution. Fidel gave him the highest rank in the army, *co-mandante*, and all the honors that go with it, an aide-de-camp, a personal bodyguard, a state Cadillac with chauffeur."

"Where does he live?"

"At Tarará, a very nice sea resort on the road to Varadero. Bayo has set up a curious kind of school for guerrillas across the road from his house. Guerrilla warfare is his specialty, you see."

"Do you think he'll be prepared to receive me?"

"Possibly. If he doesn't take to you right away, he'll shut up like a clam, but if he likes you, he'll tell you some really astonishing things, all of them true. He loves publicity. In fact, that's the one thing Fidel Castro and Che Guevara don't like about him."

I went to Tarará. When I entered Bayo's office, he was sitting behind a wide table in front of a window and looked up at me with his one eye. I wondered whether D. hadn't been exaggerating. How could this bald, corpulent little civil servant with his trim goatee have been the brains behind a revolution which (whether we like it or not) must be considered as one of the most successful of our time.

Bayo stood up to receive me. He wasn't very tall. He looked middle-aged and harmless. I introduced myself, and taking the bull by the horns I said, "I've been told that you know Fidel better than anyone."

He screwed up his eyes, and I noticed his long, dark thickset eyebrows. They looked as if they had been stuck on haphazardly, like pins into a pincushion. "Who told you that?" he enquired suspiciously.

"Everybody in Havana is talking about you and your exploits. I've been told that without your advice and assistance Fidel would never have been able to defeat Batista."

He burst out laughing, clasped my hand, and shook it. "It's true," he replied without false modesty. "I'll give you a copy of one of my books, called 'My Contribution to the Cuban Revolution.' I'll also give you a collection of poems I wrote during our struggle against the dictator. Its title is 'Fidel is waiting for you in the Sierra.' Suddenly he clapped his hands to his bulging stomach and asked me, "Do you like omelettes?" Although surprised, I replied that I did. "That's good, because I haven't had lunch yet. Follow me."

We went into the kitchen, where a lieutenant in the rebel army uniform was making coffee. Bayo introduced me. "My son Armando. He's a hero. He bombed the capital of Nicaragua and really scared that swine Trujillo."

Bayo spoke French fluently and colloquially. I complimented him on it. Since leaving Paris I had hardly once heard colloquial French and it was a pleasure for me. Bayo explained that he had been to school for a while at a French college belonging to the Christian School Brothers.

He put a huge frying pan on the electric ring, tossed in some butter, salt, and pepper, and broke six eggs. Then he stirred it all up with a spoon. While scrambling the eggs, he told me the story of his life. He came from a long line of Spanish soldiers. However far back you went in his genealogy, you found nothing but captains, colonels, and generals. His father was an artillery colonel. "We were five brothers," he said, "all five of us officers. Célestin was a pilot. He was killed in the first air accident that occurred in Spain. Alfonso and Henrique fought for Franco, and the two youngest, Joaquín, who was killed in Madrid, and myself, fought against Franco."

He burst out laughing again. Armando, who didn't understand French, asked his father to explain. "I was telling him that two Bayos fought *with* Franco, and two *against* him," he replied. "Ha! Ha! Ha!" Armando also roared with laughter.

"I was born in Cuba on March 27, 1892," Bayo went on. "My father was on garrison duty at Camagüey at the time. I went back there the other day and discovered our old house, a Spanish baroque residence. They've turned it into a museum. In this hemisphere, people will go and visit any old shanty provided it's more than fifty years old. After Spain lost Cuba, we went back to Europe and I finished my studies there. At twenty I became an officer, and at twenty-four I got my military pilot's certificate."

His outrageous behavior soon got talked about. "I was considered a Republican officer, an enemy of the King and of the clergy." The so-called omelette was ready, so we sat down at the round mahogany table.

"You're pretty comfortable here," I said.

"It was Fidel who gave me this villa. It used to belong to one of Batista's cousins. I wish I could find out where he is now. I should like to send him a thank-you card. After all, that's the least I can do. Five rooms, kitchen, air conditioning, icebox, telephone, it deserves a card, doesn't it?"

Bayo did the honors. He brought over the frying pan and doled out large spoonfuls of omelette. He took big mouthfuls, resting his elbows on the table and talking with his mouth full. He told me about his quarrels with the Spanish general staff. He was sent to Morocco in command of a squadron, and spent his time bombarding Spanish, French, and Italian newspapers with letters. He used to write, "Our mission is a disgusting one, to destroy the rebellious villages of the Rif. We are sent to blind and kill villagers."

Bayo was relieved of his command and had to go back to Spain. There he won fame on account of a duel. It was the tradition in the Spanish Air Force for the young officers to ravish any girl they fancied. One day, a captain got into a rage at a lieutenant guilty of such an excess and had him arrested. Bayo, himself a lieutenant at the time, provoked the captain to a duel and sent him off to the hospital for twenty-eight days. Bayo promptly found himself under arrest and in prison.

"I was excommunicated as well," he said. "The Church disapproved of duelling. A few days after my imprisonment, a cardinal, the Cardinal of Madrid, came into my cell. Without uttering a word he began showering me with holy water. 'What the hell's the matter with you?' I said. 'Are you trying to take the piss out of me?' The Cardinal said nothing. He began to chant away in Latin, and finally said to me, 'My son, now you are a Catholic again.'"

Two months later, luckily for Bayo, some generals came to inspect the prison. They lined up the prisoners in the courtyard and asked the usual question, "Any complaints?"

Everyone said "No," and the generals, fully satisfied, were just about to leave when Bayo stepped forward. "Might I ask what I have done wrong? I fought a duel and got sent here. If I had refused to fight, I would have been dismissed from the service as a coward. You are senior to me, tell me what I should have done." The next day, Bayo got back his freedom and his rank.

However, as he had to be punished, he was transferred to the Spanish Foreign Legion, the famous *Bandera*. "I went to my new regiment surrounded by a kind of romantic glow. My commanding officer, Colonel Franco, gave me a hero's welcome." But relations between the future *Caudillo* and Captain Bayo rapidly deteriorated. They were soon accusing one another of being publicity seekers. Bayo kept on bombarding the newspapers with his poems, while Franco was making sure he got all the credit for his officers' successes in the war they were fighting in the Rif.

"One day," said Bayo, "I recaptured a hill that was held by some Moroccans. Colonel Franco watched operations from a distance, through field glasses. He sent a message to the General saying, 'I, Colonel Franco, have captured the hill.' That evening I had an omelette cooked and sent off to the General with these words, 'Colonel Franco wishes to announce that he prepared this omelette himself.' Punishment: I was confined to barracks for one week and threatened with court-martial."

The story of the hill and the omelette was to have unforeseen consequences. When General Franco set off the Civil War in 1936, Bayo without hesitation took up arms against him. Bayo was put in command of an expedition whose mission was to retake the Balearic Islands. He landed on the island of Ibiza with three thousand men, liberated the poet Alberti and his wife, Maria Theresa Leon, and went off to Majorca, which he occupied without firing a shot. "Unfortunately," he told me, "the Fascists had some artillery. I lost four hundred and twenty men at the first landing. Italian aircraft came and bombed us in Majorca. That made me angry. I asked the Republican high command to allow me to bomb Rome. There was no reason why we shouldn't. They had damn well dropped some bombs on us. But the government was frightened, and gave the stupidest order of the whole war. They told me to evacuate Majorca and Ibiza immediately. The Fascists soon took advantage of that piece of stupidity to set up an air base there. Until then they didn't have anything you could call a base."

Bayo then became adjutant to General Batet, who was later shot by Franco's troops. He was in command of airfields and of the Air Legion, composed of French, English, and American squadrons.

It was during the Spanish Civil War that Bayo discovered guerrilla warfare. He had already noticed in the Rif that small bands of rebels, who knew the terrain and all the tricks of their special kind of warfare, could hold at bay a whole army stronger and better equipped than they. He realized that the Republicans would lose the war unless they changed their tactics. Between two campaigns he wrote a book in which he predicted, "We won't win the war with tanks and aircraft and guns, because the enemy is better equipped than we. Let us change our methods at once and form bands of guerrillas."

The Republican general staff did not appreciate the book. "Captain Bayo has gone mad or else he has turned traitor. Wanting to send men behind the enemy lines! Might just as well wave a white flag!" Once again he found himself under arrest. He took the opportunity to write another book, which the general staff simply confiscated.

His theories were finally accepted. Just before the end of the war, he received orders to train one hundred guerrillas and co-

ordinate their missions. The results went beyond all hopes. A whole
Fascist company was wiped out at the very first ambush. Bayo was
promoted to major and then colonel, and asked to form more
units. But it was too late. Franco was winning on every front.

After the fall of Madrid, Bayo went into exile, more embittered
than ever. "If they'd listened to me in time, we would have won,"
he said. "In all those three years of useless fighting and stupid
palavering I gained absolutely nothing. On the contrary, I lost my
right eye from a shell burst."

After finishing the omelette, Bayo said to his son, "I'm still
hungry. What else is there to eat?"

"Do you want some jam?"

"Good idea. I love jam. Now, where were we? Ah, yes. I know,
in exile. I went to Toulouse first. I lost my temper with the Republican leaders who had landed us right in the shit, all through
their own damn fault. I called them a bunch of old windbags. They
didn't like that very much. I told them they could feel grateful I
didn't knock the hell out of them. So after that I had to find a new
place of exile. I went back to Cuba, which I'd always considered
my second home. Besides, my mother being Cuban, I had plenty
of uncles and aunts living on the island. They were extremely rich.
They were lukewarm in their reception of me. Yes, they were willing to help me, but I would have to stop being against Franco. I
told them they could go to hell."

To earn his living Bayo was prepared to do anything. He peddled
books from door to door, wrote poems which he sold in the streets
of Havana, took walk-on vaudeville parts, composed love letters for
shy young people. "Was it then that you met Fidel Castro?" I
asked.

"No, he was only a kid in those days. Hold on, I'll get there
soon." After several months Bayo got a job as a teacher in a religious college in Havana. He was then earning $50 a month. It
didn't last long, though. In fact, after compulsory mass every
morning, Bayo used to start off his lessons by blasting the clergy.
"The priests," he would say, to the amazement of his pupils,
"should all be shot. They excommunicated me, the dirty swine!"
The parents heard about it from their children, and protested. So
Bayo was asked to leave.

He decided to try his luck elsewhere. He took his wife and two children with him to Mexico, where other Spanish Republicans had taken refuge. Thanks to these companions in misfortune he managed to secure a job as night porter at $8 a month. He then had the preposterous idea of writing a letter to the Republican government in exile. "I am at present earning my own living, $8 a month. It's not exactly a bonanza, but it's something. No use your continuing to help me. Just send me a certificate to say that I'm a good, honest Republican."

Bayo was just getting ready to bite into an enormous slice of bread with butter and jam, but he suddenly leapt to his feet and burst out with, "Do you know what those skunks wrote back? Those sons of bitches, those traitors! They said, 'Be content with the work you've found. Other Spaniards haven't been quite so lucky. You're an optimist. Bravo! Take care not to lose your job.' The sons of bitches! I wrote them another letter, and this time I said, 'You bunch of swine! Aren't you ashamed of keeping me in a job like this, me an air force colonel sunk to the level of night porter at $8 a month? You bunch of swine! Keep your lousy money and may you rot with it!' That's what I wrote them."

Shortly afterwards, the officers of the Republican army in exile in Mexico met and unanimously promoted themselves to the ranks they should by rights have held, had things been normal. Bayo promoted himself to General. "Then I should call you General?" I said.

"If you like, but I'm also a Colonel in the Mexican Air Force and a General in Costa Rica, as well as *Comandante* in Cuba. Shortly before World War II the Mexican Government appointed me professor of aerodynamics and aerial navigation at the Guadalajara air school."

So things were looking up for Franco's rebellious ex-subordinate. But he didn't enjoy Guadalajara. "I was depressed by the thought of becoming bourgeois. I wasn't doing the job I was meant for. I'm first and foremost a specialist in guerrilla warfare, and a revolution-maker. The Caribbean was infested with dictators, little *caudillos*. I was itching to knock them down one after the other, like ninepins. I was just waiting for somebody to come along and say, 'Come on, we're going to clean up Somoza or Trujillo, anyone at all, I didn't care."

One morning at the beginning of 1945, a Nicaraguan, Juan

Antonio Mesa, got General Bayo into action. "I want to overthrow the Somoza regime. I've read your books on guerrilla warfare. Would you like to train some men for me?"

Bayo accepted. He took three months' leave "for personal reasons." Arbenz, the Guatemalan Minister of War, put a plane at Bayo's disposal. He flew to San Jose in Costa Rica and set up his "school" in barracks where he began training the 276 future invaders of Nicaragua.

Everything went off satisfactorily until the day when Argüello, one of the leaders of the plot, who was supposed to give the signal to launch the attack, went over to the other side, complete with all the plans for the invasion. "I've since had my revenge," exclaimed Bayo. "I've told all about Argüello's dirty trick in a book."

As always happens in Latin America, there was just as much fighting with words as with bullets, and the Somoza agent responded with another book in which he portrayed Bayo as an adventurer with a strong thirst for money.

The Spaniard then took the offensive by publishing a book of poems. This literary battle is still going strong. The two enemies continue to bombard each other regularly in verse and in prose.

"That's Fidel and me in Mexico," said Bayo, showing me some faded yellow photographs. "He didn't have his beard then. That's Fidel and my eldest son. That's. . . ."

"How did you first meet?"

Bayo took a cigar out of his shirt pocket, and lit it while I filled my pipe. He took a few puffs and, in a nostalgic, almost pathetic voice, told me the story of his amazing Cuban adventures.

One evening he was out taking a breath of fresh air on the terrace of his little suburban house in Mexico. He was smoking a cigar just like the one he was smoking now. It was pleasant. The sun had set and a light breeze caressed his face.

Fate approached him in the shape of a tall tough-looking character. "Excuse me. I hope I'm not disturbing you," said the stranger. "My name is Fidel Castro. You may, perhaps, have heard of me. I directed the attack on Moncada fortress at Santiago de Cuba."

Bayo's voice softened. The rough guerrilla fighter could not conceal his emotion. "Fidel was like a shy little boy," he went on. "I used the familiar *tú* in speaking to him, and he answered very respectfully, like a pupil speaking to his teacher.

"But after several minutes a transformation took place. He began gesticulating, his voice rose. 'You were born in Cuba,' he said. 'So you're Cuban. It is your duty to help us.' He wanted to overthrow Batista. His plan was simple: to fit out an expeditionary force with ships and men, to make a landing in Cuba and oust the dictator. He had come to me for advice and help."

The General would have been ready to undertake this new adventure. But first he decided to question the young man. "Do you have money?"

"Not a cent," answered Fidel.

"And men?"

"No, none."

"*Hijo*, I'm ready to do anything you say. But you've got to be sensible about it. You find some men, and I'll take care of their training, I promise you."

Fidel overflowed with gratitude. "Thank you, thank you, both on behalf of myself and of the millions of Cubans who are waiting for me to liberate them. I'm going to the United States. I'll find men there, and funds, and equipment. As soon as I have them— about seven or eight months from now—I'll come back and see you." The two men shook hands and Fidel disappeared.

Less than a year later, Fidel Castro was back again. "I've been around all the Cuban colonies in the United States. I've attended thousands of meetings and discussions. I've recruited eighty-one men, all courageous and determined, and I've collected $80,000."

Bayo began to laugh. "Fidel got money from everyone. He had even managed to get $50,000 out of that stupid fool Carlos Prío Socarrás. Prío Socarrás believed that Fidel would give him the presidency if he won. 'Pinching $50,000 from an s.o.b. is not theft,' said Fidel. 'It's a good deed.' "

The General became serious again. "After that," he went on, "we talked of important matters. I explained my ideas on guerrilla warfare in greater detail. I didn't want Fidel to imagine that with his band of eighty-one men he would be able to defeat Batista's army with its tanks, airplanes, and guns." Bayo told Fidel, "Listen to me, *hijo*, if you try to fight against Batista's troops in the open, you will last a day, a week, or perhaps even a month. But you'll be defeated.

On the other hand, if you're willing to follow my guerrilla tactics, the war may last for a year or two, but I guarantee that you'll win."

"I trust you, General. Here's $3,000. Find us a training area, I'll take care of the arms and equipment."

General Bayo had no difficulty in finding a ranch. It was called Las Rosas; forty miles of it, jungle, marshland, and cliffs high up in the mountains, not far from Mexico City. The owner wanted $36,500 for it.

"I told the owner that it was catastrophic." To describe the scene, he got up, took out his handkerchief and pretended to cry. "There I was, planning to turn the ranch into an orphanage. I cried my eyes out the whole afternoon, from two o'clock till seven. At sunset, the owner, quite dazed by my words, let me have the place for $1,000. In the end I was sorry I hadn't pressed him further. He would have finished up by giving *me* money."

The telephone rang. Bayo picked up the receiver. "*Patria o muerte, Venceremos!*" he said. "*Comandante* Alberto Bayo speaking." His face lit up. He repeated two or three times, "*Bueno, hijo,* I'll expect you." As he hung up, he said triumphantly, "You're in luck. My best pupil at Las Rosas, *Comandante* Ernesto 'Che' Guevara, is going to drop in. He'll be able to help me along with my memories."

A guard came in with a coffeepot and two cups, which he put down on the table. Bayo poured out the coffee. It was greyish instead of black and had a strange taste. It's usually better in Cuba.

Bayo went on with his story. Toward the middle of 1956, Fidel Castro and his eighty-one men moved to the ranch. The firearms soon followed. There were rifles, U.S. carbines, heavy and light machine guns, mortars, and plenty of ammunition. "We had enough to arm a whole division," Bayo shouted.

"Why so many firearms for so few men?"

"The guerrilla fighter must learn how to handle every kind of weapon."

"How did you get hold of all those rifles and machine guns?"

He laughed. "The Caribbean is an inexhaustible reservoir of weapons. With money, you can buy anything you like, even jet bombers, tanks, and naval vessels. It's merely a question of dollars."

Life at the camp was run with rigid discipline. The men slept on the ground to prepare themselves for the hardships of the *Sierra.*

Bayo was the only one who had a bed, and felt quite guilty about it. "It was an old bed," he said. "At first I didn't want it. I offered it to Fidel, but he turned it down. He reckoned a leader shouldn't enjoy any special privileges. He also said that being the instructor I should take my sleeping seriously."

Reveille was sounded at five in the morning. The day began with cleaning up the quarters. Then the men washed, and after they had eaten a very frugal breakfast Bayo took them over for the rest of the day. First of all, he gave them a short speech. He recited the poems he had written the previous evening before going to bed, in honor of Fidel Castro, guerrilla warfare, and "high ideals." He spoke of a partisan's duties in the jungle. The first was that he should not risk his life without good cause; the second, springing from and qualifying the first, that he must always be ready to face the supreme sacrifice.

"The guerrilla fighter," he told them, "is like the man Littré talks of in his Dictionary. If he wants to lead a meaningful life, he must behave as though he had a long life before him, and yet discipline himself as though he were to die the next moment."

After the theory, they got on to the practical side of training. They learned to make bombs, blow up bridges and buildings, care for and transport the wounded, swim, run, climb, jump, squat in a hole for hours on end without moving, and march through the jungle and over the mountains without being seen or heard, but without ceasing to listen and observe. They studied a thousand different ways of harassing the enemy, of lowering his morale and of setting up ambushes.

Fidel found that the training was taking too long and grew impatient. "All this instruction is no doubt very useful, General, but when are you going to start teaching us how to advance under enemy fire, make an assault or an organized withdrawal?"

Bayo replied, "*Hijo*, I would be only too pleased to train your men like soldiers belonging to a big army. But there'd be no point to it, since you don't have a big army: eighty-one men. If I gave them the training you want me to, they would be killed in the first engagement. Let me do it my way. Soon each one of them will be worth a battalion."

"Perhaps you're right," agreed Fidel, "but I'll tell you frankly,

I don't like your kind of war. It's a coward's war; it's sly, all this hiding and striking below the belt."

"Don't forget, at Moncada you insisted on making a frontal attack, you were nearly two hundred strong, and you came off pretty badly."

"Well, you're the pro," admitted Fidel. "I'm only a beginner."

There was a discreet knock on the door. "*Comandante* Guevara has arrived." Bayo got up and left me alone for a moment. He came back with the man who is known everywhere, even in Havana, as the brains behind Fidel Castro, his evil genius, the *éminence grise* of the Revolution. He had the characteristic long hair and shaggy beard of the guerrilla fighter.

A few moments before, Bayo had told me that the *barbudos* had been ordered to shave. "I'm the oldest of the *barbudos*," Che later explained. "The order doesn't apply to me."

He held his black beret rolled up in his hand. He wore the usual olive green uniform and paratrooper's boots. There was a Luger hanging from his belt. He was a small, calm man, shrewd and disquieting in conversation. His voice was soft but firm. "Who's he?" he said, pointing to me.

"A friend. He's a journalist who's interested in our story."

Guevara had a rather sad, almost imperceptible smile. He nodded in Bayo's direction and said, "He's the most remarkable fellow I've ever met. At Las Rosas, our training camp, he was the toughest of us all. Throughout those interminable marches he made us do, he'd always be up front with his pack on his back and a rifle slung over his shoulder. Eight, ten, sometimes even fourteen hours of marching was quite a strain, even on young men of twenty-five like us. For Bayo it must have been a feat of endurance each time."

"I may be remarkable," said Bayo, "but Che is the best fighter I know. He's a real leader. When I gave out the grades after three months of training, he got the highest. With A's in every subject, he was easily the best."

"Better even than Fidel?" I asked.

"Fidel's name never figured in the grade lists. For one thing, you don't give grades to a commander in chief, and besides, Fidel couldn't be there for all the training. He had to slip away from time to time to get additional funds and more weapons."

I tried to get an interview with Guevara, but he excused himself. "I've got to leave, I'm in a hurry. Ask Bayo. He knows all about me, even more than you'll find in the American newspapers."

Bayo saw him to the door, and when he came back he said, "What a man! Just imagine, he's only thirty-four. Do you see what a simple man he is? He drives his own car. He doesn't like having an escort. We had to insist a good deal before he would agree to have two armed soldiers riding in the back seat. There are so many people who would like to get rid of him."

"Where does he live?"

"Not far away. He's got a villa by the sea, just as nice as mine. He uses only one room, furnished like a monk's cell. There's a cot, a closet, and suitcases; that's all you can see when you go in. The place is always in complete disorder. There are weapons, clothes, and cigarettes lying around loose everywhere. His cleaning woman takes two hours every day to tidy it all up.

"When he's not at home, he's the most efficient man in Cuba. He gives orders in that quiet voice you heard just now, and tolerates no disobedience. He would have his closest relative shot for failing to carry out an order.

"He was born in Argentina. His father was of Spanish origin, and his mother of remote Irish ancestry. His father had eccentric ideas: he was determined to give his son a Spartan education. He had read all about it in some book or other. At noon in midsummer he would give the kid ice cold baths; and he really did put ice in the water. There were enough crazy ideas to kill him, but Che didn't die, he just became asthmatic.

"Guevara had often told me how hard it was to be an asthmatic child. He felt inferior and humiliated by it. He used to tell me what a terrible disease asthma is. He was liable to get an attack at any moment. He was mad about football, and had to give it up.

"One day when he was trying to pick up a girl in a bar in Buenos Aires, an American sailor came along and proceeded to make advances to her. Che, who was then only eighteen, flew into a rage and they had a fight. According to what he told me, he would have won but all of a sudden he had an attack of asthma and had to lay off. I think he has hated Americans ever since."

Bayo picked up his drink. "Che is a truly remarkable character," he exclaimed. "I made no mistake when I gave him the best grades. It was Che who directed all the operations in the Sierra, set up secret workshops for repairing weapons and making bombs, organized supplies, trained the new recruits."

"Tell me, how did the first Castro landing go?"

"None too well. Fidel and his men embarked on November 25, 1956, on board the yacht *Granma*. According to the plan, they were to make a landing near Niquero, west of Santiago de Cuba. A friend, Crescencio Peréz, was to meet them with a hundred partisans and some trucks and guide them to Manzanillo, where other rebels would be waiting for them. Sympathizers were going to throw a few bombs in the streets of Holguín, Matanzas, and Santiago, in order to create a diversion."

That was the plan. But it didn't work out. The yacht was far too small, having been built to carry only eight men, crew included. As it was, eighty-one men were packed on board with their weapons, ammunition, food, and explosives. To make matters worse, the sea was against them. *Granma* ran into a storm. As the pumps were not in good working order, the ship began to take in water and almost sank.

On November 30, D-day, Fidel and his partisans were tossing about on the sea, seasick and still a long way from Niquero. They learned over the radio (they were able to receive but not transmit wireless messages) that the groups on the island had gone into action.

Finally, on December 2—after they had spent several precious hours fishing out the pilot, who had fallen overboard—the yacht ran aground only a few miles out of Niquero. The shore was close at hand, but because of the rough sea they had to leave behind their food and medicine and a considerable amount of equipment, including the mortars and heavy machine guns.

It took them four hours to reach dry land. "I don't know where we are," said Fidel, "but don't let's hang around. It's daylight already, and the yacht is going to give us away. We'll make for the mountains." They marched by night, hiding and resting during the day. On December 5, they stopped at a plantation to buy food. At this moment, enemy aircraft swooped down on them. They tried to hide in the sugar cane, but the aircraft strafed the whole area with machine gun fire.

After the all-clear, they took a count of survivors. There were only twenty-two men left, many of them wounded. Guevara had a bullet in his neck.

Fidel divided his force into small bands. "If we stay together we will all be massacred," he said. "We'll meet up on the mountain." Only twelve men reached Turquino, the highest peak in the Sierra Maestra. Among them were Fidel and his brother Raúl, Guevara, and Camilo Cienfuegos.

After having rested and recovered from their agonizing experiences, these twelve guerrillas started really fighting their war. Bayo had advised them to get on good terms with the peasants. "Make sure you pay for everything you take from them in cash. Promise them a better future if they help you."

One morning, Fidel Castro heard about a landlord who was guilty of cruelty. He had him arrested and tried before a court-martial, which condemned him to death. From then on, Fidel and his comrades were looked upon as the bosses of the Sierra Maestra, where almost everyone was more or less on the wrong side of the law. In order to demonstrate to the peasants that his own men were not being given preferential treatment, he did something really amazing. He accused one of his comrades of having made pregnant a young peasant girl who used to supply the rebels with food. A court-martial was held, and the "guilty" man was executed there and then by the other eleven before a crowd of villagers who had come to watch the proceedings.

Meanwhile, Batista was losing his head. Instead of realizing that he needed a milder policy, he spread terror. Murders, kidnappings, and torture became everyday events. In order to make a stronger impression, he ordered the newspapers to publish photographs of his victims, who were generally shown castrated with their testicles in their mouths. With every fresh outrage and execution, more sympathizers joined the little band in the Sierra Maestra. Fidel even had to turn volunteers away. "Go home," he said, "organize sabotage groups in your towns, make bombs, blow up the jails, the barracks, the army dumps, and the ministries." Soon these men spread panic throughout Batista's camp.

By February, 1958, Fidel was in control of the Sierra Maestra.

He christened his "kingdom" the Free Territory of Cuba. He set up a broadcasting station, Radio Rebelde.

On August 21, 1958, Fidel started carrying out a plan which Bayo had recommended in a letter. He ordered Guevara and Cienfuegos to take 250 men and open a second front. They split into two columns and descended from the Sierra by night, so as not to be spotted by aircraft. They crossed the plains of Camagüey Province, occasionally fighting a skirmish.

On December 31, the day that Raúl Castro seized Guantanamo, Cienfuegos' forces joined Guevara's at Santa Clara, the capital of Las Villas Province. Suddenly, without ever having been really defeated in the military sense of the word, Batista's army collapsed, and the war came to an end.

On January 1, at ten past two in the morning, Batista made a hurried escape from Havana in an airplane.

14

"You'll never understand how bad the Yankees really are, the dirty skunks!" Ernesto Che Guevara said to me one day. "They've behaved like bastards toward us. They've stuck a knife at our throat and told us, 'Every spare part for cars or airplanes, every grain of rice or drop of gasoline that you buy from us you must pay for in cash and in dollars. No dollars, no cars or airplanes, no rice or gasoline. Go to the Russians for them, or rot without them.' "

I was relaxing with a daiquiri at the bar of the Nacional when the "dictator" of the Cuban economy came up in his quiet, careless manner, escorted by two bodyguards. "*Que va, Francés,*" he shouted. "Drinking alone?" I asked him to join me, and as he had five minutes to spare he accepted. "But it's only a friendly conversation," he said, "not an interview. Che's opinions are not necessarily those of the government, and in no way commit the regime. If you write, 'Che said the Yankees are all bastards,' nobody will be surprised, nor will anyone give a damn. But if you write, 'Ernesto Guevara, Minister in the Cuban Government, said the Yankees are all bastards,' that'll really shake things up. You've no idea. The Swiss representative who looks after United States interests will go and see the Minister of Foreign Affairs. The Minister of Foreign Affairs will summon the French Ambassador. The Ambassador will throw up his hands and shout, 'What can I do? I don't know this journalist.' It'll cause crowds of people to waste whole days in useless discussions."

I asked him what he was doing at the Nacional. "There's a banquet," he replied. "I'm attending a banquet. Ever since our victory I've been going to banquets every day. You'd never believe it. I used to think a banquet was a way for lazy ministers to kill time. Not at all. It's work, and an odd kind of work too. The people who come to banquets expect a speech, and they all want to hear something pleasant." He shrugged his shoulders. "*Que va, Francés!* I'd be only too glad to tell them something nice. I'd like to be able to say to them, 'You want the moon? Well, it's all yours.' But I can't. Because of the Yankees, all I can offer them is blood, sweat, and tears."

He took a sip of his daiquiri. The crystallized sugar formed a sparkling pattern round the rim of his glass. "Do you know something?" he went on. "If it weren't for the United States, things would be a lot better on the American continent. It is they who prevent us from completing the Revolution. They keep on playing dirty tricks on us. From the very beginning, I told my comrades, 'You must be mad to trust the Americans.' Most of them didn't believe me. They answered, 'The trouble with you is that you think all Yankees are the same. They're not all bastards. Plenty of them are nice fellows.' Some added, 'The reason you don't like them is because you're a Communist.' "

"And what did you reply?"

"The United States is a decadent nation; they have the same ideas as their great-grandparents. They're puritans, they're stupid, and they're vicious. Finally, and this is the most important point, they are behind the times. History is progressing more and more rapidly. At first, the United States and history moved forward hand in hand. That was in Lincoln's time. Afterwards, at first imperceptibly, then more and more swiftly, history left them behind.

The United States is like a straggler from an army on the march. At every step forward his comrades leave him a little further behind. The Yankees have had it. They'll never be able to catch up with history. Others have taken their place at the head of the column."

"What others?"

"The Russians, for example. The Soviet Union is a quarter of a century ahead of the United States. Today it is the Soviet Union that is setting the pace. What sort of figure does Kennedy cut with his Cape Canaveral, which seems to have been built for nothing but Hollywood gossip columns? What does de Gaulle look like, shooting two rats a hundred miles into space? It's like a movie. Have you seen the picture 'Ben Hur?' "

"No."

"Nor have I. But a friend in Mexico saw it and told me about it. It reminded me of Cape Canaveral: the same extravagant scenery with plenty of money, plenty of publicity, and plenty of actors. And what is there left at the end of it all? You go to the movies, you sit down, and then you come out again without having gained anything at all. The Russians, they don't say much, but they send up sputniks as big as two Cadillacs to fly millions of miles round the world.

"Take another example. For the last six months, the Yankee papers, which seem to be written for senile old men, have shown nothing but photographs of their future astronauts. Did you see yesterday's papers? The Russians, they really sent their cosmonaut into space. That's what history is. It's not a Hollywood movie with 'Ben Hur' and Elizabeth Taylor."

"Why do you dislike the Yankees so much?" I asked Che.

"It's complicated. I've never liked the Yankees. Bayo must have told you about my fight with the sailor. He's a great guy, Bayo, and he's fond of me. He's sure to have told you about that fight. It was a good one. That sailor was pretty strong, stronger than me, probably. But I knew how to fight."

As Guevera talked about it, his eyes began to blaze, his face contracted, he ruffled up his hair and clenched his fists. "I was a good boxer. I'd learned in the streets, with the other kids. When you're brought up in the streets, you know, you learn how to fight. The sailor was stronger than I was, but none of his punches were effective. He just circled around me, stupidly, stretching out his arms. I punched him in the chest and back, and kicked his shins.

"Suddenly, that damn asthma got a hold of me. It's like being strangled, asthma. You can't breathe or do anything. It's worse than being hit in the belly. Suddenly I doubled up, gasping for breath. That s.o.b. of a sailor took advantage of it, to get on top again."

I suggested having some more daiquiris. "All right, a quick one," said Che, "then I've got to go."

"You don't turn anti-American just because of a fight with a sailor," I said.

"*Francés*, a Latin American can never be anything but a mortal enemy of the United States."

"Why?"

"Because the Yankees are colonialists. They reduced the whole of the Caribbean, Central America, and almost all the rest of America to the status of colonies."

"But what, in fact, have they done to the Cubans?"

"It would take hours to go through all the lousy lowdown things they've done. You ought to read 'Listen, Yankee.'"

"I've read it."

"Weren't you convinced?"

"Not quite."

"Why not?"

"C. Wright Mills tries to explain the Cuban affair," I said, "by putting all the blame on the United States. Of course, they made some grave mistakes. But you can't deny that it was thanks to the United States that the Cubans won their independence. From 1898 to 1902, they helped Cuba become a nation. They set the economy on its feet when it had crumbled after a long war, they built roads, developed the railroads, fought epidemics. . . ."

Guevara interrupted me. "Above all, they reduced Cuba to the status of an underdeveloped country. They kept Cuba enslaved. You must realize that, *Francés*." Ernesto Guevara swallowed his daiquiri at one gulp, and wiped his moustache on a paper napkin. "I've got to go off to my banquet now. Goodbye, *Francés*." He shook hands with me, climbed down off his stool and took a few steps toward the door. He turned and came back.

"Listen *Francés*." To understand the Cuban Revolution, you

did not need to come all the way over here. You could have gone to Algeria. Cuba and Algeria have many things in common. They are both enslaved countries fighting to break the chains of colonialism. The United States is just as dumb as any other colonialist power. They didn't realize that history was advancing in spite of them, against them. Imperialists should read Lenin and Marx. They'd find out the true meaning of history."

"What do you mean by history?"

"History is revolution on the march. History, *Francés*, is stronger than the United States, France, and England, stronger than Wall Street and the United Fruit Company. It strides forward relentlessly and sweeps away the old cant of the past. Today, anything that is not young and new is rotten through and through. Think of that, *Francés*, and tell yourself that all of you, Yankees, French, English, and Belgians, you're all rotten. And when you're rotten, it means that you're dead and buried. So long, *Francés*."

Che gave me a strange smile. I looked at his black eyes, as round as a cat's. He knitted his brows, deepening the furrows on his forehead. With his beard and long hair he might have been Mephisto plotting some fresh evil.

Perhaps he was just making fun of me.

An hour later, I met W. again, a South American economist who had come to make a study of Cuba. I told him about my meeting with Fidel's right-hand man. "Of course he was kidding you," he said, when I had finished. "He was making fun of you, just as he's been doing with everybody for the last three years. Che is one of those adventurers who will be remembered in the future. If he had lived three centuries ago, he would have been a pirate, right here in the Caribbean. Danger holds no terrors for him. He's not interested in wealth. He is after power. He has a superior intelligence and to gain his ends he makes use of every means at his disposal. His favorite is irony. Even the wiliest old hands find his mockery disconcerting. There are plenty of businessmen, up to every trick in the business-world jungle, who are intimidated by this comedian with his Bohemian manners.

"Guevara has perfected an infallible technique. He receives his visitors with a complete lack of formality. He unties his shoes, puts his feet on the table, cuts his fingernails, scratches his back, plays with his revolver, and flirts with his secretary. Meanwhile the Ambassador is making an effort to state his case, and Guevara lets him talk. Then, all of a sudden, just when he seems to be paying the least attention, he says, 'Excuse me, your Excellency, I think you are mistaken.' He opens a dossier, quotes figures, and ends up by completely flooring the man, whom by definition he considers an opponent."

W. had been living in Cuba almost since the beginning of the regime. He arrived in Havana a few weeks after Batista's departure. So he knows the situation pretty well, and the men too.

"Do you think Guevara is a Communist?" I asked him.

"In my opinion, he's not a Communist in the sense we mean it. He's not, or apparently not, a Party member. On the other hand, he has completely absorbed Marxist doctrine and believes that Communism will triumph in Latin America and throughout the world. That is why he has staked everything on it.

"He has done a great deal of traveling since he left Argentina in 1952. He visited Chile, had a long flirtation with the Colombian Communists, collaborated with Arbenz in Guatemala, plotted among the Mexican trade-unionists, fought in the Cuban Sierra, and now here he is in a country not his own, one of Fidel's ministers. He is really at the wheel. The master of Cuba is not Fidel, but Guevara who is his intellectual superior.

"Tomorrow, he may be president of Venezuela, or commander in chief of the Guatemalan Army. Who knows?"

W. had made a serious study of the Cuban economy. One day, he showed me a dossier containing some statistics. "Read those," he said, "and you'll understand why I disagree with Guevara. Cuba is not a truly poor country. Well before the Revolution, Cuba could be classed among the nine most favored underdeveloped countries. Admittedly, $361 a year, the average Cuban annual income, was only one sixth of the American figure. But it was not far off the Italian average, and exceeded those of Argentina, Brazil, and Mexico.

"Theoretically, the 6.5 million people who make up the population of Cuba should have no cause for discontent in their island, which is about the same size as England. The soil is incredibly fertile, yielding three harvests annually without undue effort, and the climate is fine. And yet the island never has produced all of its own food. Before the Revolution, imports of food products cost Cuba $200 million a year.

"A second and equally scandalous paradox was that the Cuban peasants lived in desperate poverty. Three quarters of them lived— or, rather, survived—in *bohios* closely resembling those of the pre-Columbian Indians, with wooden walls, daub roofs, and mud floors. Sanitation, electricity, and running water were nonexistent.

"And yet there were others even more unfortunate among these 100,000 wretches. There were the 15,000 *precaristas* who worked for the big landowners, and were left over from last century's traditions of slavery. Officially, they were free domestic servants, but in fact they were the property of their masters. They themselves owned no property and could not even call the rags they wore their own. As to their civil rights, nobody gave them a thought; some landowners, Fidel Castro's father for example, even used to entertain themselves by using them as targets, as though they were in a shooting stand at a Sunday afternoon fair."

W. left the room for a moment and came back with a sugar bowl. "Do you see this sugar?" he said. "That's what's responsible for all the miseries of this Garden of Eden. The Cubans suffer from the most paradoxical disease. They are rich, fantastically rich. Unfortunately, all this wealth belongs to the sugar cane.

"The sugar cane was first introduced by one of Christopher Columbus's companions, and has played an important role in the economy ever since the sixteenth century. In fact, for 400 years now, the Caribbean has been so to speak on the sugar standard. In the old days boatloads of slaves were shipped across from Africa in order to work the plantations, which have been fought over desperately by the French, the English, the Spanish, and the Dutch.

"Today, the sugar cane dominates the existence of some forty million West Indians, not only in Cuba, but also in Haiti, Puerto Rico, Guadeloupe, Martinique, and Jamaica. The inhabitants of these islands, these jewels set in the bluest of blue seas, owe it their existence. But they also hold it responsible for their slavery.

"What's needed to grow sugar cane? A rich soil, a warm climate, and humidity, all of which are to be found in Cuba. The island quickly became the number-one sugar producer in the world. World Wars I and II caused the price of sugar to rise at a dizzying rate, and the planters lost their heads. Planting sugar became like play-

ing the stock market. Whole forests of magnificent mahogany were
cut down to make way for the big dollar earner. From Havana to
Santiago, the whole island has come to look like one enormous
sugar cane plantation. As Sartre puts it, the smell and taste of sugar
permeate everything, from politics to cigarettes, the paper of which
is made from sugar cane fibre.

"As always happens in such cases of speculation, large companies
were formed and bought up unbelievably large estates, often for
payment in gold. Before the Revolution, the six major companies
each owned more than 54,000 acres of plantations.

"But it wasn't the American companies that controlled the majority of the *latifundios*, the big estates. They had liquidated their
property many years previously. The big feudal landlords were
mainly Cubans.

"The part played by sugar in the Cuban economy has become a
real curse. It is the main source of foreign income. Now, the international sugar market is extremely limited, total international trad-
ing amounting to little over 6 or 8 million tons a year, whereas production is about 50 million tons. Cuba alone produces between 5
and 7 million tons. How and where is this ocean of sugar to be
disposed of? Until 1960, the United States bought almost half
the sugar produced in Cuba, in accordance with an agreement—
the famous quota of 2.8 million tons—at considerably more than
the world market price, 5.41 cents a pound instead of 3.50. For the
Cuban budget, that meant an assured income of $312 million.

"The rest of the sugar was sold elsewhere if buyers could be
found, and if not it was piled up in storage. The very life of the
country depended upon it. The amount of sugar sold each year
determined all sorts of things: unemployment, road and rail traffic,
the activity in the harbors, trade, wealth and poverty, the prosperity of cinemas, and even of houses of pleasure.

"The idea of agrarian reform had commanded attention for a
long time. Many economists, several of them from Washington,
advocated a radical structural reform of Cuba's economy. In 1950,
members of an information mission from the World Bank advised Cuba to put an end to its single-crop economy. Five years
later, a report by the United States Secretary of Commerce deplored
the fact that nothing had yet been done to achieve this end."

When Castro's men were resting between ambushes in the Sierra Maestra, the conversation would constantly revert to agrarian reform, which was always referred to as *la Reforma*, the reform. The guerrilla fighters loved to make plans for the "new" Cuba. They all agreed that things would have to be changed. But how?

Fidel would say, "Ours is going to be a beautiful revolution."

Che, who conscientiously held indocrination periods every evening, would add, "You can't have a revolution without agrarian reform."

But what shape would this reform take? Castro and Guevara held diametrically opposed views on this subject. The first would say, "We shall bring justice to the country districts. We've already promised as much to the *guajiros*. The peasants have been the first to help us, and they still continue to give us information, food, and shelter at the risk of their lives. We owe them what we have promised them. The land will be parcelled out among them, and they will no longer be rent payers, but landlords."

Guevara looked upon this program as being quite out of date. He was enthusiastic about the Chinese Communist experiments in collectivization, which he had heard about before becoming a guerrilla, and was all for radical measures and for an agrarian revolution rather than a reform. If Fidel raised the objection that they had already promised the peasants to give them land, Guevara would reply, "The *guajiro* doesn't want to be a landowner. He's not concerned about that."

Che's arguments were based on a thorough knowledge of peasant life in Latin America. The poor peasant from Cuba or Venezuela bears no resemblance to his European counterpart. He is a landless proletarian working alone or in groups for another man's profit, and he is isolated from the rest of society. He is a kind of marginal man, living out his obscure life in his *bohio* as completely cut off as the Central African negro in his mud hut.

Within one and a half centuries, the Latin American republics have undergone countless revolutions. Some of these have been wars of independence, but more often they have been mere palace intrigues. Each time it was merely a question of the men in power being replaced by a different gang. Even the wars of independence brought about no real changes, except that a rich landowning caste of Creoles took the place of a similar Spanish one.

W. reminded me that before the Cuban upheaval, none of these revolutions—except in Mexico—had involved real social reform. "All men of good sense, Yankees included, believed that the time had come for a radical agrarian reform. The redistribution of land to the peasants offered a double advantage, one economic, the other political. A farmer doesn't like to have to buy food; he prefers to be self-sufficient. Consequently, after acquiring their own land, farmers would plant all they needed, and the single-crop economy would come to an end. In the second place, it is well known that a peasant who owns the land he works is no revolutionary. He is just the opposite, a cautious man, especially afraid of revolutions which might make him lose what he owns.

"In my opinion, in spite of his Marxist sympathies, Fidel sincerely wished for an agrarian reform along these lines. With the boundless pride which characterizes him, he already saw himself as a new José Martí. He spoke of withdrawing from politics after his victory, like Cincinnatus, and going back to his practice as a lawyer. But Che would return to the assault relentlessly. He would tell him that the *guajiros* did not really want to be landowners—a statement that was neither true nor false.

"You'll see for yourself if you take a trip into the country. The peasants are quite open and ready to talk. Just ask them whether they want to own land. They'll tell you that first of all they want comfortable houses, schools for their children, regular work, and sufficient food to still their hunger. That's their dream of happiness. It's the dream of a 'primitive' man, if you like, but the *guajiros* are not so advanced as Flemish or Breton farmers. Expressions like 'property deed' arouse no response in them. They are as meaningless as the words 'election' and 'proletarian.' On the other hand, talk to them about food and work, and they'll understand you.

"*Guajiros*, like the majority of Latin American peasants, are just ripe for collectivization. Che Guevara realized this. He pointed out to Fidel that in order to set up his new regime, all he had to do was to pass abruptly from a system of large-scale private land ownership to one of large-scale state ownership, even using brutal methods, if necessary. He advocated transforming the *latifundios* into cooperatives."

Little by little, and with great patience, Guevara indoctrinated Castro, who ended up, as usual, by giving in to his lieutenant. Scarcely two months after his triumphal entry into Havana, the leader of the *barbudos* launched his famous reform. The National Institute for Agrarian Reform (INRA) was set up in order to enforce the new law expropriating all estates of over thirty *caballerias* (990 acres). To the accompaniment of a big publicity campaign by radio, television, and the press, Fidel, his brother Raúl, Che, and some of the others made elaborate promises in idyllic language about the forthcoming redistribution of land among the peasants.

On October 7 and 8, 1959, a conference took place attended by Fidel Castro, Che Guevara, Captain Núñez Jiménez, and twenty-six regional delegates of INRA. I was able to read the proceedings of this secret meeting.

Jimenez was the first speaker. He reminded them that INRA was such a vital organization that the President of the Republic, the government, and the tribunals "were of no importance in comparison."* He added that the president, the ministers, and the judges were there to serve INRA.

Then, turning toward the regional delegates, he said, "I warn you that the issues discussed at this meeting are not to be mentioned to anybody, not even to your relatives and closest friends. It is you who make up the real government of Cuba. Each one of you will receive unlimited powers within his region. The army, police, navy, judiciary, local government, and the civil service will be under your orders. As delegates of INRA, you are, in socialist terminology, commissars."

After the director of INRA came Fidel, who revealed the government's true intentions concerning the agrarian reform. "We will not distribute any land, except if the peasants demand it. To keep people calm, we may hand out a few deeds, but this will be an exception. Land will become state property, though we will not tell the peasants this, so as not to set them against the Revolution. The administrator of each cooperative will be appointed by the

* INRA runs 800 single-crop cooperatives, 604 sugar-producing cooperatives and 268 "people's farms," with a total of over 7 million acres of land. It also administers 150 industrial concerns (chiefly sugar refineries and food product factories). It also set up a chain of rural shops—*tiendas del pueblo*; 2,000 of these are already operating in the cooperatives and sugar refineries, selling food products, clothing, hardware, etc.

state, since the peasants are not capable of managing an important concern. If we left them to run their own affairs, the country would be ruined."

"Wouldn't it be possible to teach the peasants to take care of their own administration?" a delegate suggested.

"You are mistaken, Comrade," replied Fidel, "for two reasons. First, because a *guajiro* cannot be educated in a month. We would need several years. Second—and here's where we get to the heart of the matter—the peasant must learn only what we have decided to teach him, and nothing else. Our main aim in the field of education should be to teach him to become completely integrated into collectives. He must get rid of his taste for individualism and his stupid love of independence."

Guevara followed Castro. "The earnings of members of the cooperatives will be limited. They will only receive part of the profit."

"That means that we are setting a maximum salary, and that the government will take the rest of the profits," exclaimed a *barbudo* in surprise.

"Indeed."

"But we promised the peasants that all the profits from the cooperative would be shared by its members. If we start talking about salaries, they'll consider themselves cheated."

"No, Comrade. You mustn't mention the word 'salary.' Go on telling them that the profits will be shared among them. Forget the word 'salary.' Strike it out of your vocabulary, and substitute the word 'profit.'

"You must get used to this idea: in our meetings, we discuss what we intend to do, and not what we intend to tell people. The counterrevolutionaries make the same mistake. They believe that we are preparing stiffer laws to supersede the agrarian reform laws we have already promulgated. They don't seem to realize that we don't need any more laws to achieve our aims. What is the point of talking about new laws and regulations, and about the old laws being out of date and abused, when we do what we want with the laws we have?"

CHAPTER 15

The headquarters of INRA took up all twenty-three floors of a glass and concrete building put up under Batista's regime on the edge of the Plaza Civica, in the center of which stands the obelisk in memory of the poet-patriot José Martí. Parked outside the entrance was a double line of brand new Russian "Gorki" trucks. They were painted dark green, and had no license plates.

When I pushed open the glass door, I felt as though I had entered one of those large, modern, international hotels. There was a big hall with a telephone switchboard and operators and a receptionist. But the porters and employees were soldiers of both sexes, weighed down with pistols, machine guns and bandoliers.

Comrade Anna-Maria Rovera, head of the press department of INRA, had given me an appointment for ten o'clock in her office on the fourth floor. I went up to one of the telephone operators, a pretty brunette with curly hair and flashing eyes. She received me

with the usual words: "*Compañero, Patria o muerte! Venceremos!*"
Then she looked at my jacket, my immaculately-pressed trousers,
my white shirt, and my tie. "Well, *Compañero*, are you going to a
funeral?"

I felt embarrassed. Obviously I should have put on a cowboy
shirt and blue jeans. I must have looked damn foolish all dressed
up in the middle of those bohemian *barbudos*. They were all staring at me. "Excuse me," I said, with a forced smile. "I've only just
arrived from France. I'm not yet used to. . . ."

"You're still impregnated with the old bourgeois customs of
your country," she said sententiously. "A good revolutionary never
wears a tie. He rolls up his sleeves and gets down to work." I promised her not to do it again, and that the next time I came I'd be
wearing a super-revolutionary outfit.

In Comrade Rovera's office, which was as big as a railroad waiting room, I created another minor sensation. I took the hint, got
out of my jacket, loosened my tie, and unbuttoned my shirt to the
waist. Right away a girl soldier came up and tapped my shoulder.
"*Patria o muerte! Venceremos!* I'm going to enroll you immediately to come and cut sugar cane with us. A good revolutionary
should help the Cuban people free themselves from the economic
ascendancy of the imperialists."

"I've an appointment with Comrade Rovera," I replied.

She advised me to wait five minutes. Comrade Rovera was on
the phone. She would attend to me as soon as she was free. "Sit
down here while you're waiting," she said. She ordered another girl
in uniform to give me her seat. I protested with some embarrass-
ment. "Take this seat, Comrade," she said.

"But I don't want to deprive a woman of her seat."

"Why not? A *muchacha* in uniform is just the same as a man.
Sit down."

To kill the time, I cast my eyes over the walls, which were covered with posters. One of them showed a dead woman wrapped
in a shroud. Only her head was showing. Underneath was written
in huge letters: ASESINO! (MURDERER!). There was another picture
that showed a worm, a *gusano*, wearing an Uncle Sam top hat. A
soldier was running the worm through with his bayonet. There
were also plenty of slogans: "Our victory is the victory of our

Latin American brothers," "We will back Fidel to the death!"
There also was a poem:

Do not force me to doubt.
Do not try to convince me
That the Cuban Revolution is Communist.
For if you succeed in convincing me,
I shall become a Communist.

Reading posters is one way of passing the time. In the metro in
Paris I always read the rules and regulations of the Seine Railroad
Company. It's very instructive, but it becomes tedious after a
while. In the INRA office, first minutes and then hours went by
with that slow Latin American rhythm that will try even the
strongest nerves. After I don't know how long, a pregnant woman
gave up her place on the sofa near Comrade Rovera's desk. I immediately took it, glad to have moved two feet forward.

I was sitting between two soldiers who were busy cleaning their
rifles. Realizing that I was getting bored, they kindly showed me a
machine gun. They gave me a careful explanation of its mecha-
nism, and in less than an hour, I had learnt to dismantle and re-
assemble it as though I had been doing it all my life. I could even
have fired it, if necessary. One of them, a blondish, slightly albino
man, said to me, "Look, there is a counterrevolutionary over there!"
He pressed the muzzle against my ribs. I pushed it aside.

"Don't point that thing at me," I said.

"All right, suppose Alfonso here's a *gusano*. Well, you cock it
like that by pulling back this little catch. Then you press here, and
Alfonso's dead. You see, it's very simple."

"So it is," I said. "You've hardly got time to press the trigger and
Alfonso is dead."

"A good thing too. You've got to kill them, the *gusanos*."

"I'm not a *gusano*," protested Alfonso.

"I never said you were. I was just using you as an example."

"Examples are all very well. But I don't like being called a
gusano, not even as an example."

"But I never called you a *gusano*."

"Yes, you did."

"No, I didn't."

"Yes, you did."

The soldiers began to fight. The noise attracted Comrade Rovera's attention. "If you want to fight, get the hell out of here,"
she shouted. I took the opportunity to remind her of my existence.
"*Compañera*," I began.

"Call me *Maqúsa*, comrade. That's what I was called in the
war."

"*Maqúsa*," I said. "You gave me an appointment for ten o'clock.
It's two o'clock already."

"Come over here."

"I'm a journalist. I want to visit a cooperative."

The double doors opened with a bang. A lottery ticket seller
burst into the room shouting out a number, "Number 24,310,
24,310! *Patria o muerte! Venceremos!* Number 24,310." He thrust
the ticket under my nose. "*Compañero*, it's only twenty-five centavos. Number 24,310 is bound to win." I gave him his twenty-five
centavos, just to get rid of him.

Comrade Rovera then explained to me, "The profits from the
lotteries no longer go to a handful of wealthy profiteers, as they
did under Batista. Now they are put toward building houses for the
people. You were saying, *Compañero*?"

"I'm a journalist. I want to visit a cooperative." The door burst
open again, and a voice shouted in my ears, "Coffee, three centavos. Coffee, three centavos. *Patria o muerte*."

Then a girl soldier appeared. Without my saying a word she
pinned on my shirt a miniature Cuban flag with a picture of Fidel
Castro in the middle. "*Patria o muerte! Venceremos!* Give me a
peso for the literacy campaign."

I tried again, for the fourth time.

"I'm a journalist. . . ."

"Crocodile-skin bags! Frog-skin bags! Real crocodile and frog-
skin. *Barato!* Very cheap." It was the voice of a souvenir vendor,
a little old man with a wrinkled face. He showed me a fawn-colored
lady's handbag. "Real frog," he said.

"Frog?"

"Yes, bullfrog. Haven't you ever seen a bullfrog? They're as big
as rabbits."

A pregnant woman with four children trailing behind her came
in like an avenging fury. She took up her stand in front of me and
began telling me her story. She had been promised a house for the

previous year. She had still heard nothing about it. It was a scandal.
"I'm afraid I can't help you," I replied. "I'm a visitor myself."
"Aren't you an official?" she said in surprise.
"No."
"What in hell are you doing, then?"
"I'm a journalist. . . ."
"Who is in charge?"
I pointed to Comrade Rovera who was on the telephone again.
She went up to her and tapped her on the shoulder. "Comrade in
charge, look here. . . ."
"Sit down over there. I'm busy just now." There was an empty
armchair next to mine, and the woman went over and sat down in
it. Her kids huddled around her like an escort. They were repul-
sively dirty.
Comrade Rovera looked up, so I leapt forward. "*Compañera
Maqúsa*, I'm a journalist. . . ."
A *barbudo* appeared out of nowhere and sat down on the desk
between her and me with a bottle of Coca-Cola in his hand.
"Where are you from?" he asked, putting the bottle to his mouth.
"Excuse me, I was speaking with Comrade *Maqúsa*."
"Where are you from?" he repeated.
"From France."
"Why are you keeping the Algerians from gaining their liberty?"
I got up and went away. In the elevator, I said to the operator,
"I'd like to visit some cooperatives. Do you have any addresses?"
"Go and see the People's Farm El Rosario, near San Vicente in
Pinar del Rio, and the Cuba Libre cooperative near Matanzas." It
was all I wanted to know. "When are you planning to go there?"
"Some time next week. Until next Monday or Tuesday, I'm not
doing a thing."

CHAPTER 16

Saturday morning. The weather was fine without being oppressively hot; real holiday weather. The thought that the central heating would still be on in my Paris apartment gave me an irresistible longing to get away from Havana. I suddenly realized that it was weeks since I had taken a day off. I felt an overpowering need to take it easy. Why shouldn't I go away for a weekend and forget about Castroists and anti-Castroists, Bayo, Guevara, and the army? Why not go swimming at one of those beaches that so many admirers of Cuba have described as "out of this world—like paradise?" After all, I had worked hard enough and, besides, Havana was empty, like Paris in August. I wouldn't find anyone in town or get anything useful done.

That much was settled. I would give myself a real weekend. The idea put new life into me. In a flash, my suitcase was packed and I was at the wheel of my hired Rambler. I didn't waste time deciding

which way I'd go. The car was pointing west, so that was the way
I went.

I passed close by the Country Club between two lines of tall
palm trees as rigid and dignified as Guardsmen on parade. I left
the last houses of the suburbs behind me and going round a bend
had the countryside there before me in all its beauty. Fields of
sugar cane stretched as far as the eye could see. Red squares of
fallow earth and the white patches of peasants' cottages stood out
like islands in a sea of green. Here and there, the foliage of palm
trees sprouting above their silvery trunks looked like parasols.

After an hour and a half, I was driving up Cabañas' only street,
bordered with a few cafés and some shops. I turned to the left,
went up a hill, and when I got to the top found myself at a dead
end. So I had to turn around. While making the turn, I suddenly
found myself looking at what might have been a picture by Raoul
Dufy. Beyond the ocher roofs of the village stretched the garden of
Eden itself, an azure bay closed in on three sides by a jutting
stretch of land covered with royal palm trees; the sky, the sea, and
the trees combining to form a fairyland of topaz, emerald, and sap-
phire glinting in the tropical sunlight. Just this side of the bay was
a charming little beach. I could see a tiny corner of tempting white
sand.

Luck was with me. Six miles from Cabañas, on the ridge above
the beach, was a motel, which seemed to have been built especially
for me.

I was the only guest, and the hotel keeper received me with
great enthusiasm. He literally clung to me, as though he were afraid
I might go away. There were ten luxurious air-conditioned bunga-
lows for me to choose from, each one with a bathroom, television,
and a terrace giving onto the beach. I enquired about the price.
"Five pesos a night," he replied. That was certainly not expensive.

"Dinner doesn't cost much either," he said. "For seventy-five
centavos you'll have such a good *arroz con pollo* (chicken with
rice) that you'll never want to eat *pollo* anywhere else. As for my
cocktails, I use the best rum in the Caribbean and lemon peel from
lemons picked in my own orchard. After dinner, you can just
stretch out in a deck chair and look at the stars in the sky and the
lights of the fishing boats in the bay. We'll fill up your glass as soon
as it's empty without you ever having to ask. It won't cost you

much. We'll make you an overall price—four pesos—and you can
drink as much and as long as you want, till tomorrow morning if
you feel like it."

Shortly afterwards, I was sitting down to a really incomparable
arroz con pollo. But after dinner, I didn't stretch out in a deck
chair. Instead, I went back to my room, turned on the television
and got into bed. There was a good Western with Spanish sub-
titles. After that came some political propaganda, the same old
thing again: *"Cuba denuncia," "Sartre,"* etc. That sent me off to
sleep, and I never even bothered to turn it off.

I didn't wake up till late next morning. I jumped out of bed and
looked out of the window. The sea was as beautiful and as seduc-
tive as ever, so I slipped on my swimming trunks and ran down to
the beach. It was like a colander, perforated all over with thousands of holes each as big as a thimble. Crowds of small crabs were
coming out of them and running about in all directions. What
strange creatures they were. Their legs and bodies were like those
of any crab you might find on the French coast, but these had
enormous pincers, out of all proportion to their size, pincers as big
as a giant crab's, as big as their own bodies.

The water was warm and clear. I felt as though I were plunging
into a bath. I dived in, rolled around, floated like a raft. I swam
across to the jetty where the fishing boats were tied up, hauled
myself up, and stretched out on the scorching planks.

Before lunch, I went for a drive across the *loma* (plain), and
up and down a hilly road, passing hardly a soul except a few groups
of *guajiros* walking along. I stopped on a little hill and noticed a
thin wisp of smoke curling up from a cottage. The country was as
tranquil and rural as possible. Two zebus were staring at me from
behind a hedge with their vacant, stupid expressions. I went down a
narrow track toward the little house, raising clouds of white dust.

The peasant was sitting nonchalantly in a rocking chair outside
the whitewashed walls of his home, smoking a long cigar. He got
up and said, *"Buenos dias."*

I apologized for disturbing him, "I was just passing by. . . ."

"Come in, *amigo*, make yourself at home."

His wife appeared in the doorway, a strong-looking mulatto with
a round face and trumpet-shaped nose. *"Buenos dias, Señor,"* she
said. "Do us the honor of staying to lunch. Please excuse us for

receiving you in such a humble home," she added. "You'll be a friend here. 'Friend' is a big word."

I made the gesture of refusing, out of politeness, and accepted only when they insisted. But inwardly I was delighted by the whole situation. There are few people who are as friendly and hospitable as the Cubans. No need for elaborate introductions. They receive you and offer their friendship as the most natural gesture in the world.

Alberto's and Juana's house was made of palm trunks covered with bark and whitewashed. The roof was made of palm leaves and daub. Like all peasant homes in this country of eternal summer it had no chimney. The fireplace was outside the building. In a corner of the main room, which was furnished with a table and bamboo chairs, an old woman had the youngest child on her knees and was busy feeding him. The child must have been about two years old. He was quite naked and greedily swallowed the rice which his grandmother was pushing into his mouth with her fingers. The sunlight filtered through the palm leaves on the roof and lit up the old woman's face.

Alberto's *finca* covered 3 *caballerias* (100 acres), which is not a large farm by Cuban standards. Cane sugar was of course the principal crop. Except for the season of the *zafra*, Alberto did not have much to do. He spent most of his time in his rocking chair. His livestock consisted of a herd of black pigs, over which he kept an unwatchful eye, and some chickens and turkeys which were allowed to run free under the banana trees. He also kept a pair of peacocks which were beautiful to look at and uttered hair-raising cries.

It was nearly time for lunch. Juana, who finished her household chores (she had hurried specially for my sake), said to her husband, "Go and fetch some *malangas* [sweet potatoes] and *plátanos* [green bananas]."

I followed Alberto into his kitchen garden. The phrase "kitchen garden" is a misnomer. To a European, it would suggest a well-cultivated plot, whereas here there was no trace of gardening. Plants grew everywhere, hopelessly tangled, in some places as tall as a man. Alberto stopped in front of some of the banana trees. He carefully examined the mauve cone that hung from each stem. I carefully imitated him, stopped, looked up. I could have gone on

looking for the rest of my life and I would never have noticed anything special. The tenth time I could restrain myself no longer.
"What are you looking at up there?" I asked him.

"I'm looking to see if the 'olive' is dry. If it is, the whole bunch
is ripe." There was another surprise in store for me with my igno-
rance of the tropics. The banana trees were high; how was Alberto
going to pick his bunch? He was not a young man, and I couldn't
see him climbing up the trunk like a young African boy up a coconut palm.

Finally, Alberto found some bananas that were just ripe. He took
his machete, which never left his side, and after two strokes the
banana tree was on the ground. "Why did you cut the tree down?"
I asked him.

"A banana tree never gives more than one bunch, but it leaves
two shoots, which grow up at its foot. Later on, each of the shoots
will give one bunch and two more shoots. Mustn't interfere. That's
what God is for."

The heart-shaped *malanga* leaves would not have looked out of
place as ornamentation in a living room. They grew at the end of
stalks two feet long. Alberto knelt down and rapidly unearthed the
tuber with his machete. The root was long, cylindrical, sinewy, and
covered with protuberances. He cut off these swellings, the only
edible part, then sliced the cylinder in two with his machete, and
threw one half away, while he covered the other with a little earth.
"In three months," he said as he stood up, "there'll be some more
malangas here."

"You don't have to take much trouble," I said in amazement.

"The earth is rich. You can plant a stick anywhere; ten months
later, it's a tree. I spend my time planting new stakes round my
sugar canes. They all turn into trees before I have time to breathe."

"You don't like working?"

"Oh, yes, I do. But I don't like tiring myself out. What's the
point? God has given me all I want except meat and milk. *Malangas* and bananas grow on their own. The pigs and chickens get
along all right. All I have to do is pick things." He laughed. "I
don't worry. Whenever my wife tells me to get down to work, I
start singing. Here is a song that never fails to make her mad:

Yo no tumba caña
Que la tumba el viento

O que la tumba Lolla
Con su movimiento."

("I don't cut sugar cane. Let the wind or Lolla's movements take care of that.")
"Who's Lolla?" I asked.
"A woman."
"What woman?"
"Any woman."

Here we were round the table in the living room. Juana brought out her very best crockery, porcelain plates marked "made in Germany." They were decorated with edelweiss and snowy landscapes, neither of which are ever seen in Cuba. "Do you have snow in your country?" asked Alberto.
"Yes, in some places."
"In the mountains, you mean?"
"That's right."
"Have you ever seen snow? What's it like?"
I gave him a little lesson about it, which he listened to with great attention. Afterwards he said, "My father told me that his father once saw snow in the Sierra Maestra. It was during a particularly severe winter. All the peasants from the *lomas* went up to see this extraordinary thing. I'd like to see snow myself some day. It's beautiful, isn't it?"
"Yes."
"My father told me that it melted more quickly than the ice cream served in a café. It's a pity, because otherwise we could have some sent. The Russians have plenty of snow in their country. I'm sure they'd gladly send us a little. It would be very instructive. We only get the wind here. Sometimes we get whirlwinds that sweep everything away. I've seen houses and carts lifted up into the sky."
It was a frugal meal: fried bananas and sweet potatoes cooked in their skins. Juana had done something special for my benefit. She'd killed a chicken which she'd cut up and fried. It was rather tough, and the flesh was dark red like that of some sort of game. There was cold water to drink. Alberto apologized for not offering us anything better. "What a shame I didn't know sooner that you

were coming. I'd have sent one of the *muchachos* to buy some milk."

"Don't you drink milk every day?"

"No, it's only for guests. It's a luxury." Alberto ate slowly. He cut up his chicken into little square pieces, which he put into his mouth and chewed carefully. But it didn't keep him from talking. "I have worries," he confided to me, with gravity.

"Worries?"

"*Seguro!* In the old days I used to go two or three times a week to watch television."

"What television?"

"In Cabañas. There's a joint there which has television. You sit down, you have a rum, and you just watch. It kills time, you know, and it's cheaper than gambling."

"Why don't you go any more?"

"*Que va!* I have worries. All the small landowners in the area are very concerned. The INRA wants us to join the cooperatives. Armed soldiers have been coming to my *finca* every week for the last three years. They survey the place, count the animals, and before leaving they always say the same thing, 'Are you a bad revolutionary?' They also say, 'If anything bad happens to you, that's your concern. You'll have to ask Uncle Sam to help you.' "

"Have they expropriated many farms in the area?"

"Yes, quite a few. You know, I'm all for the agrarian reform. As long as they take land from the *latifundistas*. But it's going too far when they go for the small landowners."

"And yet," I said, "Ernesto Guevara was careful to reassure the small landowners himself; it was at the conference of the association of sugar cane planters on February 26, 1960. He promised that there would be no difference between the peasant of the co-operatives and the independent small landholder."

"Yes, that's true," murmured Alberto, "but I'm very concerned all the same. My land is my own, and I won't part with it. In those cooperatives the land doesn't belong to anybody. You have to work ten or twelve hours a day. On my *finca* I do what I like. No need to tire myself out. God and Juana are there to help me."

The old *guajiro* cut a piece of bread and pushed it round his plate with the point of his penknife. He conscientiously mopped up all the sauce. Afterwards, he picked up the chicken bones and piled them on the edge of his plate. "Would you like a cigar?" he said.

"Yes, please." Alberto still seemed to be preoccupied. "Do you always worry like this?" I asked him.

"*Seguro, hijo!* If you were in my place, you wouldn't get much sleep either."

"But the agrarian reform only affects the big estates, doesn't it?"

"*Mira,* they also take the small ones. It always happens the same way. One morning, some soldiers suddenly arrive. They say to you, 'Get the hell out, *gusano,* we're coming to occupy.' Occupy! What does that mean? It doesn't mean anything. Why don't the soldiers say, 'We're coming to take your *finca*'? It would be more honest. As far as I'm concerned, occupy and steal are the same things."

"Why?"

"Because they pinch everything, cows, chickens, pigs, and fruit, and they never pay. They say, 'It's for the people.' When you ask for money, they give you vouchers. You can't buy anything with vouchers, not even cigarettes. They're worth nothing. *Nada!*"

I remembered having come across a passage in the proceedings of the meeting of INRA delegates on October 7 and 8, 1959 which was about expropriations. Fidel, who was presiding, promised, "The owners of estates which are seized will be indemnified with agrarian reform vouchers. They'll be paid the price they ask for . . ."

"Because," went on Guevara, "these vouchers will be worth nothing."

"Confiscated cattle will be paid for in cash," said Fidel. "It is essential that we gain control of the herds without any difficulties."

"Couldn't we pay for the cattle half in pesos and half in vouchers?" suggested a delegate. "It would be more economical."

"Don't worry about that," replied Guevara. "In a few months' time the peso, as it stands, will be worth nothing. We'll soon have a new currency."

I said to Alberto, "Do the landowners expropriated by INRA ever resist?"

"Never. They're not crazy. It's too dangerous. At the very beginning, a young farmer, about twenty-five years old, got angry because they wanted to take his land. He hadn't done anything.

There wasn't any reason for it. He shouted at them, that was all. But the INRA men came in their jeeps with their machine guns. There was a captain, a *barbudo*. He said to the little fellow, 'You're under arrest.'

" 'What are you going to do to me?' asked the young man.

" 'You'll know soon enough. You're going to die and go down to hell to join the rest of Batista's friends we've shot.'

" 'Why do you want to kill me?'

" 'Because you're a low-down son of a bitch.'

" 'Please don't insult my mother. She has nothing to do with this.'

" 'You son of a dirty bitch.'

"The soldiers put the boy up against the wall and took up their positions. In a blank voice the condemned man said to the Captain, 'Could I ask a service of you?'

" 'What is it, son of a bitch?'

" 'I am asking you not to mix my mother up in this, and not to insult her.'

" 'What do you want, son of a bitch?'

" 'In a few moments, when you finish me off, please don't aim at my face. It's for my mother's sake, when she sees my body.'

" 'Go to hell. Fire!' The young farmer crumpled up. Then the *barbudo* captain went up to the body and put a bullet through his forehead, smashing up his head. 'There, that's for your mother, you son of a bitch,' he shouted.

"Of course," said Alberto, his voice shaking with passion, "that all happened in the early days of the reform. Now the INRA men don't do any more shooting. They're not allowed to. All the same. . . . To think that I imagined the Revolution was something to make peasants richer and happier. Nothing's changed for me. I still don't make enough to buy milk for the children."

"Perhaps you'd earn more if you worked harder."

"There's no use my working. I can't sell my sugar cane. Nobody is allowed to buy it. Only INRA is allowed to, and just to annoy the small landholders they refuse. 'You only have to join the co-operative,' they say."

I said goodbye to Alberto and Juana. On the way back, I went past some workers cutting sugar cane. In long rows, wearing broad sombreros, they were moving silently forward, mechanically raising their machetes and bringing them down sharply on the juicy stems which they cut clean through. Some women and children were carrying the canes back to a cart drawn by a team of zebus. A mile away, white smoke rising straight into the sky marked the position of the sugar refinery.

I parked my car on the side of the road and went over to the workers. I was particularly struck by the eagerness with which a small boy aged twelve or thirteen was going at his work. "Do you live near here?"

"No, I'm from Havana."

"How come you're working here, then?"

"I come sugar cutting every Sunday. Don't you?"

"No."

"Why not? Every revolutionary helps in the *zafra*. Fidel said it was a patriotic duty. Haven't you read *Revolución*? Fidel and Dorticos were the first to set the example. They each worked for eight hours, bare to the waist, like all the other *macheteros*. Fidel cut four tons of sugar cane. Just think of that."

A peasant who had been listening to our conversation for a few moments took him up on that and said in a dry voice, "Don't talk nonsense. The best *machetero* in the world couldn't cut more than two and a half tons. I know that. I've been a *machetero* for twenty years. Fidel hasn't been a *machetero* for twenty years."

"It was in *Revolución*."

"*Revolución* is full of nonsense." I asked the peasant his name. He replied sharply, "*No te importa*. It's none of your business."

I went up to a *machetero* who had just stopped for a short rest, and spoke with him. He had crinkly hair and an open face. He was called Camilo. Like his father and three brothers, he had always lived in poverty. It was the same old story of the poor, shamefaced *guajiros* before the Revolution. He was a sugar cane cutter, and was employed only five months out of the year. "The rest of the time I just went hungry," he said.

"And now?"

"I'd like to join a cooperative, but there isn't room enough for everybody. You have to wait."

"Wouldn't you rather become a landowner?"

Camilo raised his face, which was covered with sweat. "Why do you say that? What's the point of being a landowner? It doesn't help at all, unless you want to get shot."

CHAPTER 17

The old bus pulled away with a sudden start, its tires scraping against the curb, and went up the main street of Pinar del Rio. We left the town behind us and headed northward. We passed the radio station, a square concrete building with a flagpole to one side. Cows were grazing peacefully in front of the station.

The road wound through tobacco fields surrounded by houses roofed with palm leaves. Occasionally, along the side of the road the rows of tobacco plants would come to an abrupt end where there were precipices, some of them 120 feet deep. What with its coconut palms, its giant parasol-shaped trees, and its zebus, the countryside was beginning to look more and more African. Rivers of ocher-colored water flowed gently down the green sides of the Rosario hills, passing through tunnels of royal palm and banana trees.

We left the Viñales valley, a remarkable geological phenomenon.

Millions of years ago it had been a huge cavern, but the roof had caved in leaving only the supporting pillars standing. Today, the plain is unbelievably fertile, always green, full of little hillocks covered with vegetation.

After Viñales, the conductor came and stood over me, leaning his hand on the back of my seat. He was young, tall, and thin, and seemed to be a nice fellow. "You're not Cuban," he said.

"That's right."

"What, then? Russian?"

"No."

"You're Italian, then?" he said, maybe because I mix a few Italian words in with my Spanish.

"No."

He smiled, hesitated a moment, then gave up. "Where are you from?"

"I'm French."

"I knew you weren't Cuban. You smoke a pipe. Cubans don't smoke pipes. Well, what are you doing here?"

"I'm going to visit the People's Farm El Rosario."

"You're a tourist?"

"No, I'm a journalist."

"I wondered what you could be doing here. There aren't any tourists in Cuba any more. That's all over. They just don't come any more. I wonder why the government keeps the hotels open." He searched through his bag and pulled out two big black cigars. "Would you like to try one of these? They're manufactured here. They're very strong though, and they'll make you sick if you're not used to them." He opened his bag again and pulled out another cigar, less frightening, wrapped in cellophane. "Take this instead," he said. "It's fine tobacco, the kind the rich smoke. It's even got a band. This one comes from here too. Pinar del Rio Province is the cigar country. *Toma*, take it.

"Do you know why cigars have bands?" he asked me. "It's quite a joke. I read about it in *Revolución*. When the Spaniards were here, the beautiful rich women used to smoke cigars. But so as not to dirty their fingers, they used to put a band of paper around their cigars. One day the manufacturers decided to sell cigars already provided with bands, and then they printed their names on them, as well as different designs."

The peasant sitting next to me, who was wearing a sombrero, pulled out his bag from under the seat, opened it, looked in, and plunged in his hand. He pulled out a hard-boiled egg and a piece of bread. He broke the egg on his knee and, observing a custom that must date back to the Arab conquest of Spain, invited me to share it. I thanked him and refused in accordance with custom, saying that I had already eaten. "*De nada,*" he murmured, and bit into his egg.

The conductor went on asking questions. "What do you think of this country?"

"Cuba is pretty," I replied.

He winked, and said, "What about Fidel? What do you think of him?"

"I don't know."

"Tell me, are there any socialists in your country, in France?"

"Yes."

"As many as here?"

"I don't know."

"Is everybody a socialist in France?"

"No."

"Ah, you're lucky to live in France. There's nothing but socialists here. Everybody's a socialist."

"So you don't like socialists?"

"I like them all right, but *they* only like the peasants who've joined the cooperatives and the people's farms. They don't like people who work outside the cooperatives. They don't like the workers."

"Why don't they like the workers?"

"I don't know. That's the way it is. The socialists give everything to the people they like: new houses, money to buy clothes so that they can go to town for the Sunday stroll. But the workers don't get anything. I want to buy a new suit," went on the conductor. "But I can't. I just don't earn enough. I work four hours a day more than I used to, and I get twelve pesos a month less. Do you think that's fair? I think the socialists are unjust toward the workers. I've been thinking about buying that suit for months now. I think about it day and night, while I work, while I eat, I even dream about it. It's become an obsession with me."

The other passengers were pretending not to listen. They might have been a thousand miles away. The soldier sitting two seats in front of me on the left didn't budge; he was sitting hunched up, with his cap pulled down over his eyes, fast asleep. Perhaps he was only pretending.

The conductor didn't seem worried. He went on in the same vein. "What's going to happen now?" he said.

"How should I know?"

"Do you think the Yankees will make a landing?"

"I don't know."

"If the Yankees land," he said, "it'll be bad. There'll be fighting and people will be killed. The Yankees have plenty of weapons. They're stronger than we are, you know." He relit his cigar which he had allowed to go out. "If it's not the Yankees, it won't be as bad," he went on.

"Why not?"

"Because the others are like us. We know them. We know they won't kill everybody. But the Yankees, that'd be bad. But I know what's going to happen, the Yankees are going to land. That's for certain, and everybody will be killed."

"What are you planning to do?"

"I don't know. If I could, I'd leave the country. I'd go some other place. I wouldn't go to the States. No, I wouldn't go there. It's bound to be just as bad as here. I'd go some other place, to your country, maybe. Everybody isn't a socialist in your country. In your country you can at least hope, that's for certain."

"What would you hope for?"

"I don't know. In that rat Batista's time I used to hope."

"But what did you hope for?"

"I don't know. How should I know what I hoped for? I just know that I hoped. Hell, I'll never know. I hoped for something, something else than this. Now we're all socialists. When you're a socialist there's nothing left to hope for, not even a new suit for the Sunday stroll."

We had long ago passed San Vicente, with its pink-tiled houses sprawling for miles along the main street. The bus stopped at a crossroads. "This is your stop," said the conductor. "The People's Farm El Rosario is four miles away. There's no other way to get there, so you'll have to walk."

The sun was beating down mercilessly. To avoid the melted tar that stuck to the soles of my shoes, I had to walk along the edge of the road. Halfway to El Rosario I passed a large building under construction: a model stable which would accommodate several hundred head of cattle. After an hour I caught sight of a group of new houses, spaced at regular intervals, each with its front door painted a different color. A wide lawn surrounded them.

I felt very hot and the road seemed interminable, so to cheer myself up I began whistling any tune that came into my head. I finally came to *Madelon*, that marching song of the French Army during World War I. Suddenly I heard some girls' voices behind me, singing the same song, but to Spanish words.

I turned. It was a group of girl soldiers between thirteen and sixteen years old, all armed to the teeth. They had been resting behind a hedge when I went past whistling. Now they were marching along in step, in double columns, and singing:

"Patria! Patria!
Milicianas adelante! [Forward, soldier girls!]
Milicianas a marchar! [Soldier girls, forward march!]"

When we got to the administrative building, they practically mobbed me. They shook me by the hand, kissed me, and congratulated me. "Bravo, Comrade. You're a true revolutionary."

I was quite taken aback, and raised my eyebrows in astonishment. "Why am I a true revolutionary?"

"Because you were singing our anthem."

"I couldn't have. I don't even know it."

"Come on. Don't give us that stuff, Comrade."

"I don't understand."

"Stop joking. You were whistling something just now."

"Yes, *Madelon*."

"No you weren't. It's the soldier girls' anthem."

This little encounter proved extremely useful. It was the best possible introduction I could have had to the manager of the people's farm. The girls dragged me along to the office, shouting to the manager, "*Patria o muerte! Venceremos!* Comrade, here's a true friend of our people, a foreign revolutionary. He came here singing our anthem."

The manager was a fat little man between twenty-eight and

thirty with a round face and a fine black moustache. "What's that, *compañeras?* Singing your anthem?"

"*Si, si, si.* He was singing:

Patria! Patria!
Milicianas adelante!
Milicianas a marchar!"

I was anxious not to tamper with historical truth and modestly corrected them, "Excuse me. I wasn't singing. I was whistling it."

"Yes, yes, that's true. He wasn't singing, he was whistling," said one of the girls.

"But he was whistling in tune," said another. I only wished my wife could have been there. She always runs out of the house when I start singing that song in my bath.

The manager dusted off a chair for me. "Sit down, Comrade. You must be tired after your walk. No, no," he said generously. "Don't trouble to show me your letter of introduction. I can see who you are. The INRA only sends us real revolutionaries, true friends of our glorious and courageous people."

I leaned back with a sigh of relief, as I was beginning to get anxious, because I didn't have a letter of recommendation from the INRA.

The manager shouted to the girls, "Go and get him something to drink. There's cold Coca-Cola at the *tienda del pueblo.*" I was a guest of honor.

The office was an austere room with two tables, a few chairs, and an iron cupboard. The walls were covered with propaganda posters. "What can I do for you?" asked the manager.

"I'm a journalist," I explained. "I would like to see how the peasants on this farm live."

He enthusiastically launched into a regular dissertation. "This farm covers an area of 37 thousand acres. It was formerly the property of Batista's son. They only grew cattle fodder, which didn't allow the 600 peasants who worked it to live decently. They had to live on bananas and mangoes and lived in huts built of daub without any modern conveniences.

"Less than a year ago I was still a student. My ambition was to be an architect, nothing to do with agriculture, you see. Then the INRA sent me here. I got down to work right away. Everything

had to be started from scratch; there was nothing here before, no
running water, no electricity, no milk, no school, no doctor, nothing.

"At first the *guajiros* were skeptical. They thought it was all a
joke. They never thought we would keep the promises Fidel had
made in the Sierra. But when they saw the INRA trucks loaded
with bags of cement, bricks, construction stone, and tiles, they
understood. They set to work of their own accord. In four months
we built houses for everybody. Every one of the 120 families has
its own home.

"After that we tackled the vital agricultural problems. We gave
up the single crop system and started producing corn, cotton,
beans, tobacco, and fruit. We also started raising poultry and cattle.
The friendly countries helped us: China sent us tractors and the
Soviet Union sent 'Gorki' trucks."

He then explained that a people's farm should not be confused
with a cooperative. "You can compare it," he said, "with a Soviet
sovkhoz. The land does not belong to the peasants but to the state,
that's to say the country as a whole. The cooperatives, which are
the equivalent of *kolkhozes*, are the property of the farmers. They
pay for their water, electricity, fertilizers, seeds, etc. The peasants
on the people's farms are housed free. Water, electricity, seeds, and
fertilizer are all paid for by the state. In addition, they receive a
salary of thirty centavos an hour, on an average, 3.30 pesos a day.
This allows them to buy food and clothing."

With the manager's authorization, I visited a house selected at
random; it turned out to belong to a tall gangling fellow called
Oscar Jaime.

The village looked like something out of a Western. *Monteros*
wearing big sombreros had tied their horses to the wooden porch
rail of the office. The men had swarthy sunburnt faces and wore
long machetes at their belts. We passed a huge shed. "Come and
see," said Oscar. "*Esto es algodón.* It's cotton. That's what we're
harvesting now. See how good it looks." A mountain of white fluff
filled the place. Some men were putting it in sacks, others carried
them out to a truck. "We have a hundred *caballerias* of cotton.
We also grow potatoes. Have you ever seen potatoes? They come
from Poland and Czechoslovakia."

The Jaimes' house was perched on a little hillock. On a brass plate screwed above the door these words stood out clearly: *"Esta es tu casa—Fidel."* "Read it: This is your house—Fidel," said Oscar proudly. "Fidel gave it to me himself. He came here specially to hand over the new houses. He also gave out furniture, pots and pans, plates, forks, and knives. Fidel is the father of the whole nation."

The house was a bare minimum of bricks and stone. The whitewash covering the walls did not hide the cracks. The floor was of cement. The windows had no glass, only plain blinds designed to keep out mosquitoes at night. But they could get in through a crack under the roof; there was no ceiling separating the room from the roof. There were no doors inside, only openings. There was a minimum of furniture: a wooden table, two rocking chairs, and four varnished bamboo chairs. The beds looked quite comfortable. In spite of everything, it must have been a palace for the Jaimes.

"We used to sleep on the ground," Oscar said. "On straw. We lived in a cardboard hut. When it rained, the walls melted away like sugar." He gave a forced laugh to hide his emotion. He showed me two colored photos hanging behind the table in the living room. They were of Fidel Castro and Camilo Cienfuegos, rifle on shoulder, in the Sierra Maestra. Beside it was a colored lithograph of a horseman of the 1880's saluting a crinolined belle. "I can never be grateful enough to Fidel for all he has done for us. He's made men of us," said the peasant. It was all very naive, no doubt, but you couldn't help feeling moved.

Little by little the room filled with onlookers. They politely took off their hats and stood bunched in the corner. The five Jaime children (two girls and three boys between fourteen and eighteen years old) stood behind the table. Oscar and I sat in the rocking chairs.

My host told me about his life in the days before the Revolution. He spoke in a loud voice, but calmly, without passion. "Our master didn't pay us. In order to survive we went into the neighboring haciendas during the sugar cane *zafra*. We earned quite a lot during harvest time. The more cane we cut, the more we earned. In the evening we would buy rice and beans with our earnings. We had to eat a lot for the *zafra*, otherwise we could never have stood the strain. Peddlers came from town to sell us shoes and clothing. On those days there would be kerosene in the lamp. In fact, life wasn't bad.

"Then suddenly work would come to an end. At first we would tell our wives to spend less. We'd take on badly paid jobs. We'd do anything for a few pesos. The peddlers disappeared, since we had no more money for them. They only came at *zafra* time. Afterwards they deserted us. We would start eating less and less rice and beans. And then the day would come when we bought nothing at all. We went on a diet of sweet potatoes and bananas. Instead of drinking coffee, we just sucked sugar cane."

One of the visitors said to Oscar, "You haven't told him about medicine. We had to see to it that we didn't get sick outside of *zafra* time. If we did, there wasn't any money to buy medicine with. And the doctor wouldn't have come all the way out here for nothing. Now, if we fall sick, we get free medical treatment."

"How much did you earn during the harvest?" I asked him.

"I worked fourteen hours a day, Comrade. I made a peso and a half. I was a good *machetero*."

"How many children have you?"

"Five, Comrade. I have five children."

"How did you survive the rest of the year?"

"We had food for six months and went hungry the other six."

I asked another, "How about you?"

"I have six kids. I earned a peso a day. May I tell you something?"

"Go ahead."

"I'm forty-five years old. Do you know when I first tasted milk?"

"When?"

"At the beginning of last year, when they started the agrarian reform. In Batista's time my kids didn't know what milk was. Milk, that was something for the rich, not for *guajiros*. Now we have milk and meat, and we eat all the year round. We don't go hungry any more. May I tell you something?"

"Go ahead."

"The agrarian reform is justice."

A man in a green uniform with a Luger at his belt suddenly appeared in the Jaimes' living room. His name was Antonio. He was a strong, red-faced, talkative man. I took him for the political commissar, because all the villagers immediately stopped talking.

Antonio sat back in the rocking chair which Oscar had respectfully risen from. He looked me over carefully while the mistress of the house brought coffee. Being a new guest, I was honored by being given a real cup. The others had to make do with the Cuban method of drinking from cups made by cutting and rolling up pieces of paper. When my cup was empty, it was refilled and passed on to Antonio, who emptied it in one draught.

He then drew himself up in his chair and, in a peremptory tone, reminded us of the misery in Cuba under Batista's dictatorship. He expressed himself entirely in statistics which he produced with the speed of an adding machine. He spoke in a sarcastic tone of voice: "Did you know that 89.5 per cent of the men, women, and children in this village couldn't read or write, 98 per cent didn't have decent homes, 91 per cent were employed only 3 months a year?"

Then he asked me questions about France. "Tell me, *Compañero,* do pineapples grow in your country?"

"No."

Antonio smiled and turned toward the audience. "You see. Fidel was quite right. Cuba is the richest country in the world. And avocados and mangoes?" he asked me.

"They don't grow in my country either."

"And apples and pears?"

"France," I said, "produces apples and pears with the best flavor in the world."

"Impossible! Apples and pears don't grow in Cuba, yet. All right! It's the Yankees' fault, theirs and their puppets'. But thanks to our friends, the Soviet Union, Czechoslovakia, China, East Germany, and Poland, our children will eat the best apples and pears in the world."

The day was drawing to a close. The sun was about to sink behind the purple mountains. I went back to the *oficina.* A Chevrolet with a long aerial was parked between two horses tied to the rail. The front doors were open and the two policemen sitting on the front seat were talking to some riders who had dismounted.

There was a crowd in front of the "people's store." The shelves were filled with canned foods—ham from Poland, corned beef from Russia, beans and peas from Czechoslovakia. "Our *tienda* is a great blessing," said Oscar. "Before the Revolution, the storekeepers used to exploit us mercilessly. We paid twice as much for everything as it cost in town, and the weights were rigged too. But we couldn't do anything about it. We had to go to them."

"Why?"

"Because they gave credit. You could buy up to 100 pesos worth and pay later."

Like the rest of the peasants, Oscar would get into debt during the dead season and pay up during the zafra. Because of the usurious rates of interest (30 to 40 per cent), repayment never ended. It was a vicious circle.

"With the money we made at the *zafra*," Oscar told me, "we paid off the debts and part of the interest. We'd repay the rest the following year—with still more interest, interest on interest. In Batista's time I was still paying up for my grandfather who died when I was only five."

We drank an orangeade at the *tienda*. Oscar was worried about me. Where was I going to spend the night? I suggested telephoning for a taxi. "We don't have a telephone yet. Come and have supper and stay with us. You can go back tomorrow with one of the trucks taking cotton to Pinar."

After dinner a soldier half-opened the door, and without looking in announced, "Movies at eight o'clock. Everyone meet at the school."

I questioned Oscar. "What kind of movies are they?"

"Educational movies. You'll see. They're very good."

"Do you have to go?"

"No. Nobody *has* to. We're all free here. But all good revolutionaries go to educational movies."

The school yard was already full of people when we arrived. A screen had been fixed to the wall. The children sat in a row in front and the peasants stood behind them. The entire audience was surrounded by a ring of armed soldiers.

We were to be shown two short films: "May First in Moscow" and "The Epic of Fidel in the Sierra Maestra." To start off, the soldier who had summoned us made a speech. He was a thin man with jerky gestures who shouted. "At first," he said, "Fidel and his comrades numbered no more than twelve. They succeeded in defeating Batista's army which was large, well-trained, and well-equipped. If they could do it, Comrades, the six million people of

Cuba can stand up to all the imperialists in the world. We are not alone. The friendly socialist countries are on our side, and will support us to the end."

Later the soldier passed on to the tasks confronting the peasants. He asked questions to which the crowd responded in chorus. "If you meet an old man of ninety-nine who can't read, what do you do?" he asked.

"Teach him," shouted the audience.

"And if you meet a *gusano*, what do you do?"

"Send him to the firing squad."

"Bravo! Otherwise you would be counterrevolutionaries. And a counterrevolutionary is an agent of the American imperialists, a traitor who wants to re-establish Batista's tyranny. Which of you wants to be a counterrevolutionary?"

"None of us."

"Why don't you want to be counterrevolutionaries?"

"Because a counterrevolutionary is a traitor who must be shot."

"Why are counterrevolutionaries traitors?"

"Because Fidel said so," shouted the audience.

"And Fidel is always right," concluded the soldier.

"Yes, Fidel is always right," they shouted back, wild with enthusiasm. "Fidel is always right!"

"Napoleon is always right!" echoed in my mind. I was thinking not of the victor of Austerlitz, but of a character from George Orwell's "Animal Farm," in which the farm becomes a sort of co-operative run by the pig Napoleon. Napoleon organizes regular meetings to which all the animals are invited; each time they condemn the "traitors," the pig Snowball and his "accomplices." "Snowball is a traitor!" the speaker regularly announces.

"Snowball is a traitor!" the crowd repeats obediently.

"Why is he a traitor?"

"Because Napoleon said so."

"Napoleon is always right."

The story of the *guajiros* bears a tragic resemblance to Orwell's fable. Like the animals on the farm, the Cuban peasants work just as hard as before, and are not really any happier. But as a result of propaganda, they now say they are better off and that they have become free.

Before the Revolution, Fidel promised them, "Each one of you will own the land he tills and will be his own boss." "Men promise much that they may give little," wrote the disillusioned Vauvenargues. Three years after Castro's victory INRA has distributed only 33,000 property deeds, although 500,000 peasants had put all their hopes in the agrarian reform.

The *guajiros* have merely changed masters: the INRA has replaced the *latifundista,* and Señor Foreman has been succeeded by Comrade Manager.

Last week I was talking to some peasants from the Cuba Libre cooperative in the province of Matanzas. Theoretically, every member of this community owns at least 65 acres of land. But he cannot do what he likes with this land; he can neither sell it nor rent it, nor leave it in his will. Though the land belongs to him, he can sow only the crop prescribed by the INRA delegate.

Cuba Libre covers an area of 1,300 acres and produces good crops of sugar cane, beans, and grains. It yields a good crop, but at the end of last year, when the profits were distributed, the seventy-one "cooperators" received only one fifth of what was owing to them. "Where are the other four fifths?" they asked in surprise and disappointment.

The superintendent was not in the least disconcerted. "Carefully reread the rules and regulations of the cooperatives. It says that 80 per cent of the profits will be used to build houses."

"But we all have houses."

"Ah! Not houses for you, but for the peasants on poor cooperatives. If you have any objection, you are always free to leave. You are quite free to withdraw from the cooperative whenever you wish. But I must warn you that a *guajiro* leaving a cooperative takes nothing with him."

"That's unfair," said one of the cooperators.

The superintendent grew angry. "Comrade, you have no right to speak of the agrarian reform in those terms. It was Fidel who promulgated the reform and Fidel is always right."

The peasant bowed. "That's true, Fidel is always right."

18

The classroom was not luxurious, but it was clean. The pupils had tables and chairs of white wood, and the teacher had a desk and an armchair. Behind him was a painted wooden bookshelf on which were displayed Fidel Castro's speeches, Jean-Paul Sartre's book on Cuba, *Guerrilla Warfare* by Che Guevara, as well as the works of Lenin and various politico-social works dealing with Marxist problems.

The teacher was one of the young girl soldiers who had given me such a warm welcome the day before. She was called Yolanda. She was eighteen years old, small, with a good tan and long black hair. She wore a tight-fitting pair of khaki fatigue trousers with large side pockets, and a shirt that set off her well-formed breasts.

Her father was a technician in a canning factory in Havana. He had wanted her to continue her studies beyond the average level in Cuba and had sent her to the university. "I'm going to be a chemical technician," she said. "For the moment the universities are shut, but they will probably reopen next year. In the meantime, I have joined the Literacy Brigades like many other students, both boys and girls."

She described how she had first of all attended a two-week course at the "Alphabetisors'"* training center, which had been set up in what had once been a millionaires' luxury hotel at Varadero. The instructors came from the Rebel Youth Organizations (an amalgamation of Castroist and Communist youth movements). "They were not the only ones," she added. "There were also some Chinese technicians belonging to the *Junta de Planificación.* They used to listen to the instructors, and then put in a few words themselves, to remind us of the importance of our task and to elaborate a few details."

After her two weeks of training, Yolanda was solemnly presented with a pair of paratrooper's boots, a pair of Army fatigues, a U.S. Army belt, a black beret, a Czech machine gun, fifty rounds of ammunition, and two brochures entitled *Alfabeticemos* and *Venceremos.*

"Ah!" she cried. "I will never forget that ceremony at Varadero. We assembled in the hotel's main hall, along with soldiers who had come especially from Havana. What a fine revolutionary ceremony! What splendid patriotic speeches! Fidel's own representative, a real *barbudo* from the Sierra, reminded us of our unswerving duty and brought tears to our eyes."

"What unswerving duty?"

"It is all contained in that slogan we have engraved in our hearts: *Patria o muerte! Venceremos!* Then," she went on, "we all left the Varadero Center singing the anthem of the soldiers of the Literacy Brigades."

"The one I was whistling yesterday?" Remembering the applause I had got the day before, I began to sing *Madelon.*

"No, No! Not that one. I'll sing it for you. This is our anthem. It's beautiful. Listen:

Forward march the Brigades to war,
To fight against illiteracy,
The worst enemy of the people.

* I hope the reader will excuse this rather literal translation of the Spanish word *Alfabetisador,* which is at present all the rage in Cuba. (Author's note.)

How do you like it?"

"You sing well."

"No, not me. I mean the Literacy Brigades' marching song. How do you like it?"

"Well, it's very catchy," I said.

"You haven't heard the best yet," she said. "The chorus is the most moving. Listen to this:

Cuba mine, I'll make you
Educated, yes, yes, but never, never enslaved."

Yolanda was sent straight to the El Rosario farm, where a literacy school had just been set up. Her pupils were *monteros* who spent most of their time on horseback out on the plain or up in the hills. They could attend classes only in the evening, so they didn't begin till after the movie ended.

I sat down at the back of the class. Yolanda handed me *Alfabeticemos* and *Venceremos*. I got out my pen and paper, and there I was back at school. Almost all my classmates had bristling whiskers. One of them, in military uniform, had hung his Garand rifle over the back of his chair. Another one was nervously crumpling a cigar butt between his fingers. No doubt he was once again feeling like a schoolboy who is afraid of being caught smoking.

Our young teacher, Yolanda, laid her machine gun on her desk and announced in a firm voice, "Comrades, we will turn to page sixty-six of *Alfabeticemos* and to page two of *Venceremos*. We will begin with the more advanced comrades. *Compañero* Ramón, what do you know about the Revolution?"

A toothless old peasant, with hollow cheeks and disheveled hair, stood up and recited in a monotonous voice, "The Revolution wins all the battles."

"Very good, Comrade Ramón. Now tell me about the Cuban Revolution."

"The Cuban Revolution had to fight many battles before it could consolidate itself. Throughout these struggles, it was able to triumph thanks to the courage and steadfastness of our people and to the help furnished by the numerous friendly peoples and governments." He hesitated, stared at the ground, scratched his beard and started off again mumbling, "The . . . er . . . the . . . er canceling. . . ."

Yolanda quickly came to the rescue. Without even looking at the text, which she knew by heart, she went on for him, "The can-cel-ing of more than a mill-ion. . . ."

"Yes, that's it, Comrade Yolanda. The canceling of more than a million. . . . I remember now. Sorry. The canceling of more than a million tons of sugar from our quota on the North American market constitutes the first act of economic aggression unleashed by the forces of imperialism, which hoped to weaken our resistance. But the friendly countries, such as the Soviet Union and the People's Republic of China, hurried to buy our sugar which the United States Government had turned down."

"Very good, Comrade Ramón. I see that you have understood our Revolution perfectly. Now let's move on to the comrade beginners. *Compañeros,* we are going to read the first letter of each of the following words: Organization of American States, OAS. I repeat, OAS. Now, all together, with me, OAS."

Yolanda kept religiously to the instructions she had been given at Varadero. She did not stray one iota from the contents of the two brochures.

Alfabeticemos and *Venceremos* are both the gospel and the manual of arms of this new form of popular education. The first thing Cuban illiterates learn is not A B C, but the initials of the Organization of American States. In the second lesson, on vowels, they take as examples of "A," "E," "I," "O," and "U" the names Cuba, Fidel, Raúl and Camilo (Cienfuegos).

The pupils then move on to the initial letters I, N, R, and A. The following expressions are used to practise the newly learned letters: "agrarian reform," "the land belongs to the peasants," "the agrarian reform advances," and so on.

After about sixty lessons, the student (this is the title officially given to the Cuban illiterates who are learning to read) is allowed to write a letter to Fidel Castro, running something like this: "*Comandante* Fidel Castro, I am glad to have learned to read and write. You said that he who did not study was a bad revolutionary. I am very grateful to the Revolution and to you for having given me this opportunity to advance myself."

A student who reaches this level, which is equivalent to a diploma, will not only have learned to read and write. He will also have mastered the short dogmatic texts contained in *Alfabeti-cemos* and the 365-word glossary with which this book concludes. I have made a random selection of definitions in this novel manual of basic Spanish:

Aggression: Provocation or attack.

Agriculture: Cultivation of the land.

Algeria: North African country. French colony fighting with all its strength for freedom.

Anti-imperialist: One who is against imperialism, against the oppression of the weaker countries by the stronger.

A.P.: Associated Press. American information agency serving U.S. imperialist interests.

Barbarity: Cruelty, ferocity, lack of culture.

Brigades, international work: Groups of voluntary workers from different countries, who come to cooperate in the task undertaken by the Cuban people.

Companies, foreign: Associations for commerce and negotiation formed with capital from other countries for the purpose of gain and exploitation.

China: Asian country that has carried out a social revolution.

Disarmament, world: Proposal made by the Soviet Union to put an end to the international arms race, eliminate weapons and prepare the ground for peaceful coexistence.

FBI: American institution whose purpose is to investigate crime and to practise political persecution.

Wars, just: Those wars which support the people in their struggle for independence and national sovereignty.

To entrench oneself: To take cover from the enemy.

The next two definitions, on page ninety, came across better in the original Spanish:

Máximo: Lo mas grande.

Máximo Líder de la Revolución: Jefe superior de la Revolución (Fidel Castro).

The Public Relations Service of the Ministry of National Education was run by a charming young woman. She received me very kindly, offered me a seat, asked after my health, went back to her typewriter, and forgot all about me for two hours, at the end of which time she suddenly remembered I was there and asked, "What do you want?"

"Some information on the literacy campaign."

"Ah yes! Of course. I have just what you need." She got up, cast a glance over the metal filing cabinets ranged along the wall, went to a drawer, opened it, searched about inside, shut it, and said, "It's not there. Where can that envelope be?"

"What's it like?"

"A large yellow envelope. It's full of statistics and interesting papers. Where is it now? Not in that drawer, not in that one. Ah yes! It's over there." She opened another drawer. Same business. At the eleventh drawer she exclaimed triumphantly, "Here it is! I knew it wasn't lost. Take it. You can keep it. I've got another one somewhere. I'll look for it later on."

The poor girl was in quite a state. I asked her to come for a cup of coffee with me. "It'll fix you up," I said.

"I guess I really do need it," she sighed. "Public relations is such a tiring job."

The Castro people have long been familiar with the propaganda system inherited from the Americans. In the epic days of the Sierra Maestra, Fidel secured the services of a New York public relations agency. For a few hundred thousand dollars this office organized his personal publicity, launched propaganda campaigns, mobilized the commercial radio and television, distributed information bulletins, news items, and photographs of Castro and his men to the press, and also gave the *líder máximo* publicity suggestions. It was they, for example, who advised him to grow a beard and give his partisans the evocative nickname *barbudos*.

In the café, the woman from the Ministry of Education repeated that she was overwhelmed with work. "I have to write up bulletins for the press, news items for visiting journalists, and so many other things that I don't know where to turn next. No doubt you are aware that we are right in the middle of Education Year."

I knew it only too well, and I couldn't help thinking of my little friend Jesus, the lottery ticket vendor, who wasn't going to school because it was Education Year. "Who's responsible for this campaign?"

"The Minister, Comrade Armando Hart. He's a great guy. You should meet him. He's twenty-seven, tall, handsome, and eager, with a boundless admiration for Fidel. You should see the way he treats those tottering old university rectors. He shouts at them as if they were children. The rectors are terribly frightened. They bow to the ground and reply, 'Yes, of course, Mr. Minister.' 'You may count on me, Mr. Minister.' 'Naturally, Mr. Minister.' The other day, he gave a good lesson to a teacher who had once flunked him in an exam. He summoned him to his office in the morning, kept him waiting till the evening, and then, when he received him, gave him a piece of his mind. That teacher got what he deserved."

"Isn't twenty-seven a little young to be Minister of Education?"

"That depends on the minister. With Armando it has worked out well. He studied at the University of Havana. Then he went to Communist China, where he studied literacy methods. He has promised Fidel that by the end of the year there won't be a single illiterate left on the island."

This is the best possible propaganda argument the Revolution could have. It shows how in three years the Cuban revolutionaries have succeeded in accomplishing what generations of bourgeois governments could not or would not do. In Latin America, where there are 70 million illiterates out of a total population of 220 million, education is regarded as an inaccessible luxury. And yet, for a man of the people, it means at least as much as wealth, for it implies the ability to escape from his state of servility and attain a higher social status. In Cuba, all possible means have been used to insure the success of the *Año de la Educación:* radio and television never stop talking about literacy, there are posters which say, "You, who can read this, do not forget that there are others who cannot. Go out and teach them how to read." The newspapers publish installments from *Alfabeticemos* and *Venceremos.* Activists from the Rebel Youth Organizations go about telling the children in the streets, "What are you waiting for? Make yourselves useful. Go and help the old who cannot read or write. Teach them how to read."

The Castro people have an easy game here. During the half century between Independence and Revolution, only one new school was built in Havana. During his first month in power, Fidel Castro saw that work was begun on thirty-seven new schools. The number of classrooms in the island has increased from 18,000 to 25,000. It is a real victory.

The young woman confirmed what Father Z., the teacher from Belén College, had already told me. "Education Year is also working a radical change in teaching methods. Hart has ordered the closing down of all educational establishments, public as well as private, from April 15 to December 31. He has dismissed 35,000 reactionary teachers."

"Who's going to replace them?"

"Students chosen from among the healthy and dynamic elements in the Rebel Youth Organizations."

"Do you think they will know how to teach?"

"Of course," she replied. "Anybody can teach. All you need is a good textbook. In any case, the new teachers will not be sent off into the wilds without a minimum of training beforehand. Czechoslovakia, the Soviet Union, and the People's Republic of China have each sent us several hundred technicians. Their mission is to train future teachers. In addition, they have put at our disposal special technicians who are collaborating with Armando Hart on the revision of school textbooks. They are working day and night. There are so many things to change, especially in history and geography."

"What is there to change in history and geography? The Nile still flows through East Africa and out into the Mediterranean; 1492 is still the date of the discovery of America. These are established facts, they are indisputable."

"Yes of course, but next year, Cuban school children will know the truth about the Chinese Revolution, about life in the Soviet Union, the role played by the United States in Latin America, etc. I went with Armando Hart on an inspection tour in Camagüey, and we visited a college. After touring the buildings, we brought the teachers together and gave them some new directives.

"The young Minister read out the following declaration: 'Every lesson, every lecture, and every exercise must serve the cause of the Revolution. Even mathematics must play its part.'

" 'Excuse me, Mr. Minister,' objected one of the teachers, 'I have been teaching mathematics for the last twenty years. To be quite frank, I have never yet come across revolutionary mathematics or counterrevolutionary mathematics. I have only had experience of plain mathematics. Whatever our opinions or those of the Government may be, two and two still make, always have made, and always will make four. It's a universal law.'

"The ardent young Hart appeared annoyed. 'You don't seem to understand. When I say that mathematics must play a part in the service of the Revolution, I'm not joking, you know. I mean it in all seriousness. The very future of the Revolution is at stake. In the problems you give, instead of saying: 3 cats + 7 dogs = 10 animals, you must say: 3 cooperatives + 7 factories = 10 revolutionary projects. Just think about it. How will the children get interested in the Revolution if you're always talking to them about cats and dogs? It's the same with your problems about taps. It's ridiculous to talk to them about taps flowing and discharging x gallons of water per hour. Talk to your pupils about sugar production and sales.'

" 'That's all very well, but it's easier for a ten-year-old to understand problems about cats and dogs and kitchen taps than political economy.'

" 'That may be, but you will obey my directives. From now on, all the examples you use must be drawn from the Cuban people's struggle and that of their supreme leader, Dr. Fidel Castro. Search through his speeches for ideas to present to the children you are entrusted with. Never miss an opportunity to attack the greed of the Americans and of their flunkeys the *latifundistas*. Turn your pupils into real revolutionaries and real socialists. Teach them to follow the torch that our supreme guide is carrying across the American continent. Never begin a lesson without writing in large letters across the blackboard, *Patria o Muerte! Venceremos!* "

CHAPTER 19

"*Abajo los Judas que atropellan a la Juventud!*" "Down with the traitors who insult youth!"

For some hours, several dozen excited young hooligans had been demonstrating against the staff at La Salle Academy. Organized by the leaders of the Student Revolutionary Committee, they had gathered in front of the college walls and were brandishing banners covered with war slogans and shouting death and destruction to their own teachers.

There were a few reporters on the scene—from Castroist newspapers, of course—to whom they handed the text of a petition addressed to the government, as follows: "We accuse those in charge of the academy of trying to turn it into a center of counter-revolutionary indoctrination. In particular, we denounce the unjust and capricious attitude of Brother Barnaby. We want to know how long the Cuban people will tolerate these criminals. We hope that the Revolutionary Government will finally put an end to their vile activities directed against both Christ and their country."

I managed to slip into the college, and asked to see the principal. "That's quite impossible," I was told by a teacher wearing a cassock, Father D. "He is having enough trouble with the authorities as it is. If he gave even the briefest interview, it would immediately be considered an act of provocation, and he would be attacked more violently than ever. You know what I mean. But if you like, we could talk."

Father D. ushered me into his office, an austere room with a table, a metal filing cabinet, and three deal chairs. There was a large poster on the wall showing the face of a small boy. A large caption read: "Parents, send your children to the nearest catechism class. It depends on you whether they are to grow up as Christians or as Atheists."

"These are strange times we live in," said the priest as he sat down. "The Castro forces are destroying family life with their new education. They are turning every little Cuban into a spy or informer. In every school or college, whether private or state-run, there is a Revolutionary Watch Committee. They are real Soviets endowed with discretionary powers and loudly supported by the press. Their membership is drawn from the Rebel Youth Organizations that have united with the Communist Youth Organizations.

"These sweet, virtuous little angels keep a card index on their teachers and classmates. The information is sent on to *Comandante* Rolando Cubela, President of the Federation of University Students (FEU), who, in turn, passes it on to G-2.

"There is a member of the Committee in every class, who comes to school armed and in uniform. A boy fifteen years old interrupted a history lesson one day. He drew his pistol, took aim at the teacher, and threatened to shoot him on the spot if he persisted in teaching that the United States had declared war on Spain in order to come to the help of the Cuban rebels. The teacher was not in the least disconcerted. He gave the boy a good slap and sent him out of class. The next day, at the Committee's intercession, the history teacher was dismissed without pension or compensation. A few weeks ago, orders were given for a general toughening up. Hardly a day goes by without *Revolución, Hoy* and the other Government papers accusing members of the Committees of being too soft. Yesterday, for example, *Revolución* devoted a whole editorial to this Academy."

Father D. rummaged through the stack of newspapers on the table in front of him. "Here's the article," he said. "It says, 'The patriots at La Salle Academy must go into action without delay. What do they mean by their conciliatory attitude?' As a result, the Revolutionary Committee approached the principal the very same day. 'The situation has become intolerable,' they said. 'Counter-revolutionaries have infiltrated us and are attempting to sabotage the Revolution.' 'Who are they?' 'Both teachers and students. We are here to demand that these worms be expelled.' 'Before expelling them, we'll find out how everyone feels. Both teachers and pupils will vote by secret ballot.' When the votes were counted, there were sixty in favor of expulsion and four hundred and twenty against. 'That settles it,' said the principal, 'the majority is opposed to expulsion.'

" 'In that case, we give you warning that we shall now turn to direct action.' That evening, a bomb went off in the cloakroom. There was more noise than damage, but the newspapers took the opportunity of denouncing 'the criminal activities of a counter-revolutionary clique.' "

Father D. sighed. "Well, you know the rest of the story: sixty boys—all members of the Committee—supported by soldiers from outside, are demonstrating in front of the college gates. Tomorrow morning the press will play up the story. Tomorrow evening, under the pretext of restoring order, the authorities will expel a few of the four hundred and twenty who voted 'no' last week. Brother Barnaby will probably be sent to prison. At all events, he expects to be."

A sad smile spread across his wrinkled face. "What are we to do? Things are very, very difficult; not only for the Christian schools, it's the same for all the schools on the island. Cuban education is following the pattern of the Communist-bloc countries. Their principle is: indoctrinate, indoctrinate at all costs, and as quickly as possible."

"Is Hart, the Minister, a strong enough man to carry such a policy through?"

"Armando Hart is only an administrator. He merely carries out the orders of the thousand or so Russian, Polish and—by far the most numerous—Chinese specialists, who are assigned to the Ministry. They are responsible for the idea of school-towns. Not even Hitler or Stalin went as far as they are going. The first of these schools is now being built on the steep slopes of the Sierra Maestra. It's called Camilo Cienfuegos. It's been built by the army. From January 1, 1962, 20,000 children will live and study there.

"This enormous boarding school was conceived, in theory, to cope with the problem of the wide dispersal of students in the mountainous region. In practice, it will mean that the children will be regimented from the age of six on. In this way, the new regime will be able to control thousands of young minds, under conditions that exclude almost all risk of nonconformist contamination.

"Castroism is extremely farsighted. It is investing human capital for the future. Even now, children between the ages of eight and fourteen all think alike. They have been turned into monsters of fanaticism. I know some who send in a detailed report to G-2 on their parents' activities every week.

"We priests, of course, are the fly in the ointment. As long as there are priests in Cuba, the masses will continue, if not to follow us, at least to listen to us. That is why we have to be crushed by any means. Let me tell you a true story, which took place recently in a Catholic boarding school in Havana. Thirty soldiers forced their way in at three o'clock in the morning and invaded the children's dormitories, waking them up with bursts of machine-gun fire at the windows and ceilings. The children were forced to get up, and the soldiers led them off to G-2 Headquarters, where 'specialists'—we have plenty of specialists of every sort these days—lectured to them. They said, 'You saw the priests throw stones at the soldiers and spit on a photograph of Fidel, didn't you?' The boys answered 'no.'

"A sign was hung around their necks: *Actividades conspirativas*, and they were photographed, full face and profile. After they had been fingerprinted, they were threatened with being sent to *La Cabaña*. They continued to refuse to level absurd charges against their teachers. The eldest of the boys were then seized; the soldiers lined them up against the wall and pretended to shoot them. Eight hours of moral torture finally broke the boys' resistance. They all signed a petition accusing their teachers of taking part in counter-revolutionary, anti-national activities. The document was published in the press next day. It allowed the government to imprison or exile the priests and take over the boarding school.

"You see," explained Father D., "Fidel Castro wants to set up a national Cuban church independent of Rome. He has promoted an association 'For Cross and Country,' which has the real aim, even if it is not openly declared, to prepare for this schism. A large number of priests have been asked to condemn Rome and the Cuban episcopate. Not one has agreed. That's another reason why Fidel has declared war on us.

"Fidel's attitude is quite unjustified. Ever since the beginning of the 26th of July Movement, we gave him our full support. If the Castro brothers were not put to death by Batista after the Santiago tragedy, it is entirely thanks to the personal intervention of the Archbishop, Msgr. Péres Serantés.

"At the beginning of 1958, one year before the triumph of the Revolution, all priests signed a petition condemning the crimes of Batista's dictatorship. On March 2, the same year, the bishops of the island sent out a pastoral letter which was read in all the churches. They demanded the constitution of a national democratic government."

"When I went to INRA," I said, "I was shown a pastoral letter signed by Msgr. Diaz, Bishop of Havana. His Eminence explained in very human terms why the agrarian reform should be supported."

"That's quite correct. Msgr. Diaz's words were: 'If Catholics who want to be worthy of that name understood the full implications of Christ's twofold commandment to love God with all one's heart and one's neighbor as oneself, they would willingly accept the necessary changes. Let those who are blessed with riches and who set great store by their Christianity decide for themselves whether their conscience can allow them to go on living in peace before the tears, the poverty, and the desolation of those of their brethren who have nothing.' The Castro people continue to distribute this letter to foreign journalists, but they take good care not to mention that since then Msgr. Diaz has been beset with every kind of difficulty, imprisoned several times, threatened with exile and even tortured."

Father D. sighed again. "We have become serpents to be crushed underfoot, and they never miss an opportunity of proving our worthlessness. During Holy Week, they sabotaged the electricity in the Church of Jesus of Miramar. On Sundays, the police give fines to motorists who park in front of churches. Prison chaplains are no longer authorized to visit prisoners. The national printing press has just published a book called *El hombre del campo* [*The Countryman*], in which there is one chapter under the signature of José Martí recommending parents not to baptize their children. José Martí, however, never wrote anything of the sort.

"Have you heard about Fatima's latest miracle? It's very edifying. Cuban cinemas were going to show a short film on the Virgin and the miracles of Fatima. The ICAIC* censors hesitated for a long time. They considered the film an instrument of clerical propaganda. But they didn't dare to ban it. So they decided to adapt it. They cut out all the religious scenes, and thereby achieved the miracle of showing a film on Fatima without ever mentioning the Virgin.

"There are new accusations, new insinuations, new provocations every day. On February 11, 1961, we celebrated a mass in the chapel of our Academy commemorating the thirty-third anniversary of the foundation of Cuban Catholic Action. During the service, the Revolutionary Committee mobilized some INRA soldiers and had our buildings surrounded. When mass was over, and the students and their parents prepared to leave, they were prevented by gunfire. The siege lasted for twelve hours. It wasn't until eleven o'clock, after the Papal Nuncio had gone to see the president of the Republic, that it was finally raised.

"At Santiago de Cuba there is another La Salle College. Every year they celebrate Catholic Students' Day with a mass and a banquet. On the last occasion, March 7, 1961, at half past six in the evening, soldiers burst in on the students with machine-gun fire and shouts of '*Abajo los aliados del clero fascista*,' 'Down with the allies of the fascist clergy.' Of course, several fights broke out. On March 8, 672 students who had taken part in the mass were expelled from the college, once again on the pretext of restoring order.

---

* Cuban Institute of Cinematographic Art and Industry, whose director, Mr. Guevara (not to be confused with Che Guevara), has been a member of the Communist Party since 1952.

"The Castro forces attack us on every front. If you have time, go down to San José de las Lajas near Havana. I'll send you to some Christian trade unionists who will tell you a very illuminating story." Father D. fell silent; he became absorbed in the contemplation of his long hands, calloused like a peasant's. "What do you think about all this?" he asked me. "Don't you think it's shameful for men to behave like that?"

"I was at the movies the other evening," I said. "They were showing one of the latest Hollywood productions, about two young delinquents and a beautiful woman, rich and idle. After the word END a note from the ICAIC appeared on the screen, informing the spectators that 'This film portrays the life of American youth, debased by capitalism and imperialism.' But that didn't particularly surprise or shock me. It was afterwards, during the newsreel, when they showed pictures of Cuban priests and prelates while the recorded voice of Fidel Castro announced, 'To betray the poor is to betray the people.' "

"To betray the poor," murmured Father D. "Isn't it shameful to accuse the clergy of such ignominy?"

"The Castro people," I said, "reproach the Cuban clergy with being largely composed of Spanish priests. They gave the Catholic University in Havana the insulting nickname of Yankeelandia."

"It makes me want to weep," said Father D., "when I'm called a foreigner. Of course, most of us *are* of Spanish origin." His voice rose in indignation. "But isn't Castro himself the son of a Spaniard? When the Madrid Government handed Cuba over to the United States it was only the clergy who remained at their posts. If the priests had gone back to Europe, and if other Spanish priests had not come out to work in this country, the island would now be American. We'd all be speaking English now. If Cuba has remained an independent nation, it is largely thanks to the clergy."

"Were you born in Spain, Father?"

"In a village in the Basque country," he replied. His long pale face lit up in a smile. "Do you know the Basque country?" he asked.

"I'm afraid not."

"My home was only a few miles from the French border. There was a little stream close by that cascaded down the mountain side. When I was a boy, I used to bathe in the clear water. I used to go fishing, too." He brightened and chuckled softly to himself. "I hardly ever caught anything. I had a long feud with a trout which spent its life hiding between a flat stone and some reeds. I was determined to catch him. It became a question of honor. But the trout never moved, he remained quite indifferent to the flies and worms I dangled on the end of my line. In the evening, at supper, the whole family used to tease me about it, and I got more and more angry. I caught him in the end, after goodness knows how many weeks of trying. It was only then that I noticed the trout was blind. They have trout in the streams here, too. But I've never had time to go fishing.

"In the old days, when I used to make the rounds of the *bohios* every week, baptizing here, bringing consolation there, the peasants received me with joy. They always seemed glad to see me. We were on familiar terms, but they never failed to start their sentences off by addressing me respectfully as 'Father.'

"Although poor and needy, the *guajiros* had managed to preserve, over centuries of hardship, that nobleman's dignity which is so characteristic of Galician peasants. Particularly during the *zafra*, their season of prosperity, some of the gestures they made had a nobility that belonged to a more ancient civilization.

"Ah! *zafra* in the old days! The roads and lanes were a fever of activity. Carts loaded with cane followed one another for miles. Round the *bohios*, the avocados and mangoes would be ripening on the trees. The peasants lived in poverty, but they knew happiness of a sort. You should have heard with what pride the *guajiros* talked about their children. 'Father,' they would say. 'You should see our *muchacho*, he's. . . .'

"Now everything has changed. In theory, the Revolution has freed men from poverty. So it should have made them happier. But the *guajiros* have become unhappy. They are both ashamed and afraid. They're afraid of being denounced by their neighbors and their own children. They're afraid of themselves. They run away when they see me. 'Priest' has come to be synonymous with 'plague' for them: both bring only trouble. So they keep as far away as possible, from sheer terror.

"I was walking along the road recently near San José de Las Lajas, the place where I suggested earlier you go and do some research, when I met some soldiers. The sergeant shouted out to his men, 'Well, what do you say to the *gusano en sotana*, the earth-worm in a cassock?' The soldiers hung their heads without replying, and the sergeant got angry and shouted, 'Traitors! Don't tell me you're on the clergy's side. Because that's what I'll think if you're not careful. Come on, what do you say to the *gusano en sotana?*'

"Timidly, as though committing some sacrilege, they took up the chorus: '*Cuba si, clero no! Down with the Church and I shit in your mother's face.*' Excuse my using such language, but it's the truth." The priest blushed, passed his hand across his brow as though he were feeling ill.

"Father," I said, "are you all right?"

"Yes, perfectly." His voice seemed weary.

"Father, you should go and lie down."

"No, no. I'm quite all right."

"You're tired, then."

"No," he replied, shaking his head, "there's nothing wrong. I'm just worried; not about my fate. I'm a Spaniard by birth; they'll just exile me at the very worst. It's the others, those who will stay behind that I am worried about. You're a journalist. You haven't spent your life among the Cubans. Their troubles don't concern you personally. Whatever you may do, you will never come to feel quite like one of them, not to the extent of weeping for their suffering. You'll soon be leaving for your own country and one day you will forget Cuba. But it's different for me—don't think I'm being proud. I'm one of them, Cuban just like them, sharing the misfortunes and sorrows of Cuba."

I filled my pipe. Father D. cast a sad glance towards me. "In winter," he told me, "they used to make pipes in my village in the Basque country."

"Do you expect to go back there?"

"There? Perhaps. Where else should I go when I am thrown out of Cuba? At least I'll be left in peace there. I'll be free to pray and serve God. I won't be insulted, people won't run away from me saying that priests are dressed like crows and, like crows, bring bad luck."

CHAPTER 20

For anyone who is used to even a minimum of liberty the atmosphere at Havana University is intolerable. At the entrance the students are searched by soldiers and must show their identity cards. Along the corridors there are large posters inviting them to denounce their counterrevolutionary fellow students to the Watch Committee.

The whole place was more or less deserted. Only in one corner of the courtyard, close to the office of the FEU, a few boys and girls in uniform were talking. They were all armed. But for them, the university would have been a desert. "We're on vacation," explained Rufo, the student who acted as my guide, "a compulsory and everlasting vacation." Rufo had done his pre-college studies at La Salle Academy. It was Father D. who asked him to show me round the lecture halls, corridors, and gymnasiums.

Together we climbed the steps of the monumental stairway that led up from San Miguel Street to the university's Doric façade. The soldier sitting on a wooden stool at the top of the stairs asked to see our papers. Rufo had warned me, "Pretend you don't know me."

The soldier looked at my passport mechanically and said, "For enrollments, go to the building at the back and to the right."

Rufo joined me shortly afterwards and laughed. "Fortunately, he can't read. We've been sent soldiers from the country; they are the staunchest Fidelists, but the most ignorant, too."

He waved his arms in a wide circle. "Look at that—what a thriving university." His voice was bitter with irony. "Most of the departments have closed down. The Science, Chemistry, Agriculture, and Architecture departments have been 'on vacation' for several months already, and will no doubt continue to be so for a long time to come. Castroism is eternal, since, apparently, it is all the future. Ah well! Just take a good look around you. Castro's eternity has already begun here. There's the revolutionary paradise for you."

"Why has the university closed down?"

"There are no more teachers. Castro had some of them shot and a good many more imprisoned. Those who escaped fled the country."

"Are there really no teachers left?"

"Oh yes, a few; in the Law School there are three. There used to be about forty. Castro has vainly been trying to replace those who left. He inserted some 'help wanted' ads in the daily papers: 'Wanted for Havana University: professors of science, chemistry, etc.' He soon realized that qualified teachers were harder to come by than out of work seasonal laborers. So he cooked up some new solution. He appointed government engineers and retired judges as science and law professors."

"What are you studying?"

"In theory, engineering. For the moment, it's best not to think about getting a diploma. Unless I forge one myself."

"How old are you?"

"Twenty-two."

"Why don't you like Fidel? I mean, apart from the fact that he's holding up your studies."

Rufo sighed, threw up his hands with a gesture of despair. "It would take so long to explain."

"Father D. told me that you are a practising Catholic. Is that why you are against Fidel?"

"Yes, but there's plenty else besides."

"What, for example? Your family? Have they suffered under the regime?"

"Why do you want to know? What's it got to do with you? You came to take a look at the university under the Castro Revolution, didn't you? Why bring me into it?"

"It's of great importance, I assure you. Obviously, it's shocking to find policemen and informers in a university; but I'd like to understand your personal reasons for opposing Fidel. You don't run any risk by telling me. Your name won't be published."

"I'm not afraid to die."

"Well then, answer my question. Has your family suffered under the Castro regime?"

"Not in the least. My father works on the administrative staff of a department store. The Revolution didn't affect his life very much."

"Well then?"

After walking for some time we finally paused by a low wall. On the other side of it began the *vedado* district with its well-kept streets, private houses, and luxury stores. It was toward evening, and a cool breeze coming in from the sea brought us the smell of eucalyptus and jasmine.

I stood in front of the young man and insisted, looking into his eyes. "Well then?"

"*Bueno,* I'll tell you. And if that doesn't satisfy you, I'll introduce you to some friends, some of them Catholics, some not. They too will tell you what they have learnt and how they feel about things. First of all, let me ask you a question. It's you who have been doing all the asking so far. Now it's my turn."

"OK. Go ahead."

"If, when you were a student, the police had burst into the lecture hall to arrest your friends merely for not thinking like Fidel, would you have remained a Fidelist?"

"Of course not."

"Well, then, there you are. You've answered for me. At first, the university was 100 per cent Fidelist. Fidel seems to have forgotten completely that the students once supported his movement to the hilt. Without our efforts and our blood—don't forget that plenty of us were killed by Batista's police—Fidel Castro would never have succeeded in overthrowing the dictatorship. What could he have done all alone with only his handful of wretched, underfed, badly equipped *barbudos* against Batista's powerful, well-armed divisions? The legend he has built up since then is quite untrue. He did not win by force of arms. He only won because thousands of boys and girls risked their lives day and night in order to dynamite barracks and public buildings, collect information and generally undermine the morale of Batista's troops. Batista's army melted away without ever having really fought. That's when Castro found himself victorious.

"I don't think that Fidel really ever has forgotten these things. He knows only too well what we have done and what we are still capable of doing. He knows that Havana University has always been a stronghold of the struggle for liberty and democracy. He's well aware that we have always resisted oppression of every kind, and above all he knows our contempt for danger and for death. That is why he's so suspicious of us, and why he is just as much afraid of us as he is of his original army, the real *barbudos* of the Sierra. He disbanded his former comrades for fear of having to answer to them one day.

"Fidel let no scruples interfere with his determination to bring us to heel. He turned his attention to the university even before the victory celebrations were over. Do you want to know how he set about trying to make the students submit?"

"Yes, of course."

"*Bueno.* Tomorrow evening at nine o'clock, I'll come and pick you up at your hotel. I'll get you to meet some members of the old FEU."

"The old FEU?"

"Yes, the real FEU, the Union which existed when the Cuban Revolution was a real revolution of the people. The FEU that exists now, well, that's something else again. It's just the university branch of G-2."

Rufo came to fetch me at the agreed time and took me to the old city. After threading a labyrinth of alleys we finally arrived in front of a house built in Spanish colonial times, with tall rectangular windows protected by crisscrossed wrought-iron bars. We went in through the wide entrance and up a monumental stairway with marble steps and mahogany bannisters to the second floor. We stopped in front of a dark wooden door on which were two iron knockers shaped like lions' heads. Rufo pressed an electric bell.

A woman of about thirty opened the door for us. It was Rufo's sister, the wife of a well-known lawyer, Mr. O. Mrs. O. ushered us into the dining room. The curtains were drawn, and the air conditioner was making a humming noise.

There were six young people (two of them girls) standing side by side with their backs to the mahogany sideboard. Rufo introduced them. "Emilio, fourth year law student; Léonel, fifth year medicine; Juan, second year engineering; Lázaro, fourth year medicine; Lidia, third year chemistry; Vilma, second year law."

We sat down around the polished table, lit up by a lamp that hung from the ceiling. They all looked at me in silence. At length, Léonel, a chubby boy with glasses, spoke to me. "Rufo told us that you were interested in Havana University. What do you want to know?"

"The truth about your conflict with Castro."

"The struggle didn't come out into the open until the end of 1959. Until then, Fidel had been content to act more subtly. He had the student organization infiltrated by activists from the Communist and Rebel Youth movements.

"Then Fidel struck suddenly, in October, on the day of the university elections. The students were to elect seventeen representatives to run the FEU. There were two opposing lists, one headed by Pedro Luiz Boitel, a leader in the student section of the 26th of July Movement, and the other by *Comandante* Rolando Cubela. Do you know Cubela?"

"I met him in the bar of the Casa Vasco." He was a man of 180 pounds or so, one of the heroes of the war against Batista. After fighting beside Fidel Castro in the Sierra Maestra, he invaded Las Villas Province and took over the township of Santa Clara.

"Cubela isn't a student," explained Juan. "It was Fidel Castro who sent us that little surprise, thinking that a soldier of his stamp would be able to keep us in line."

"But don't you have to be a student in order to run for election to the FEU?"

"Of course. Cubela got over that problem by enrolling in the medical school."

The enormity of such a procedure was only too obvious to me. It was as though after the liberation of France, de Gaulle had placed a general at the head of UNEF, the National Students' Union. I could easily imagine what an uproar such a measure would have raised among Castro's admirers in France.

Léonel continued with the account of these elections. "Fidel, of course, favored Cubela, and joined the campaign himself at dawn on voting day, October 17, 1959. An article by him appeared in *Revolución*, inviting Boitel to withdraw and the students to unite in order to elect Cubela to the presidency unopposed. Boitel refused, and the polling went on as usual. Cubela won with 52 per cent of the votes."

Léonel turned scarlet, and his eyes sparkled behind the thin lenses of his glasses. "A few days after his defeat," he went on, "Boitel found himself in prison. He was accused of conspiracy, and sentenced to thirty years of hard labor. They obviously didn't think that was enough, because they tried him again for another 'act of conspiracy' and he got twelve additional years. There's a third trial pending now."

"Was Boitel a genuine student?" I asked.

Juan leapt to his feet and shouted in my face, "How dare you ask that? Of course he was a genuine student. He was in his last year of engineering."

"Relax," said Rufo. "What are you getting worked up about?"

After this incident, Léonel went on with his story. The first meeting of the new FEU administration was held on February 8, 1960. The first thing Cubela did was to attack an anti-Soviet demonstration which had been organized by some Catholic students in protest against Mr. Mikoyan's visit to Havana on February 5. "I have here," he declared, "a resolution to exclude these saboteurs from the FEU and from the university."

There were violent protests from the opposition which was massively represented in the public gallery. Before the booing and the serious threats of violence, Cubela judged it wiser to withdraw his project. But it was only a postponement. The following month, during a quieter meeting (not surprisingly so, as the seventeen administrators of the FEU had an armed guard to protect them),

Cubela made this announcement: "We're going to set up special tribunals to try counterrevolutionary students."

Finally, on July 15, 1960, Cubela introduced three battalions of soldiers into the university and dissolved the University Council, a traditional body composed of the rector and deans. Fidel and Raúl Castro appointed a four-man *Junta Superior de Gobierno* to take charge of the university. At the same time, a Revolutionary Watch Committee was created.

"The very first thing the Committee did," Rufo said, "was to divide students and teachers into three categories: 'revolutionaries,' 'neutrals,' and 'counterrevolutionaries.' The luckiest in this third group were merely ordered never again to set foot inside a lecture-hall; the rest were sent to prison. The 'neutrals' had their names plastered all over the walls of the university buildings. They weren't described as 'neutral,' but as lacking enthusiasm. The Fidelistas have their own brand of humor." Rufo began to laugh, a dry, humorless laugh that was taken up by the others.

"There are now no 'neutrals' in the university," said Juan. "They are all 'revolutionaries.'"

"Why's that?"

"It's easier that way if you want to pass your exams and get a diploma. If you don't belong to the first category, you don't get a certificate. That means no exams and no diploma."

"What does a student have to do to belong to the 'revolutionary' category?"

"In theory, nothing. But in fact, you have to demonstrate your enthusiasm for the Revolution. You must join the army, volunteer to cut sugar cane every Sunday, and memorize Fidel's speeches as well as the revolutionary songs that are sung in the bus on the way to the training areas or the sugar plantations. In every bus there's at least one representative from the Watch Committee taking down notes on each individual."

The seven students burst out laughing again, but there was something sad, hollow, and even sinister about their laughter. Lázaro was the first to recover his seriousness. He spoke in a low voice, as though making a confession. "We already have our martyrs, you know. Three thousand of our fellow students are in prison. In Havana alone, there are eighty students serving thirty year sentences. Julio Antonio Yebra, a fifth year medical student at Havana, and Porfirio Ramírez, president of the FEU at Las Villas, have been shot. After their execution, the members of the Castrist FEU voted motions of congratulation."

There was no bravado in Lázaro's words, no false boasting. In his quiet confidence I could detect scarcely a trace of that triumphant tone young Spaniards so often use when talking about heroism and death. "You should write that we have our martyrs. It's something that the French should know." His voice was trembling and there were tears in his eyes. "There was a time when France gave us courage. But that's all over now. There's nothing to hope for from that quarter. What a change! French intellectuals are more pro-Castro than Cuban Castrists themselves. They howl louder than the wolves. They should be told that on this Caribbean island students are dying for the sake of freedom."

Lázaro grew more excited with every word. His voice grew louder and more bitter. "Why have the French intellectuals stopped up their ears? So as not to hear our martyrs singing the Marseillaise in face of the firing squad? That's no lie—it's easy to check on. In Camagüey during Holy Week some students demonstrated, shouting 'Vive la liberté' and singing your Marseillaise. The soldiers opened fire on them. Several were wounded, some of them mortally."

The young man fell silent. He was pale and his lips and cheeks trembled. He looked at me; the other students looked at me, fixedly and seriously, as if they were waiting for an explanation from me. "Ah!" Lázaro burst out. "I can't help wondering just what *are* the ideals of the French intelligentsia?"

CHAPTER 21

Some twenty miles from Havana stands the little town of San José de Las Lajas, on the Carretera Central, which is like the backbone of Cuba, running from one end of the island to the other, linking all cities. San José is an industrial town, the majority of the men being employed either on a public works project or in an electric appliance factory. As I got off the bus, two men came quietly up to me. "Señor Franco?" They were the trade unionists whom Father D. had spoken about. I got into their car and they drove me to the other end of town, to a small isolated cabin. There were two more men and a young woman, also active local trade unionists, waiting for me.

Introductions were soon over. Juan, one of the two Cubans who had come to meet me, said, "I was on the Committee of the Christian trade union set up at the public works project. Listen to what happened on Passion Sunday, day of the feast of St. Joseph, patron saint of our town. A large number of parishioners, many of them employed on the project, were taking part in the religious service which, as in previous years, was being held in the Church of San José de Las Lajas. Everything went on quietly until it came to the Elevation of the Host.

"Then, just as the server was ringing his small bell, and all heads were bowed in prayer, there was a sudden burst of gunfire. Soldiers came crashing in, shooting at the candles and saints, and shouting, '*Muerto a los gusanos con sotana!* Kill them! Shoot them!'

"They rushed at the choir boys and pushed them around. They slapped the priest and then turned their attention to the altar, which they proceeded to smash with the butts of their rifles. Then one of them suddenly shouted, 'The nuns, let's undress them!' They all joined in, 'Let's undress them!'

"In the first row of the congregation a dozen nuns, who had been kneeling ever since the riot started, stopped counting their beads and threw terrified glances around them. Some of them stood up and tried to run away in spite of the heavy robes that hindered their movements. But the soldiers soon caught them. 'Strip the nuns!' the soldiers shouted again. The sisters fell to their knees. A tall Negro was the first one to get to them; he grabbed one of them wildly by the collar of her robe and pulled. The heavy material gave way with a long, sinister ripping noise.

"Now that the first moment of panic was over, the faithful began to react. They were enraged by the attack on the nuns, and quite a battle ensued. They used their fists and even picked up the prayer stools and started hitting out at the soldiers. But the soldiers, being younger and better armed, had too much of an advantage, and they beat up the parishioners systematically, using rifle butts and candlesticks. Some broke the arms of statues of the saints and used these as clubs.

"The incident had enormous consequences. The next day it was headlined in *Revolución*, *Hoy*, and *El Mundo*, which were all bitterly indignant at 'the inadmissible provocation on the part of clerical elements in the pay of Yankee imperialists.' Not the soldiers who had invaded the church were found guilty of provocation, but the parishioners, the choir boys, and the nuns.

"That evening, when they left the factory after work, the workers of San José found the gates closed, and two soldiers armed with

Czech machine guns standing guard at the exit. The workers were
ordered to the dining hall, where a meeting was to be held. In the
dining hall, its walls covered with the same slogans ceaselessly
churned out by the Castro Revolution, the tables had all been
pushed to the back and the benches lined up in rows.

"Everybody sat down, and the trade union delegate and his
assistants then made their appearance with a certain amount of
solemnity, filing in in order of seniority. The atmosphere was tense.
Everybody knew what the meeting was about, especially as many
workers still showed marks of the previous day's battle. As they sat
in silence, packed together on the benches, the workers wondered
how the members of the all-powerful Watch Committee were going to react.

"The trade union delegate in blue-grey shirt and olive green
military trousers, a revolver and cartridge belt at his waist, stood up
to address the workers. He began in a sober, dry tone of voice, but
he soon got carried away. 'Comrades, you are well aware of the
regrettable incident in church yesterday morning. Counterrevolutionaries, traitors to their country in the pay of the Yankee imperialists, indulged in a most detestable act of provocation. They
made a cowardly attack on Cuban patriots. Some of these Judases
are here right now among us. Here is a list of their names. The
demonstration they made yesterday upon the orders of the *latifundistas* has enabled us to unmask them.

" 'Comrades, we must throw out these lackeys of North American imperialism, these *gusanos* whose only thought is to undermine the Revolution. Comrades, we are now going to have a show
of hands to decide whether we can continue to allow these vermin
to practice their vile tricks among us or whether we should eliminate them. All those in favor of the necessary purge raise their
hands.' "

The men who gave me this account had themselves taken part
in this *acto revolucionario*. "What do you think we did?" asked
Juan.

"You raised your hands of course."

"Yes, we raised our hands. Everybody raised his hand. Even the
accused voted their own expulsion. There you see the full horror
of the situation. Can you imagine at a trial the accused sitting on

their own jury? Can you imagine them sentencing themselves to
the maximum penalty?"

"What happened after the vote?"

"The accused were excluded from the CTC, the Confederation
of Cuban Workers. The point is that a worker who does not belong
to the CTC loses his job and is condemned to unemployment."

The *Censo Laboral* law, promulgated on April 14, 1960, by the
Castro Government, places all employment under the control of
the CTC. Juan explained the system to me, "Let's take an example.
Tonio is looking for work. He finds out that there is a job open at
Woolworth's, a nationalized business, and at Gustavo's store, a
private business in San Rafael Street. What does he do?"

"He goes to Woolworth's or Gustavo's."

"No. First of all he must go to the CTC. When he gets there,
he says, 'Look, Comrade, there is a job going at Woolworth's and
one at Gustavo's. I would like to try for one of them.' He shows
his papers, tells his life story, talks about his family, his activities,
his opinions as a union member, about politics, about everything
in fact. He is asked why he wants to work at Woolworth's or at
Gustavo's. He replies that he's looking for work and that Woolworth's and Gustavo's offer good jobs. Above all he mustn't say, 'I
want.' That would seem suspicious. The CTC official makes a note
of the information. Then he says, 'Comrade, we're going to check
what you have told us. Come back in a week and get your notice.'"

"What does this 'notice' mean?" I asked Juan.

"Either the acceptance or refusal of his candidacy. In order to
have work, Tonio must get a 'favorable notice.' If he doesn't get
it, he can go back home and starve. If he does get it, he has now
only to go to the Ministry. Once again he must tell them all about
his life, past and present, give an exact account of his family and
opinions. Once again he is told, 'Comrade, we are going to check.
Come back in a week.' Finally, Tonio has everything in order. He
goes to Woolworth's or Gustavo's and says, 'I want to work for
you.'"

"What if Woolworth's or Gustavo's don't want to hire him?"

"That's impossible," replied Juan. "They have to take him on."

"And that's not all," said Pablo, one of Juan's friends. "Supposing
Tonio wants to change jobs one day. Suppose, for example, he
marries a girl from Matanzas and wants to go and live with his

parents-in-law. Before leaving his present job, he has to apply for permission from the Ministry."

"In this way," concluded Juan, "the government is able to exercise strict control over the workers."

"What about the trade unions?" I said.

"They're all rotten. The government and the Communists infiltrated them long ago."

"How did they manage to do that?"

Juan and Pablo did not answer immediately. They just looked at one another. "I think we can trust you," Juan finally said to me. "We're going to take you to see Pedro, one of the founders of FON.* He's in hiding. The police are after him. He'll tell you how the Communists succeeded in gaining control of all the levers of power in the unions. *Vamos!* Let's go!"

We went out into the courtyard where a Chevrolet was parked. Juan opened the trunk. "Get in there," he said.

"Why?"

"So you won't see where we're going."

"Is that really necessary? Couldn't you just blindfold me and let me lie on the back seat under a blanket? I won't move."

"*Chico*, we believe you, but orders are orders."

I had no choice. Fortunately I'm quite small. I settled down between a five-gallon can and a tool box. "Careful," said Juan. I made myself as small as possible, and the lid came down with a bang. It was hot and dark inside my prison. The smell of gasoline was intolerable. I had to clench my teeth to keep from throwing up.

The car started off, slowly at first, and then gathered speed. I was bounced about as though in an open boat. After a few moments I began to make out the shapes around me, enabling me to change my position and lean against the spare tire, which made things more comfortable. A thin ray of light filtered in through a crack, showing the dancing specks of dust. But I got a headache watching them, so I closed my eyes.

I dozed off, and don't know how long the drive lasted. I was awakened by the jolts of the Chevrolet. Somebody came and opened up the trunk. It was Juan. "*Cómo va?*" he asked.

* National Workers' Front, the workers' section of Castro's 26th of July Movement.

I emerged from my prison half-stunned, and rubbed my eyes. I had a splitting headache. "Where are we?"

"We're there," replied Juan. "Do you need anything?"

"No, I'm OK. But I could do with a good *ron con soda.*"

Pedro went to get me a drink from the cottage that served as his hiding place. He was a small wiry man.

"I'm a friend of David Salvador," he told me. Salvador is the former Secretary-General of the CTC, the Confederation of Cuban Workers, who was imprisoned in *la Cabaña* for "reactionary, counterrevolutionary, and deviationist plotting."

Ten weeks before the end of the Batista regime, the Communist Party officially joined the 26th of July Movement. On Castro's orders, the trade unions under Communist control immediately combined with the FON to form the FONU.* After the victory of the Fidelistas, David Salvador, the uncontested leader of the former FON, was elected Secretary-General of the CTC, despite the opposition of the Communists who only controlled three unions out of thirty-five.

The Communist leader Jesus Soto was determined to seize control of the remaining thirty-two unions, and used tactics that were very simple and met with Che Guevara's and Raúl Castro's approval. The Communists levelled charges of collaboration with the Batista regime against all those trade unionists whom they wanted to eliminate. Once these men were imprisoned, they were immediately replaced by active members of the Communist Party. The unions reacted to this threat by forming the Cuban Humanist Workers' Front, and all the union secretaries signed a manifesto that demanded "the completion of the revolution without prejudice to the rights of the individual."

The tenth Congress of the CTC opened on November 18, 1959. Salvador's supporters clearly outnumbered Soto's: he had 1,700 "humanist" delegates against Soto's 220 Communists. Nevertheless, Soto claimed four out of the nineteen seats on the Executive Committee. Salvador turned down this claim, but Fidel Castro came to the rescue. On November 20, having surrounded the conference hall with soldiers, the *líder máximo* took the microphone. He spoke for several hours and brought his speech to a close by saying:

---

* *Frente Obrero Nacional Unido,* National Workers' United Front.

"Not to vote for Soto and his supporters is to act as a counter-revolutionary and splitter."

Jesus Soto was elected President of the CTC, while his three confederates became Vice-President and Directors of propaganda and external relations.

The cleaning-up process was started immediately and was hustled along as fast as possible. Among the first victims was Manolo Fernández, Secretary-General of the Entertainment Workers' Union. Jesus Soto accused him of having betrayed the working class and the Revolution from the very beginning. Manolo Fernández was expelled without being given a chance to defend himself. Threatened with arrest, he took refuge at the Chilean Embassy.

The elimination of David Salvador proved more difficult. The first step was to replace the Minister of Labor, a personal friend of his, with an active Communist, Augusto Sánchez. Realizing what this measure implied, the Humanist leader went straight to the President of the Republic. "What should I do?" he asked him.

"Go away."

Salvador resigned on the spot. Shortly afterwards he was arrested by G-2 and locked up in *la Cabaña*.

"I too shall end up in *la Cabaña*," said Pedro. "First I was thrown out of the union, then I was almost arrested. I succeeded in escaping and since then, as you see, I've been in hiding."

"What have they got against you?"

"Being against Castro."

"Pedro's not the only one who's anti-Castro," broke in Luis, who had been following the conversation. "All the workers are against the Revolution."

"Why?"

"We were happier before. Thanks to a very advanced trade union organization, we had gained considerable advantages—an eight-hour working day, for example."

"Do you realize," put in Pedro, "that the average salary in Cuba used to be well above that of the other Latin American countries? It even approached the United States average." Luis used to earn 300 pesos a month, plus an additional 40 to 50 pesos for overtime. Now he earns under 250. A worker in the Tropical Brewery used to get 560 pesos a month, and a cleaner in the Polak Brewery 200.

Workers in many other countries would be envious of these salaries.

Luis added that workers used to be entitled to thirty days of paid vacation a year, over and above the nine public holidays. "Now we get a total of only two weeks," he said bitterly, and working himself up he went on, "We've lost the advantages of the collective bargaining contracts we had established between employers and employees. We've lost everything, even the right to strike."

"My sister works in a cigarette factory," said another worker, a thin boy with glasses. "Three months ago, the workers in her factory threatened to go on strike. They wanted a cut in their work hours. Twelve hours a day is a long working day for rolling cigarettes. The union delegates, instead of backing the workers, sided with management. They accused some of the workers of instigating 'a counterrevolutionary demonstration with the object of sabotaging production.' They declared that the women were whores who went to bed with Americans. That's quite untrue. My sister's never been to bed with an American. Finally, they called upon the workers to vote on a motion by acclamation.

"The next day, *Revolución* published the motion. The workers of the cigarette factory 'unanimously' announced their indignation over the activities of 'a minority of traitors' and promised to work for an extra hour each evening to 'demonstrate their allegiance to the Revolution.' "

" 'Increase production,' " said Juan, "has become the regime's daily theme, incessant and murderously boring." I had noticed the same myself. Everywhere, on factory walls, in shops and offices, posters and notices are displayed announcing: "We have increased production." There is even one—this is no exaggeration—in the most luxurious of the brothels still tolerated by the regime.

"Working overtime is very profitable," said Juan. "Stakhanovites are covered with laurels."

"Not with money, though," said Pedro.

"Honors are less expensive," laughed Luis. "The bricklayer who lays most bricks in one day gets his photo in *Hoy* and *Revolución*. But it doesn't earn him an extra cent."

"It's a serious matter," Juan added, "if you don't keep up production rates. There's a textile factory at Bauta, twenty miles north of Havana, where all the machinery is American-made. Since it has been impossible to get spare parts for the last two years, several looms have come to a standstill. The manager, who was appointed by INRA and doesn't understand the first thing about textiles, has accused the workers of sabotage and imposed fines on them. Sometimes he penalizes the workers when the cotton thread breaks— and the cotton is of very poor quality."

"*Este pais es un pais de locos,*" said Luis. "It's a country of madmen." "Madness," echoed Juan. "Instead of seriously attending to business, this manager wastes his time on absurdities. His latest effort is pretty macabre. The founder of the factory, a former American named Dayton Hedges, who became a Cuban citizen, had himself buried in a corner of the factory compound. The manager had Hedges' body exhumed and replaced by that of a soldier who had been killed in an accident. He had Hedges thrown onto a garbage dump."

"What a curse!" burst out Luis.

Carlos, a friend of Pedro's, is a skilled workman in an electrical appliances factory. He showed me his latest weekly pay slip. It read as follows:

Gross salary for 60 hours: 65 pesos
Deductions:

Taxes	1.80
Industrialisation funds	3.00
Mothers' fund	2.20
Pension contribution	3.00
Union fee	2.60
Miscellaneous	2.00
Inspection	6.40

Net: 44 pesos

Before the Revolution, Carlos earned more than 50 pesos. "And," he added, "I worked only forty hours a week." Now, Carlos starts work at seven in the morning and works until eleven. He has lunch at the factory and is back on the job at one. At five in the afternoon he is free to leave, theoretically at least.

"In fact," he went on, "it's only the end of our *paid* working day. We have to stay on the job another two or three hours. In theory, again, nothing forces us to stay on the job. We are merely invited to contribute to the production increase on a free and voluntary basis.

"But anyone who refuses to put in the extra hours or asks payment for them is accused of counterrevolutionary plotting. Then G-2 takes a hand, raids his home, questions his neighbors, rakes through his past and makes all kinds of difficulties. If the obstinate worker persists in taking a stand, the union delegate convokes the workers to 'vote' for his expulsion. That's already been the fate of sixty workers in my factory. They're now walking the streets. After their dismissal, forty of them were 'placed under G-2 supervision.' That means they were sent to *la Cabaña* prison."

Hardly a week goes by without the workers being invited to contribute a full day's pay "voluntarily and spontaneously." The causes or, rather, pretexts are legion. They must contribute toward buying tanks and airplanes, or take part in financing "Education Year," they must help toward the improvement of livestock or buy sandbags for the protection of public buildings in civil defense. Finally, every worker must subscribe to a fund for paying the soldiers who are recruited from among the factory workers and who do their training or stand guard during working hours.

There is nothing written down in black and white to enforce these contributions. The law even goes out of its way to specify that salaries are free of any deductions. At the beginning of the regime, in an attempt to win the support of the workers, the government increased almost all wages by 20 per cent. But a few weeks later the workers had to "volunteer" to give up this increase for the sake of the Revolution.

In theory, there is only one obligatory contribution, 3 to 5 per cent toward old age pensions. There is a second, optional one, according to the written law. It's not a "tax," but a "participation" (of 4 per cent) in the Cuban industrialization fund. But if a worker decides not to participate, he must send in a special written request for exemption to the Ministry of Labor. "You can imagine," said Carlos, "that no reasonable man would dare to embark on such an undertaking. Two of our comrades were stupid enough to do so. G-2 immediately discovered that they were engaged in counterrevolutionary activities with connections in Miami. They were brought before the Revolutionary tribunal and condemned for treason to thirty years of forced labor."

"Every day," Luis told me, "we have to buy *Hoy*, the Communist Party daily paper. The union delegates who sell it come through the factory, handing a copy to every single worker. "*Toma!* Here, take it!" they say. On the first and fifteenth of every month they also hand around the Communist magazine, *Mella*, the CTC paper *Vanguardia Obrera*, the INRA magazines and *Verde Olivo*, published by the psychological warfare sections of the Agrarian Reform Institute and the army.

The union delegates are handed as many copies as there are workers in the factory. When a worker is absent, his newspapers are set aside for him. Thanks to this ingenious system, no copies remain unsold.

The young worker must also "voluntarily" join the army. Those who do not bow to this optional obligation are noted by the union delegates who are also the leaders of the factory Revolutionary Watch Committee. The information gained on "counterrevolutionaries" is handed on immediately to G-2.

Even the soldiers are not entirely free from trouble of this kind. Carlos was taking part with the rest of his platoon in a training march in the forest. They lost their way, and after vainly wandering about for several hours they met a priest of whom Carlos asked the way. The next day he had to appear before the Committee. "You are guilty of having dealings with the enemy. You dared to speak to a *gusano con sotana*. Don't do it again. Next time you'll pay for it. Meanwhile, in order to prove your repentance, you must make a pro-Revolutionary gesture. You will contribute a week's salary toward the fight against illiteracy."

CHAPTER 22

It was a huge palette-shaped swimming pool full of sparkling, crystal clear, ultramarine water. The red-vested butler ushered me to one of the deck chairs set out on the tiled terrace below the house. "Would Monsieur like to drink something while waiting for Monsieur?" he asked. I was in Miramar, the silk-stocking district of Havana, at the home of Mr. Dupont, the French business-man I had met on the plane.

Dupont appeared almost immediately, smiling, and holding out his hand. "Would you like to have a swim?" he asked, following a normal custom in tropical countries.

"Unfortunately I don't have my swimming trunks with me," I replied, casting a longing look at the pool.

"There must be some in the house that would fit you, but God knows where. If my wife were here she would find some. But she stayed in France and I have to live as a bachelor, that is to say, badly. Fortunately, I've still got José."

"He certainly has style."

"He's got other qualities as well, and above all, absolute devotion to me. That's a rare thing to find in a country where employers are all made out to be exploiters. While I was away, four *barbudos* came and set up their quarters here. They arrived a few weeks after my departure for Europe and gave José a lot of trouble. They asked him why I had left Cuba. He replied that I had gone for a cure, as I had done in previous years. They said to him, 'That dirty capitalist could have got cured in Cuba. We've got perfectly good doctors here.' The butler told them that it wasn't a question of doctors, but of climate. The *barbudos* wouldn't believe a word of it. They told the poor boy 'From now on, everything in this house is the property of the people.'

"They brought along their sleeping bags and fixed themselves up in the living room and in my wife's bedroom. They amused themselves by carving their initials on the furniture and writing *Venceremos! Patria o muerte* all over the walls. When I got back, I found the villa in a hell of a state. The terrorized butler had taken refuge in the cellar. I found him trembling all over, not daring to come out, half dead from hunger. When he saw me, he shouted: 'Monsieur, Monsieur, what a terrible tragedy! They've taken your house and both your cars.' "

"Had the *barbudos* taken your cars too?"

"I had a Buick and a Dauphine. Some civil servants from INRA drove them off to the Ministry of Commerce."

"How did you get your things back?"

"As far as the house was concerned, it was quite simple. I'm over six feet tall and weigh two hundred pounds. I got a hold of those *barbudo* squatters and threw them out with a few good kicks in the behind. It didn't take more than five seconds."

"Didn't they protest?"

"Well, no. They were so surprised at seeing me back that they didn't have time."

"What about your cars? Did you get them back?"

"Yes, eventually. But I first had to fight passivity and ill will. They tried to wear me down. But I come from Brittany, so I'm more stubborn than all the Cubans put together. Every morning at eight o'clock I would turn up at the Ministry of Commerce. I pestered everybody until lunchtime. Then I went to INRA and repeated the performance till evening."

He was sent from one office to another. Everywhere he was told to be patient. "It'll come out all right," he was told. "After all, what have you got to complain of? You haven't been shot." Sometimes a peevish employee would shout at him: "Serve you right you loud-mouthed profiteering bastard. With all you've stolen from the people, you ought to shut up."

"I always replied very calmly," went on Dupont. "I took care never to get excited or say anything in the least offensive." He would reply, "I haven't got a loud mouth, and I'm not a profiteer. Everything I own is the fruit of my labor. I wore myself to the bone for thirty years. I built part of my house with my own hands."

"What about the furniture?" they would say.

"The furniture was willed us by my wife's aunt."

"Why is it Empire furniture?"

"Because that's the period it dates back to."

"What period?"

"The Empire."

"What was that?"

"The Empire was the period of Napoleon's reign."

"Napoleon was a dictator, wasn't he?"

"If you like."

"Why do you have furniture that belonged to a dictator?"

"That's not it. My furniture didn't belong to Napoleon. It was made by cabinetmakers who lived during his reign."

"Lobo* also had Napoleon furniture. He admired Napoleon. Do you admire this guy Napoleon?"

"That has nothing to do with the case."

"Yes it does. The people confiscated Lobo's furniture, and Lobo admired Napoleon. If you also admire Napoleon, this dictator, this oppressor of the workers, you will have your furniture confiscated too."

"It's not a question of furniture. I came about my cars. They've been stolen."

"Your cars. They were given you by Batista."

---

* Former sugar-king of Cuba, who has been a refugee in New York since the Revolution.

"That's not true. Batista never gave me anything. On the contrary, he sent me to prison for six months."

"Why did he send you to prison?"

"For giving supplies to Fidel."

Then the employee would soften and ask Dupont to come back next day. "I'll look into your case myself. You'll get your cars back tomorrow."

But the next day he would be sent to a different office. "I can't do anything for you," he'd be told. "Go and see so and so. He'll help you."

One day, Dupont saw his Buick in the courtyard of the Ministry. "That's my car," he shouted.

"No it isn't, it's the Minister's."

"It's my car, I recognize it."

After an hour's discussion, he decided to take possession of his own car himself. "Right there in the courtyard," he said, "in front of the petrified guards, I opened the trunk, took out the radio transmitting and receiving equipment the Minister had had installed, and then I climbed into the front seat. Now, there's only my Dauphine to get back."

"Where is it?"

"Goodness knows. There's such confusion in the ministries that nobody can tell you anything."

The butler brought drinks on a silver tray. Dupont poured me a very stiff double Scotch. "Can you still get Scotch in Cuba?" I asked in astonishment.

"No, I brought this bottle over from Europe. There's nothing like it left here. When I think how this used to be a land of milk and honey. . . . Castro and his rabble have messed everything up."

Dupont told me that even Castro's warmest partisans have been quite upset by the waste and disorder they have found. "The Revolution," he said, "has turned disorder into an institution. Have you heard the story about the Japanese experts?"

"No, I haven't."

"The INRA had asked them to study the possibilities of stepping up Cuba's rice production. It was a question of increasing the yield per acre. The experts spent six weeks in Havana. Dressed in their city suits and bowler hats they went to INRA every morning.

They spent a good deal of their time waiting. The moment they spoke of getting down to work, they would be told, 'Don't rush things. It'll get us nowhere. In any case, the Revolution is going forward.'

"When the seventh week came around, the reserved and polite Japanese finally flew off the handle. They said to Núñez Jiménez, 'You are attempting the wrong revolution. If you want to save the Cubans from starvation, you must first teach them how to work.' Jiménez replied by citing the Chinese as an example. The Japanese experts laughed in his face. 'The Chinese work sixteen hours a day. They don't leave their offices, workshops, or fields every five minutes, like the Cubans do, to go around the corner for a rum with their friends.' "

"What did Jiménez say to that?"

"He threw half his employees into prison. The rest took the hint. Instead of going round the corner, they had their friends call on them at their offices, and drank their rum there. So much easier. On the other hand, you've got to admit that the higher officials have made an effort to get on the ball."

"And is it working out?"

"It would be if they had the right man in the right place. But it's just the reverse. With the object of having trustworthy men to run the administrations and public services, they've appointed street-sweepers as managers of electronic factories and art students as directors of agricultural cooperatives. Here's a case in point that I happen to know a lot about: The man in charge of the importation of pharmaceutical products is a *barbudo*, a nice guy, honest and conscientious, quite a bruiser, who did wonders in the Sierra Maestra. Unfortunately he was by trade a clerk at a dry cleaner's. Suddenly he found himself head of an extremely important public service.

"When the appointment was made, he was told, 'Dry cleaning and pharmaceuticals are just the same thing, it's all chemistry. You'll see. You'll learn fast. You're just as bright as the next guy. There's no reason why you shouldn't do just as well as your predecessor.' His predecessor was an M.D. and a Ph.D. in chemistry. The former clerk bought himself a book on chemistry up through high school level, and did some studying every evening.

"One day he was told, 'We've got to economize on foreign currency. Cut down your imports by 20 per cent.' He replied, 'Sure,' and cut imports of each product by 20 per cent: 20 per cent less aspirin, 20 per cent less penicillin, 20 per cent less everything. That was how Cuba went on importing Vichy water and Alka-Seltzer.

"Somebody in the Government realized what was happening. He had the *barbudo* come to see him and said, 'You weren't told to make a uniform reduction on every product. Make a selection.'

" 'Sure,' replied the *barbudo*. He went back to his office, got out his list of imports, and what do you think he did?"

"Stopped the importation of Alka Seltzer and Vichy water, presumably."

"Not at all. He just cut out two products out of ten. He began at the top of the list, took hold of his pen and scratched off the first two products. Then he counted up to eight and crossed off the next two, and so on. Result: Vichy water and Alka-Seltzer are still imported, but not penicillin."

Mr. Dupont told me what was happening in agriculture. Before the Revolution, Cuba was very well provided with livestock: 5.5 million head of cattle. The island filled its own need for milk, cheese, butter, and meat. It even exported condensed milk. Now there's a shortage of butter.

"Why?"

"Because the Cubans ate the dairy cows and spared the beef cattle. In three years, 60 per cent of the cows have been sent to the slaughterhouse. One of the cooperatives in the Matanzas district took great pride in their pedigreed herd of Sainte Gertrude bulls and cows. While making a tour of inspection there one day, Fidel said, 'These animals serve no useful purpose here.' All the breeding bulls were sent to the slaughterhouse. The cows were given to Venezuela in an attempt to win favor with President Betancourt, who at that time went in for cattle breeding.

"It is Castro who is primarily responsible for all these absurdities. His recklessness drives Guevara out of his mind. He has the annoying habit of going about with a book full of checks payable by the state treasury in his pocket. If he likes the look of a project, however hopeless it may be, he says without a moment's thought, 'OK, boys, go ahead. Here's the money,' pulls out his checkbook and signs a check for one, two, or three million dollars. Afterwards it's Guevara who has to straighten out the budget.

"Last year, Fidel, who often goes fishing in the swamps on Zapata Peninsula, said, 'The Dutch drained the Zuider Zee, we'll do the same with Zapata.' Dutch specialists were hired at great expense. Che Guevara is furious about it, apparently. He said to Nuñez Jimenez, 'Fidel has gone quite wild. This idea of his will cost a fortune. There are plenty of more urgent projects the money could have been spent on.' "

23

From the day of my arrival, wherever I went, I was asked the same question: "Are you going to interview Castro?" And I always had to answer no. An interview with the leader of the *barbudos* had never figured on my agenda. I came to Cuba to see how people lived under the Revolution and to share their daily life. Yet without ever having looked for an interview, I got one, quite by accident, in an elevator in the Habana Libre Hotel.

It was four o'clock in the afternoon. I was coming down from the twenty-fourth floor, where I had been visiting a friend. At the twenty-third, the elevator stopped, the door opened and in came a crowd of *barbudos*. I had no difficulty in recognizing the tallest of them: Fidel.

I looked up (otherwise, my modest five feet five only afforded me a limited view of him), and introduced myself, "Fidel, I'm a French journalist."

He offered me an enormous hairy hand to shake. "*Encantado!*
Delighted to meet you." He dug his hand into a pocket of his
military shirt and pulled out two cigars. He kept one for himself
and stuck the other in my mouth. "*Toma!* Here." Then he asked
me, "What paper do you work for?" I told him. He went on questioning me. "How long have you been in Cuba?"

"About a month."

"Have you seen a lot?"

"Yes, quite a lot."

"Would you like us to have a little talk together?"

"I'd be delighted."

When we reached the ground floor, the elevator came to a stop
and the operator opened the door. Fidel stood aside to let me pass.
"After you."

"No, no."

"I'm a Cuban and you're a foreign visitor. So I have the pleasure
of asking you to go first."

"*Muchas gracias.*"

"*Con mucho gusto.*"

Fidel took me along to the cafeteria. At that time of day there
were few people there. They all stood up and applauded. Fidel
thanked them with a gesture of his hand and asked them to sit
down again.

We sat down side by side at a square table with a yellow plastic
top and four chromed steel legs. A waitress in a black dress and
white apron came across toward us from the bar at the end of the
cafeteria. Fidel ordered two beers without giving her time to reach
our table.

"The strong man" of the Revolution drew in deeply on his
cigar, which he held right in the center of his lips as though it were
a clarinet. He raised his chin when he let out the smoke. "Excuse
my asking," he said, "but have you a press card?"

"Of course. Here."

He refused to look at it. "I believe you. Tell me, where have you
been in Cuba?"

"More or less everywhere, except to the Eastern provinces."

"Ah! You must go to the *Oriente*. That's where everything
began."

"I intend to go there."

"Have you visited any cooperatives?"

"Yes, I have."

"Which one?"

"El Rosario."

"El Rosario," he repeated. "I'm very fond of El Rosario."

"Yes, it's a fine agricultural achievement."

"And a social one, too."

Fidel half-emptied his glass in one gulp. Seeing him there in front of me, I had the feeling that I had known him for a long time. It seemed to me that I had spent all my life looking at that long, irregular face, with its black pupils and its beard, bushy in some places and sparse in others. Even the harsh intonations of his hoarse voice seemed familiar.

"You're exactly as you appear on television," I told him.

He burst out laughing, gave his cigar a few more chews and replied, "I'm a revolutionary, not an actor."

Fidel, who was certainly doing more questioning than answering, asked me if I had read "Listen, Yankee." I replied that I had. "The author is an honest American," was his comment. "He came and spent a few weeks among us. He saw and understood. It's an excellent book. I've had it translated. What do you think of it?"

"I think that in "Listen, Yankee" C. Wright Mills behaves like a passionate pamphleteer rather than a cool, impartial sociologist."

"When faced with a revolution you cannot, you have no right to remain impartial. You have to take sides. That's what Mills did, and he did it with honesty. Mills explains," Fidel went on in a more excited tone, "how the Yankees will never succeed in making themselves a present of Latin America. They imagine they're being generous with their subsidies. But their $100 million, $200 million, or even $1,000 million handouts bring them no returns. The reactionary governments could be bought with far less money. All these millions of dollars they hand out only go to enrich a handful of privileged people, and the large working masses don't profit from them at all.

"Mills' other great merit lies in having destroyed the myth of United States–Latin American solidarity. Our living in the same hemisphere does not mean that we have identical needs or customs. The American racist from Alabama has nothing in common with the oppressed Indian in Bolivia. The first believes himself superior to everybody because he is likely to live to the age of seventy, whereas the second does not believe in anything; the existence he leads hardly leaves him time, and he dies of exhaustion, starvation, and shame before reaching the age of thirty-five.

"Quite frankly, we in Latin America are very far removed from the North Americans. Our true brothers, the people who resemble us like two peas in a pod, are the men who are working themselves to death at the bottom of South African mines, the Harlem Negroes beaten up by the American police, the Chinese."

A crowd of onlookers had collected in front of the cafeteria, which was separated from the hotel lobby by a glass partition, and stood there watching us in silence. They were simple folk, young for the most part. There were a few peasants, recognizable by their large hats and rough features, some porters in uniform, three soldiers, two girls.

"Do you remember the story about the chickens?" said Fidel suddenly.

"Chickens? What chickens?"

"You must have read that story in "Listen, Yankee." We had to help the peasants find a way out without taking too much time over it. We advised them to breed chickens. Breeding chickens is easy: you just build a coop out of banana palms, buy two hens and a cock and give them a little corn. Then, after a few weeks, the hens lay and soon you have your chicks. The chicks grow, and when they're big enough to eat, you kill them and roast them over a wood fire. Afterwards, you stand on the roadside and sell roast chicken to passing tourists."

"Tourists are hardly very numerous just now," I said.

"That's the Americans' fault. Just because we have done away with a few traitors and criminals, their press insists on describing our country as a slaughterhouse where blood flows like wine."

"You must admit, though, that there has been a good deal of bloodshed in Cuba."

"When you make a revolution, you are obliged to kill. It's inevitable, otherwise the revolution would not take place at all. The French Revolution went through the same phase. What about the Reign of Terror and the guillotine? A writer from your country—I can't remember his name—went so far as to say that there was a satanic aspect to the French Revolution. When you think of the thousands guillotined during the Reign of Terror, we must seem like choirboys."

"If Robespierre had put a stop to the executions and given 'laws instead of blood,' as a French saying has it, my people might well have got away without Napoleon."

"Well, my opinion is that the French were not yet ready to make full use of their Revolution."

"Why don't you hold elections, as you promised when you came to power?"

Fidel shrugged his shoulders before replying. "What nonsense you talk! Elections in Cuba! Nobody wants them. In this country there have never been true elections. All the elections that have taken place were rigged. They were just jokes to make those stupid Yankees believe that a president elected by the people necessarily acts democratically. In reality, all our presidents were *caudillos*. In Cuba, as in the rest of Latin America, elections have always been a kind of trap. Parliamentary democracy in this part of the world became the symbol of a social-economic system that was archaic and obsolete.

"In any case, elections might well prove dangerous to the Revolution. They would make us put the clock back to the colonial days and waste precious years in unprofitable argument. A representative who is electioneering often talks bunk; he's thinking about his re-election and not about his country. The Revolution has no time to waste on absurdities. It does not progress by means of parliamentary speeches. It needs to go forward, like a bicycle; as soon as you stop pedaling, it falls down.

"Look! A revolution is a revolution. None of us ever tried to make out that it was a game of canasta between deputies. When you make a revolution, you forget about rules and appearances. You go right ahead, whatever the price."

With that Fidel got up and shook hands. "There, I think I've given you something to write a good article with. Goodbye!"

CHAPTER 24

All that was left of the car was a smoking pile of jagged, twisted scrap metal. A body lay stretched out on the sidewalk beside it, the face cut to ribbons, the belly ripped open and limbs torn off. A few minutes earlier, this had been a passer-by going about his business. Now it was just a fearfully mutilated corpse. Another victim of the attempt was writhing and groaning face upwards on the ground, a young man, apparently. His guts were oozing out of his torn belly. A crowd gathered around them, some soldiers came running on the double, machine guns and rifles cocked.

The bomb had exploded under the car just as the two victims were passing. For a moment, the sound of backfiring and horns was drowned by the din of the explosion. Then there was a noise of broken glass, finally some shouts, and everybody in the street where I happened to be started running toward the scene of the blast, while a thick cloud of smoke rose to the sky.

Now there was a total hush. The onlookers were fascinated by two trickles of blood flowing off the sidewalk and into the road. The soldiers tried to widen the circle, saying in low voices, "*Por favor, Compañeros,* move back, stand off!"

Near the wounded man and the body stood a young man with his back to the wall, his hands clasped behind his head, guarded by a soldier. He had hazel eyes and fine hair, and was wearing a white T-shirt and light-colored canvas trousers.

"What's your name, murderer?" said the soldier. The boy kept his teeth clenched. He stuck out his chin and looked the soldier straight between the eyes. The soldier gave him a blow in the kidneys with the butt of his rifle. "Are you going to tell me your name, you bastard?"

"It's got nothing to do with you."

"Suppose I loose off a burst into your belly, you'd soon tell me your damn name, huh?"

"Go ahead, chicken." He was very pale, and his cheeks were trembling, but he went on glaring at the soldier, who turned round to glance at the crowd, as if looking for encouragement.

Somebody shouted, "Send him to the firing squad, the murderer!" "That's right, shoot him! Shoot him!" The young man grinned at them. "The firing squad!" screamed the crowd.

"Why not kill him right away?" a woman asked.

The soldier shrugged his shoulders. "I'd ask for nothing better, myself. Unfortunately, it's against orders. He has to be tried first. But you needn't worry, he'll end up in front of the firing squad."

"Send him to the firing squad," chanted the crowd on the other sidewalk.

A groan from the wounded man stopped their shouting. "He's in pain, poor man," murmured a woman.

"It wasn't him I was after," said the young man.

"Shut up!" the soldier said.

"I didn't mean to kill anybody, I only—" His words were cut short by a blow to the belly that doubled him up.

A priest made his way through the crowd. An NCO tried to turn him away. "Get away. We don't need you. You're nothing but a murderer's accomplice. Get away!"

"He's dying," replied the priest in a low voice.

"That's your fault, you bastard."

"Don't shout. It's my duty to help this poor wretch."

"Listen here, murderer, get out, do you hear me? You'll do as I say, if you know what's good for you."

The wounded man let out another groan. The priest turned toward the NCO. "Please, I beg of you."

He crouched down. The dying man opened his eyes. "Father," he murmured. The priest took his hands between his own, as if to warm them. "Father, it hurts." He began to toss about, groaning more loudly. Beads of sweat ran down his face and glistened on the stubble of his beard. "Father, Father."

The priest passed his hand across the man's forehead, gently stroked his hair and spoke to him in a soft voice. The dying man grew more peaceful. He smiled, opened his eyes wide and gazed at the priest. Gradually he succumbed. His limbs became more and more relaxed, his eyes dimmed, his breathing weakened and stopped.

With a reverent gesture, the priest slid his hand down and closed the dead man's eyes. He made the sign of the cross and began to speak over him the prayer for the dead. A woman in the front row of the crowd knelt down. Another followed suit. The NCO who had tried to turn the priest away also crossed himself, furtively.

There were now two corpses on the sidewalk. Some policemen were busying themselves around the bodies, which had been covered up. They were making marks on the ground with a piece of chalk and carrying on an animated conversation.

The crowd was silent. Everybody seemed dazed, fascinated. Indeed, there's nothing so bewildering as the sight of a man dying. Death is such a simple thing; a yawn, a stretch, and that is all. Always, it remains the same inexplicable mystery.

CHAPTER 25

The women were elegantly dressed in low-cut dresses, dazzling with jewels. The fine glasses arranged in descending order before each blue porcelain plate glittered in the light from the Venetian chandelier. Servants in white livery fluttered around the ten diners, filling the glasses with a Mouton-Rothschild at just the right temperature. The roast was duly presented on a silver platter before being carved.

I was seated at the right of Mrs. V., the lady of the house, a handsome young woman with fine features and hair drawn back in a chignon. She sat very straight on her high-backed chair, making sure that nothing was amiss.

"How do you find the roast?" she asked me. "I know the French are a bit hard to please in such matters." I said I found it superb.

Mr. V. presided over the other side of the table. His greying temples, long aristocratic face, and striped tie gave him the air of some teenager's heart throb in an English movie. He was a splendid host, carrying it off with that elegance composed of casualness and affectation that is so characteristic of Latin Americans of the old school. He spoke French with a studied refinement I considered a tribute to France, and he talked of literature. What did I think of the latest Prix Goncourt? Why wasn't Malraux writing any more?

On his left, Mrs. D., petite and charmingly plump, with a round face framed by recalcitrant curls, spoke Spanish only. Her remarks were at times somewhat surprising. She asked me in dulcet tones, "Did you hear the explosions last night?"

"What explosions, Señora?"

"Why, they shook the whole of downtown Havana! Woolworth and the other big stores were burning for hours; it was fantastic! Bombs going off all over the place—the police didn't know where to start."

"I'm afraid I didn't hear a thing. My hotel's a long way from the city center and I went to bed early."

"It was my husband who organized it all," she added with a touch of pride.

My right-hand neighbor, Miss S., daughter of a South American ambassador, pointed out a strapping fellow with thinning hair, sitting on the left of the hostess. "D.," she explained, "is the *coordinador*, the leader of the Havana network of the MRP, or People's Revolutionary Movement. I expect you know that the MRP is the most effective of the anti-Castro resistance organizations. The gentleman opposite me is M., one of D.'s principal lieutenants; his wife is to the right of Mr. V., and to her right you see Mr. R., who used to be a reporter for *Revolución*. The girl to the left of the *coordinador* is his secretary; she's a student and her name is Maria."

I took a quick look around the spacious dining room, which was decorated with taste. A crystal vase filled with magnificent red roses dominated the Regency console against the far wall, flanked by a glass cabinet with a display of silver plates. Beyond was a cosy nook formed by a divan, a coffee table, and some Louis XV armchairs. The servants, quiet and assured, moved to and fro, and the scene struck me as unreal.

The whole thing had begun suddenly and unexpectedly. The previous week, at a cocktail party given by a certain embassy, I had been chatting with Miss S., whom I had already met at similar occasions in Havana. Standing in a corner of the room, by French windows opening on to a park, we talked of films, books, and travel. The tone of the girl's voice changed abruptly as she announced, somewhat dryly, "The *coordinador* of the MRP has told me to say that he would be glad to grant you an interview. When would you like to see him?"

I leapt at the chance. Two days later, Miss S. sent me one of her father's messengers with a note "to be destroyed immediately" which read, "I shall call for you on Tuesday at eight P.M. Black tie, if you've brought one."

I am sorry I cannot give an exact description of the property belonging to Mr. and Mrs. V. to which Miss S. drove me. Castro's police could too easily identify it.

I was roused from my thoughts by M. He was a thin man with a turned-up chin, and he spoke in a hoarse voice, fiddling nervously with his bread. "If you're interested," he suggested, "you might like to watch some of our fireworks. We've got a few good shows coming up. Would you care to have a list, so that you can choose?" He screwed up his beady eyes and added, "Are you afraid?"

"It's astonishment I feel, rather than fear," I replied. "You are showing me an entirely unknown picture of the clandestine. I always imagined that people who carry out terrorist attacks, risking a violent death at any moment, spent most of their days in hiding or disguise. The other day, in order to introduce me to a trade union leader whom G-2 were after, some anti-Castro workers made me travel in the trunk of their car.

"Yet here you are, the heads of the underground, sitting peacefully round this lovely table. We're enjoying wonderful food and chatting amiably. I'm blaming myself for not having brought Mrs. V. flowers. But who ever heard of a journalist going to visit outlaws with a bouquet in his hand?"

There was a general burst of laughter. M. brandished a revolver and put his knife between his teeth. "Now do I look like a proper terrorist?" he asked.

D., the *coordinador*, said to me, "Basically you're right, of course. But anyone who chooses to be clandestine has to accept it as a regular profession. With time, he acquires certain habits. In the end the routine becomes more dangerous than the police investigations."

"What does it matter?" interrupted M., scowling. "Sooner or later we'll all be hanged on the nearest lamp post. You can count on it—unless, of course, Castro falls soon."

"Hell," murmured V., "before he died at the hand of an assassin, Umberto I of Italy said of threatened attempts on his life, 'Those are just occupational hazards.'"

"How right he was!" nodded D.

"Are you a fatalist?" I asked him.

"Not exactly. I don't give myself up to fate bound hand and foot; I fight. I am simply resigned to being arrested one of these days. For the moment the other side is the stronger. Those who survive will take my place. I haven't the slightest illusion about my chances of getting out unscathed. One day the police will be bursting into my bedroom while I am asleep, or else I'll get picked up on the road, quite stupidly. Now I've gotten used to the idea, it gives me comfort in some way. I always look on the bright side, am ready for anything, and never complain."

"Have you had any rough times?"

"Now and again. There are bound to be some. The other evening one of our best friends, Armando, was going back into the room where he had spent two days in hiding. Some militiamen and cops from G-2 were waiting for him. Without allowing him time to switch on the light, they jumped on him all together. Armando fought like the devil—he managed to draw his revolver and kill four of them, but finally they got him.

"Armando was a good fellow. Wasn't he, M.? He came back from Miami because he liked a fight. There was no one like him for putting plastic bombs in the air conditioning. He was a real artist."

"Forgive me if I seem indiscreet," I said, "but how is it you manage to talk so openly in front of the servants?"

"Oh, they're not ordinary servants. They belong to our secret commandos. They're here to protect us rather than to lend distinction to the dinner. Presently, after you've gone, they'll fade away quietly, though not before washing the dishes and putting everything away. The V.'s can go to bed with an easy mind. If the police question them, they can say they retired early."

I turned to M. "What did you do before you joined the opposition?"

The *coordinador's* assistant looked at me questioningly. "You mean when I was a civilian, I suppose?"

"Yes. What did you do in civilian life?"

M. was silent for a moment, then in a quiet voice he began to talk of his past. Now nearing forty, he came of a simple family in one of Havana's populous suburbs. His father had brought him up on middle-class lines. "Perhaps it sounds rather silly to say that I learned to respect other people's property and to do no harm. I went in for the law and became a judge—only in a small way, a magistrate at petty sessions. The people I dealt with were in modest circumstances. Although it was my job to apply the law, I twice rebelled against it. The first time was because of Batista, and now because of Castro. Cuba today has become Communist and totalitarian!" He stopped, looking rather sad. Clearly it went against his grain to admit to a Communist Cuba. "It's not Cuba any more, it's something else," he declared.

"What is it then?"

"I wish I knew."

D. broke in, with his deep, commanding voice. "Cuba will soon be free again. It will change into something entirely new, like a man who recovers from a serious illness."

"I don't think so," said M., shaking his head. "Cuba will never be free."

"What makes you say that? The news is fine; the Castroists are getting rattled, our friends abroad are preparing for a landing. Castro's days are numbered!"

"I'm sure we shall win, but I don't believe in a free Cuba any longer. We're a nation of slaves—always have been and always will be. When Batista went we had our chance of freedom. Castro destroyed it by terror and there are still some Cubans prepared to thank him."

"If Voltaire were alive," said V., "he would have reason to say again: 'Trembling, each of us kisses the hand that enchains him.'"

"Yes," said M., "as free men, the Cubans are done for!"

"*Francés,*" M. said to me, settling himself in his chair, "let me tell you why Castro has reduced the Cubans to slavery. You don't mind if I use your first name, *verdad?* No need to be all formal just because I used to be a judge! With the folks who came to see me in those days it was first names all around. I never made believe it was the Royal Court of England! Anyway, what the hell! We're at war, aren't we? Don't let's waste time bowing and scraping."

"Well said!" the others approved. "First names it is. No more standing on ceremony."

"*Bueno,*" went on the ex-judge. "Do you know Calle 49 in the Kohly district?"

"That's where Yurikrushenko lives—the real chief of the Cuban police."

"*Caramba!* You knew it!"

"It's common knowledge."

Officially, the head of the political police is a Cuban, Ramiró Valdès. But since the spring of 1961, Castro, on the advice of Che Guevara, has discreetly set up G-2-H, a kind of super-police instructed to watch over G-2 and carry out certain top-secret missions. Yurikrushenko, a Russian "technician" and former henchman of Beria, is the man who runs G-2-H.

"Since Castro came to power," M. explained, "justice has ceased to function. The police can raid any house at any time, day or night, and arrest whom they like. No pretext is needed. Those who protest are answered in Castro's words: 'A state of war exists in Cuba, resulting from the Revolution. It is the Revolution that makes the laws.'

"In accordance with that principle, thousands of Cubans have been arbitrarily seized and imprisoned. There are 20,000 still in prison without the right to legal assistance. Not even the chaplain can visit them. Only their wives are allowed to see them, and that only once every three months."

"But surely, courts still exist?" I said.

"They call them courts! In fact, they're simply courts-martial composed of ignorant peasant *barbudos*. When a defendant appears before them, they first listen to the indictment. The man on trial is theoretically entitled to a lawyer, but in practice this safeguard is denied him. The *barbudos* content themselves with asking, 'What is your reply to these charges?' Then they say 'Guilty' or 'Not guilty.' If he's convicted, the accused may appeal—to another court-martial sitting the same day.

"A young man I knew was charged with the attempted assassination of a Castro officer. The only witness was the intended victim. The court condemned the boy to death. Two hours later, shortly before midnight, the appeal court met. At one A.M. it confirmed the sentence of capital punishment and at three A.M. the young man was shot."

The ex-judge paused to swallow some wine. "On December 21, 1959," he continued, "Castro's government published the *Ley Fundamental*, which conferred the right to shoot 'counterrevolutionaries.' "

"What does this law mean by 'counterrevolutionary?' "

"An earlier decree, of July 7, 1959, gives the term a very broad interpretation. A *contra-revolucionario* is a criminal in general. He may be a terrorist who blows up a barracks or a tippler who after five or six rums in a café announces, 'Fidel is wrong. If I were in his place, I. . . .' "

A loud voice came from the other end of the table. It was R., saying, "An anti-Communist is a counterrevolutionary too. In a four-hour speech on March 26, 1960, Castro delivered a slashing attack on the radio and TV commentator Luis Conte Agüero, accusing him of inciting the Cubans against Communism. I can still remember one of his phrases: 'Your attitude,' he said to Agüero, 'proves that you are a counterrevolutionary.' "

R. must have been about forty. He had a handsome face and delicate hands. "If you like," he said, "I'll tell you all about the Agüero case." Without waiting for my reply he went on. "Every day at noon, Dr. Luis Conte Agüero used to appear on the CMQ television channel. He was accustomed to giving his own views on current affairs. Often he stressed the growing influence of the Cuban Communist groups. His attitude displeased the leaders of the Revolution, especially Raúl Castro.

"On March 25, 1960, Agüero found armed militiamen in his office, who prevented him from giving his broadcast. The management of CMQ lodged a formal protest. The militiamen countered this by saying that the technicians and journalists of the station 'rejected the protest.' On the following day, Fidel Castro made a personal TV appearance and condemned Agüero."

"What happened to the commentator?"

"He took refuge in a friendly embassy and from there he managed to get abroad.

"Before the press was brought to heel, there used to be twenty daily newspapers in Havana, six television networks and a number of broadcasting stations.

"The Castroists began by setting up cells among the typesetters and technicians. Before long they printed or broadcast only material authorized by their trade unions—whose allegiance is Communist. When the management objected, the workers asked the authorities to nationalize the paper or station. By this means the papers, one after the other, came under government control, or simply closed down."

"How about censorship?"

"It isn't really censorship. The newspapers have to toe the line to some extent, particularly regarding their vocabulary. I expect you've noticed it: 'Sister countries' means those of the Communist bloc; 'the legitimate government of Viet-Nam' means Ho Chi Minh's government.

"I worked with *Revolución* up to mid-1960. Once, to mark the occasion of 'Journalists' Day,' Armando Hart, the Minister of Education, gave us a talk on our mission under the Revolution. 'The impartiality of the journalist,' said he, 'is a myth. The only solid foundation for objective reporting is alignment with the publicly expressed opinion of the millions who support Fidel. If he does not so align himself, the journalist becomes a defender of the oligarchy that has been keeping the people in slavery and poverty.' "

We took our coffee near the swimming pool, seated in wicker armchairs and rocking chairs. Two servants appeared with trays of refreshments. Mrs. V. filled the glasses.

"A *votre santé*," she said to me.

I replied, "*à votre santé*," while the others said, "Chin-chin."

V. had the lights switched off and we were silently watching the moon's reflection in the water. It was a beautiful spring evening, calm and peaceful. The faintest of breezes made the tree tops tremble, their dark shapes standing out against the clear night sky, and carried invigorating whiffs of eucalyptus to us.

Seated close by me were the *coordinador*, his assistant, and Maria. D. puffed on a cigar. "By the way," he said, "I hope you received the note of welcome I sent you the evening you arrived in Havana?"

"So it was you who sent it!"

My remark seemed to please him enormously. Then he said, "What would you like me to talk about? My network, perhaps?" When I nodded, he went on. "We have at our disposal—I am speaking only of the MRP—about five hundred men divided into watertight cells of three, four, or five at most. They're well trained and armed. While awaiting the signal for the general uprising, they keep their hands in with sabotage, for which we are well organized; we put our bombs where we like and take care there are never any casualties. Incidentally, the explosives are always placed by employees of the target undertaking—Woolworth's, for example."

"Isn't it rather risky for them?"

"Not particularly. Woolworth's has 300 clerks, supervisors, etc. All are reputed to be good revolutionaries; most even belong to the militia. In these circumstances, how can G-2 conduct a serious enquiry? Whom can they suspect? Whom imprison? Yet the police are obliged to chalk up some successes. Thus all they can do is to arrest employees selected at random. This way sincere Castrists are sent to *La Cabaña*—which is fine with us because, once in prison, the true revolutionaries themselves have a taste of the mistreatment and torture they refused to believe existed."

"Where do the arms and explosives come from?"

"Mostly from abroad."

"Are you in touch with the rural *maquis?*"

"Naturally. Are you interested in meeting them?"

"Yes."

D. appeared to be impressed. He went on smoking and drinking but his eyes never left my face. M. and Maria were looking at me too, with astonishment, or perhaps with fright.

"What section of the *maquis* would you like to visit?"

"I don't care."

"The most important is at Escambray. For a year now, 3,000 youngsters have held the whole mountain area. They are headed by Captain Duque, one of Fidel's former officers. Unfortunately, you would never get through. The Sierra Escambray is completely surrounded by 50,000 Castro troops. I think your best chance would be the Sierra Cristal, at the far end of Oriente Province. If you get through, you'll meet some first-class men."

"Right, that's where I'm going."

"Quite sure you know what you're doing?"

"Quite sure."

"Why do you want to go into the Sierra?"

"Well, I've visited cooperatives, factories, and schools. I've talked with militia, policemen, padres, students, and with you. I'm still missing *maquisards* from my collection. If I don't meet any my report will be incomplete."

D. nodded gently. "I understand," he said, but I was sure he did not.

"As you wish," he said.

"What do I have to do?"

"Above all, watch your step. We're not in France or the United States, you know. We're not safe anywhere. The worst can happen at any moment."

"I'll watch my step."

"All you have to do now is wait. In a few days we'll send Maria to you with a message. If anyone asks you about her, just say she's your latest conquest—you met her in a bar somewhere. Lastly, and most important, do exactly as Maria tells you, and don't ask her too many questions."

CHAPTER 26

"*Buenas tardes*," said Maria as she came running into the bar, breathless, with tousled hair and shining eyes. She smiled at me. "I'm terribly sorry to have kept you waiting. I ran all the way." The *coordinador's* secretary had telephoned that morning, four days after the dinner at the V.'s house, to make this date with me.

"Would you like a drink?"

She shook her head. "Not just now, perhaps later. I'm not thirsty at the moment." She smiled again, saying, "You're lucky. The *coordinador* has taken a special interest in you."

"You mean it's all arranged?"

"It's all arranged."

"What do I do?"

"You start from Guantanamo."

"What? The American base?"

"No, no! The town of Guantanamo—it's quite separate from the base."

Right. I'll go to Guantanamo."

"You take a bus to Santiago—it's an overnight trip, but comfortable: air conditioning and aircraft-type seats. In Santiago, you hire a car from any garage. If they ask questions, say you're spending a week at the seaside with a pretty *muchacha*. It's about 50 miles from Santiago to Guantanamo, and it's a good road."

"What happens when I get there?"

"Be in the café close to the central square at half past noon, next Saturday. Smoke your pipe—don't forget that, because the man who will be looking for you knows you're short and that you smoke a pipe."

"*Bueno*, I'll be smoking my pipe."

"The *coordinador* has asked me to insist that you take no action on your own initiative. Do exactly what the Guantanamo contact tells you. Don't try to find out his name: first call him 'Tomás.' He will call you 'Maxime.'

"Wait in the café till 1:15. If you see nobody, go away and try again on Monday." She gestured with her hands. "Well, there you are! That's all I have to tell you. And now, please, I should like a little rum with Coca-Cola."

Maria was sitting under a wall lamp, the soft light casting a halo around the clear regular lines of her face. A slender gold chain supported a tiny glittering medallion at her throat. Noticing my glance, she took it off and showed me the medallion. "That was my fiancé's," she said. "They shot him six months ago. His mother gave it to me."

"Had you been engaged very long?"

"Eighteen months. We were about to be married."

I could not help saying, a moment or two later, "You're beautiful. Your eyes are fascinating."

"My fiancé liked them," she said.

"What did he do?"

"He was a university student."

"Why did you join an anti-Castro set-up?"

"To avenge him, of course! I used to take no interest in politics. I didn't want him to get mixed up either. But he had been doing it for years, first against Batista, then against Fidel. I knew something would go wrong one day. But he said it was his duty.

"One morning some G-2 men came and took him away from the

university, and no one has seen him since. A few weeks later his parents read of his death in the newspapers. They asked the *Cabaña* authorities where he was buried, but they refused to tell. So of course the parents imagined all kinds of things, for instance that he had been mutilated. Why was the body not returned?

"I was acquainted with one of my fiancé's friends. I went to see him and I said, 'My fiancé is dead and I have decided to take his place.'"

It was noon when I arrived in Guantanamo, at the wheel of a hired Rambler. The café was easy to find. Inside was a busy scene, the numerous customers crammed against the mahogany bar. I sat down at a table near the door, ordered a big orange juice and lit my pipe.

At 12:40 a kind-looking man with greying hair sat down opposite me. As if we were old friends, he greeted me with a *"Salud, Maxime."*

I answered in the same way. *"Salud, Tomás."*

"How's business?"

"Fine, thanks."

"And how's your son? Still flourishing?"

I have no children, but I entered into the game. "Yes, he's very well. He had a cold last week, but luckily shook it off."

"I'm glad to hear it."

I offered him a drink. He stood the second round. Just like two old pals. After about a quarter of an hour of this play-acting, Tomás said, "Let's go and eat. Where's your car?"

"In the square."

Once in the Rambler, Tomás apologetically asked to see my press card. "Just a formality—security and all that. You understand?" I started the car. "Well now," said Tomás as he handed back my papers, "so you want to go into the Sierra?"

"Yes."

"You mean that?"

"I mean it."

"You've thought about the risks?"

"I have."

"Chico, what you want to do is very risky indeed. For some days now the Communists have been jumpy. They've had such losses

in Escambray and Cristal that they've decided on the big stuff. All the militia in the Santiago and Guantanamo area are mobilized. A lot of them were scared, but the Communists had no hesitation in shooting fifty men as a warning. Raúl Castro came to Santiago especially to attend to the matter."

"When did he come?"

"Tuesday. He left again yesterday. The fellows were shot on Thursday. So you see, *chico*, your plan really is dangerous. It's not so easy to get through the lines as it used to be. You'll need a lot of luck to succeed—a hell of a lot, believe me!"

"Does a guide come with me?"

"Sorry, my boy, I can't give you anyone. If the Communists catch one of my lads they'll shoot him as sure as I'm sitting here."

"And if I go alone?"

"You can always try. After all, if you run into any trouble, that's your affair."

"There won't be any trouble."

"How do you know that?"

"There won't be any trouble."

"*Chico*, if they catch you, they'll shoot you too."

"They won't shoot a journalist, it would cause them too much bother afterwards."

"OK, so they won't shoot you. But, *chico*, they'll keep you in prison a long while and they'll sure give you a hard time. But if you're set on going. . . . You'll have to leave very early tomorrow morning. Take the road that leads to Baracoa."

"Where will your boys be?"

"They'll be waiting for you somewhere between Guantanamo and Baracoa. Don't worry about them. They'll find you all right, if you get through the militiamen. Don't forget the password. They'll speak to you, sort of casually, about Maxime, and you must say, 'I've got a toochache and I'm looking for a dentist.'

"Meanwhile, go take a walk at the seaside. There's a first-rate beach quite near here, with a hotel and a restaurant. Get into bathing trunks, swim, eat, sleep—and not a word to anyone."

"*Bueno.*"

"Drop me off here."

"Don't you want me to take you home?"

"No. Just leave me here and go for a swim."

"Thanks a lot, Tomás."

"*De nada, chico!* And don't take too many risks—it's not worth it."

"I'll be careful."

"*Que Dios te acompañe!*"

I left the beach, drove through the streets of Guantanamo— empty on a Sunday morning—and took the only road that crosses the Sierra. My Rambler, like all the American cars in Cuba, was no longer in the prime of youth; it wheezed and limped, accelerated feebly, and an alarming clanking, like old iron, drowned out the engine noise. I had to stay in second gear.

At the exit from Jamaica, a small town at the foot of the mountains, I was stopped by two militiamen who asked for a lift to their camp, which was along my route. I was glad to take them, feeling that with two loyal revolutionaries aboard I might find it easier to pass the lines.

My poor Spanish with its revealing accent meant that I had no hope of being taken for a Cuban. So, when my passengers asked if I were a Czech, I answered at once with the universally known Russian affirmative "*Da.*" I went on to cook up a romantic tale about a date in Baracoa with *una muchacha linda,* a pretty girl. Of course the simplest road would have been along the coast, avoiding the Sierra, but I was late and hated to keep pretty girls waiting. The soldiers saw my point, but stressed the dangers of my undertaking.

"*Mira,* the mountains are unsafe! There are bands of *gusanos* hanging about near the road. They're just savages. If they find you they'll cut you to ribbons."

"I know, I know—but a date's a date."

Yes, they agreed, love was sacred.

The road wound upward laboriously between clumps of giant cacti, their branches standing like chandeliers against the clear sky. As we climbed, the landscape grew more and more like that of wartime Algeria. All bridges were guarded; there were armored cars at every crossroads, and we passed military camps surrounded by barbed wire and machine-gun defenses. We overtook an endless column of militiamen, marching in fours with rifles slung on their backs. They were hot and sweating and covered with white dust. A

few wore sombreros, the others the regulation black beret. They
were kept in line by NCO's of the regular army, in uniform, with
olive-green caps.

At the check point marking the limit of the "unsafe area," my
two companions went to the duty sergeant and explained about my
sentimental journey. The sergeant, an honest *barbudo*, said guile-
lessly, "I ought not to let you through. It's dangerous—the *gusanos*
will probably kill you."

"But I've got a date."

"Sure, I know. You're a Czech, aren't you?"

"*Da!*"

"On your way, *Compañero*. But don't say I let you through. Tell
them some other story." He winked. "When I think that there's a
pretty girl waiting for you while I'm wasting my time here! What
wouldn't I give to be in your place."

And so I drove on, this time alone.

I was wondering where the underground fighters would show up.
"Somewhere between Guantanamo and Baracoa" was pretty vague,
since the distance was a good 120 miles. It was as if someone had
fixed an appointment for me on U.S. 1 "somewhere between New
York and Providence, Rhode Island."

I hardly noticed the countryside, although it was certainly magnificent. Over the narrow, winding road giant bamboos joined in a
splendid Gothic arch. The bad road surface held my attention,
however. The surfacing, thin enough at best, had disappeared al-
together in places, leaving a sort of jagged gravel on which the tires
shrieked and skidded at every turn. To cap it all, the air was hot
and heavy, without the slightest breeze. A storm was surely about
to break and no one from the underground army had yet put in an
appearance. I was beginning to lose hope.

Suddenly, as I rounded a bend, I had to step on the brake to
avoid crashing into a tree that blocked the road. The car lurched
and stopped sideways on the road. In less time than it takes to tell
the tale, men swarmed out of the ditches and surrounded the car,
their weapons trained on me. They were wearing uniforms of sorts.
Their hair was incredibly long, and, with their unkempt beards,
they looked like Fidel Castro's one-time partisans. But they were
reasonably clean and did not appear overtired or ill-fed.

The one who seemed to be in charge ordered me out of the car.

He stuck the barrel of his American submachine gun in my stomach and searched me from head to foot without ceremony. "Who are you?" he asked.

I showed my press card and said, "I'm a French journalist."

He studied my papers with great care. Then, with an air of innocence, he remarked, "Ah! So you're French? You must know Pigalle, the Folies Bergères, Maxime?"

I jumped at the last word. "Maxime! I've got a toothache and I'm looking for a dentist."

He shook me by the hand. "My name's Julio," he said. He was small, thin, and bony, with hollow cheeks swallowed by his beard, and his eyes were a deep black. A hunter's cartridge belt of worn leather held up his trousers of blue-grey cloth, so threadbare that black hairs showed through at the knees. His two-pocket shirt, with shoulder straps, was in better shape. He was well armed: aside from the submachine gun, a short-barreled revolver dangled by his right leg and there was a dagger in his belt.

He broke into a nervous laugh. "To think we took you for an enemy! No one believed you would come this far. We spotted you miles away through the glasses, and were afraid you were a Communist *agent provocateur*. My men wanted to shoot you down. I thought an ambush was better. Just as well!" Julio became serious again. "Don't let's waste any time, *hombre*. How long can you stay?"

"I told the hotel in Santiago that I was spending the weekend at the seaside with a *muchacha*. Might as well cash in on the Frenchman's reputation as a woman chaser! No one will worry if I don't get back tonight—but I ought to return tomorrow, or Tuesday morning at the latest."

We set off. Julio kept up his chatter, while letting his glance travel from a group of flowering aloes to a clump of banana trees, from the top of a solitary breadfruit tree standing in a tobacco field to a group of royal palms at the edge of a stream.

When we reached the valley, the guerrillas spread out in a fan as we crossed a field of *malangas* with their heart-shaped leaves. Soon a white patch surrounded by banana trees announced the presence of a *bohio*. The farmer greeted us from the threshold of his hut with its walls of coconut-palm trunks and its roof covered with palm branches. Julio whispered to me, "That's Jorge. Don't tell him anything. He never asks questions, anyhow. The Communists wanted to evacuate him but he refused to leave his farm, though he has sent his wife and four children to an aunt in Santiago. One of these days the Communists will come back and they'll certainly shoot him. I've told him so a hundred times, but he just laughs. He's convinced they won't do him any harm—says he'll pretend he knows nothing. Well, that's OK with me. But the Communists aren't fools, are they?"

In Cuba each of the opposing parties has its pet name for the other. To Fidel's supporters their opponents are *gusanos*, earthworms, while Castro's men are all dubbed Communists by the underground fighters of Oriente and Escambray.

The *bohio* consisted almost entirely of a simple large living room. Opposite the door, behind the square table, hung a colored portrait of Fidel Castro, still bearing in the left-hand corner the name of the magazine from which it had been cut, *INRA*. Julio was furious. He spat on the floor and cursed Jorge. "Aren't you one of us? How the hell do you have the nerve to stick up a picture of that cowardly murderer in your house? If I were you, I'd rather be buried in a dunghill!"

"It's meant for the others, for the militia," said the farmer. "If they come and they see Fidel's photo, they'll think I'm on their side. Anyway, I've always believed in Fidel. *Fidel es siempre el mismo Fidel!* He's still the same old Fidel! He can't have changed. He doesn't know what's going on. *Fidel no sabe nada!* He knows nothing. He's a prisoner of the Communists. If he were free, believe me, he'd be with us out here in the Sierra. Believe me, *Fidel es siempre el mismo Fidel!*"

Again Julio spat. He shrugged his shoulders and appeared to calm down; then he broke out once more, "That murderer has sold Cuba to the Communists. Will you never understand?"

"I assure you, *Fidel no sabe nada! Nada! Fidel es siempre el mismo Fidel!*"

"*Tonterias!* Poppycock!"

"It's not poppycock, believe me, Julio."

"That's enough. Instead of talking nonsense, let's eat." It was a frugal lunch: green bananas fried in pork fat, with boiled *malanga* roots, washed down with fresh water and coconut milk. As we ate, Julio told me some of his story. He was now in his fourth year in the underground. He had begun by fighting under Fidel Castro's orders in the neighboring Sierra Maestra.

"Before that," he said, "I was a medical student at Havana University. I gave up everything to follow Fidel. At the end of the war I was a Captain: that's a high rank in Castro's army—the highest is *Comandante*. A Captain under Fidel is like a General in your country."

After Batista fell, Julio was personally appointed by Fidel to an important post near Holguín in northern Oriente, supervising land reform measures. "Over there in the Sierra Maestra," he went on, "the land reform was the great dream of us all. Since then, unhappily, Fidel has completely changed. Sometimes, when I think back to those days, I weep tears of anger. Can you imagine that? Tears, at my age!"

Julio stopped talking to swallow a mouthful of *malanga*. Then he continued his tale, apparently feeling a compelling urge to justify his revolt against his former chief. "It was some time before I understood. To start with I was like Jorge; I thought that Fidel could not change. But why didn't he keep the promises he made in darker days? I asked for explanations, and each time I was told, 'Don't you bother your head about that. Fidel knows what he's doing.'

"Then the police—not Batista's but the new police, our police—imprisoned some of the comrades who had fought on Fidel's side. We were told they were traitors. Now I was really puzzled. I went to Havana and saw Núñez Jiménez and Rolando Cubela and told them what I was thinking. When I got back home again near Holguín I found two policemen waiting to arrest me. I drew my revolver, fired, and took to my heels.

"A few days later I returned to the mountains, where little by little other friends from the old days joined me. Now there are over a thousand of us here in Sierra del Cristal, all determined to give our lives to overthrow Fidel and his gang of Communists."

"And afterwards, what will you do?" I asked.

"Afterwards we'll make the Revolution, the real Revolution this time! Whatever happens, we can't go back on the land reform or on Fidel's earliest achievements; they are irreversible."

"And after the Revolution, what will you personally do?"

"I've no idea. Maybe I'll become a doctor, as I always wanted. Yes, afterwards I think I'll be a doctor."

"Unless you get knocked off first," broke in Jorge.

"What makes you think I'll get knocked off?" asked Julio.

"*Hombre*, who knows what fate has in store? Tomorrow, maybe we'll all be dead. Dead and buried. *Hombre*, who knows?"

Julio pulled out his revolver and kissed the barrel. The others followed suit. I asked why they did that. "Because it's safer, *Francés!*"

"What good does kissing your revolver do?"

"None in particular."

"Then why do it?"

"In the Sierra, when anyone speaks of death you must always kiss your gun. It's bad luck if you don't. My grandfather, who fought with José Martí against the Spaniards, always did it, except once— and that was the time he was killed in an ambush."

The guerrillas looked down at their plates as they ate. Julio swallowed his food in large mouthfuls washed down with occasional draughts of coconut milk. Jorge bustled about, refilling plates and glasses as they were emptied. I motioned to him to stop. "No more for me, thanks."

"Don't you like it?" he asked anxiously.

"Sure I do, it's fine, but I'm not hungry any more."

"So you like my food, Frenchman?"

"*Si, éste me gusta mucho.*"

"I'm glad. You see, I was a bit scared because Julio told me, 'We've got a Frenchman coming. The French are a bit difficult about their food—they're used to good things—so you make an effort!' Well, I did what I could. Usually the wife does the cooking. Boy, can she cook! You ought to taste her steak and onions with gravy. It's so good the kids and I finish it off and lick the plates and pot clean. *Caramba*, can that little woman cook!"

The meal drew to an end. Julio finished off by cleaning his plate with a piece of bread. Then he wiped the blade of his knife and stuck it back in his belt, boy scout fashion. "Are you ready, *Francés?*" he asked. "*Anda!* Let's go!"

The two guerrillas who had stayed outside during lunch were waiting for us in front of the wooden fence of the farmhouse. They had saddled some small stocky horses. "I've chosen this dappled mare for you," said Julio. "She's quieter than any grandmother. She'll get you there without hurrying, but as safely as a mule."

We rode off across the valley through fields of *malangas*. The red earth, damp from a lunch-time shower, was heavy and stuck to the horse's hooves. Soon we were climbing a narrow track up the mountain. As for my mare, she was docility itself; butter would have melted in her mouth.

Julio's mode of riding was to lean forward over his horse's mane, one hand on the pommel of his saddle. From time to time he would stand up in the stirrups and look back at his men, strung out in a long line behind him.

Suddenly, sun and sky were blotted out by a wall of darkness that enveloped us completely. I could no longer see a yard in any direction. There was no time to shelter before the storm was upon us; the sky was alive with lightning and I could sense the nervousness of the animal beneath me. The rain pelted down with the violence of hail and in a fraction of a second I was drenched from top to toe. What garment could possibly stand up to such treatment? Luckily, it was all over in a few minutes; soon the sun was burning down as hot as before.

Julio, riding ahead, looked around and burst out laughing at my discomfiture. "*Hombre!*" he cackled, "*te gusta la vida de guerillero?*"

A quarter of an hour later, when I was just starting to get dry, we were overtaken by another tropical storm as heavy as the first, and I was soaking wet again. I was beginning to feel distinctly uncomfortable, for it was a long time since I had been on horseback and I was becoming saddle sore.

Then, fortunately, we reached the summit area. Julio signalled with his arm and we all dismounted. Two men led the horses into a nearby cave while another unpacked a radio set and some ammunition from a rucksack.

"We will camp here tonight," said Julio to me, "but you'll sleep down below, in the *bohío*."

"Why can't I stay here too?"

"Because you're unarmed. An unarmed man is a liability to guerrillas."

The band of fighters had now dispersed among the crags, and I was left alone with Julio and one of his men. "What's your name?" I asked the latter.

"Mind your own damn business!"

Julio laughed heartily. "Pedro," he said, "is a real tough guy. He's a good boy and a real pal, but now and then he flies off the handle."

Pedro had a peasant's head with a face that looked as if it had been hacked out of a piece of wood. A Garand rifle was slung across his back and a surplus U.S. Army canteen hung at his hip. "Why did you come out into the Sierra?" I asked him. He made a sweeping gesture with his hand as though to say, "If you only knew. . . ." I asked a more precise question. "What's your quarrel with Fidel?"

"Fidel's a traitor!" said he with some vehemence. "He is a traitor and a bastard. *Caramba!* On the day when they shoot him I'd trade my wife for the privilege of being in the firing squad." Pedro stole quietly away and took up his post some fifty yards from the cave. He slipped between two rocks, unslung his rifle, loaded it, cocked it, and put it down in front of him.

Julio lay on his stomach among the dust and stones, and lowered the peak of his fisherman's cap. "Come here," he said. I flattened myself down at his side. We were on the very edge of a cliff with a sheer drop to the vast green, red and ocher carpet of the valley. Far off was the silvery thread of a river winding sluggishly through fields of sugar cane to lose itself where the mountains closed in again. The road was also visible, a lead-colored ribbon snaking along the flank of the Sierra.

Julio adjusted his binoculars, watching the road at the point where it turned behind the mountains. "Everything OK?" I asked.

"Those cowards won't come today, either!" he exclaimed.

I was surprised. "Don't they ever attack you?"

"Oh yes, they send a few planes over from time to time. Big planes, B-26's that come and make a lot of noise. It's enough to make you deaf. Maybe that's what those Communists are trying to do."

"But don't the planes drop anything on you?"

"Sure, they scatter bombs all over the mountain, but we don't come out of our hiding places, so they simply blow holes in the rocks. We're lucky they don't have any napalm like Batista's planes had. The noise is the only inconvenience—you've no idea what a racket those B-26's and their bombs kick up! It often really scares our newer recruits, but after three or four bombings they take it philosophically and, like everyone else, just take cover and wait until it's over."

"And what about the militia?"

"Oh, several batallions sometimes come up, with artillery and aircraft, looking for us. But they always draw a blank. We see them coming for miles and get away. No matter how much they rummage around, they never find anything. We know the Sierra better than they do."

"Don't you ever fire at them?"

"We're not that stupid. It would be the best way to get spotted."

"So the militia doesn't really bother you?"

"The soldiers are like the aircraft—their bark is worse than their bite."

"Yet on TV I saw pictures of prisoners captured in the Sierra."

"*Mentiras!* All lies! Those gutless militia were beating around in the mountains for a couple of weeks without finding the slightest trace of any of us. But they had to show that the operation was not a total failure, so they arrested a bunch of peasants down in the plain and for good measure they threw in a few people released from jail especially for the purpose. I know that for a fact—Jorge has a TV at home, and he recognized friends who had been locked up in Santiago for quite some time."

Our talk was growing less and less like an interview. I did not need to press Julio for confidences. He spoke softly, his glasses always trained on the end of the road, and he talked about the war, his war. "*Esta guerra es mi guerra,*" he murmured, "I will win it."

"Are the others former supporters of Fidel like you?"

"Some of them."

"How do the recruits train?"

"I teach them myself what they have to know, when everything's quiet. They get their training gradually, over a longish period. We do a lot of marching—ten or fifteen hours at a stretch, stopping for only ten minutes every four hours. My boys are wonderful. They can march night and day and they can run for long spells, upright or bent double. They jump and climb like goats. They can make bombs, blow up bridges, and mine the roads."

"Do you often lay mines?"

"Yes, because it's a good method for being left in peace. The militia are terrified to think that when they leave their barracks they may go up like carnival rockets. And mines are such fun! Gustavo enjoys them like a schoolboy. He knows how to make an oildrum into a device that will send a truck to kingdom come! He's a real artist when it comes to mining a road."

"Where is this Gustavo?"

"On guard, out front. Would you like to talk to him?"

"Yes."

Julio whistled. A head appeared above a rock; Julio raised the butt of his rifle twice, and a few minutes later Gustavo sauntered up, along a line of pine trees bordering the crest.

"Gustavo," said Julio, "tell the *Francés* how you make a mine."

"It's easy. You just take a can, some explosive, and a length of wire. The most awkward part is the detonator. Sometimes you can find them ready-made, by taking them out of grenades, for instance. Otherwise you have to make them yourself. Want me to show you?"

"No, I don't have the time."

"Too bad. We could have blown up a bridge. That's a show you don't see every day—it's better than the movies."

"The other day, thanks to Gustavo," said Julio, "they made us a present of a cannon, a small mountain gun towed by a jeep. There were four guys in the jeep when it drove over the mine. They're all dead. We could have picked up hunks of the jeep 200 yards away. But the gun was unharmed. We took it away, just to scare the militia some more."

"Where is it now?"

"Hidden in a cave."

"Do you use it?"

"No. A cannon fired from the Sierra can be spotted. It's like calling out to the Communists, 'Here we are; take good aim.'"

Gustavo took an empty condensed milk can from his pack. "Look," he said, "here's how you make a grenade. Watch closely, it's easy. The best thing is a length of lead pipe, otherwise any old can will do. Stuff it with the hardest things you can find; bits of scrap iron, pebbles, anything at all. Then pack it well—that's very important. Cover it all with dynamite. Before you put the lid on, don't forget to make a hole in it for the fuse. All you've got to do now is put a match to the fuse and throw the grenade. It does plenty of damage, believe me.

"A week or two ago we were bored to death and looking for some way to liven things up. Not far away there was an advanced post of the militia—some silly little asses who thought themselves real tough guys, with their berets and cowboy belts. So I said to Julio, 'How about paying them a little visit? For us it will be as good as going to the movies, and as for them, they'll stop pretending they're heroes.'

"We went over there one evening about the time the main feature starts. We surrounded the camp and threw in a lot of fruit juice cans stuffed with things that make a lot of noise and flame.

"*Caramba!* I never saw such a riot in my life! Smoke and flames all over the place, and the militiamen rushing about in all directions, screaming as if they were being castrated. They were firing their submachine guns at random and killing one another—absolute bedlam. We had orders to be careful, but all the same we stayed behind the banana trees to watch. We didn't shoot—we didn't want to kill them, only to scare the pants off them. We had thrown our Molotov cocktails and fired a few rounds into the air; we had paid for our seats, so we watched the show. Boy, what fun we had! *Caramba, Francés,* we were all doubled up laughing! We were so amused that Julio got worried and said, 'Come on, let's beat it, otherwise they'll be the ones to laugh.' He was right, of course. We couldn't risk being caught by reinforcements. The next day the militiamen had stopped playing heroes. They were kind of slinking along, their berets in their pockets."

"Were many killed?"

"No, just three or four were knocked off by their own comrades. Our Molotovs couldn't kill them. In any case, Julio didn't want us to shoot those little idiots. He said they were nitwits who didn't know what they were doing. When there's any choice we kill only the officers."

"And the men?"

"We try to take them alive. We strip them and paint the hammer and sickle on their asses and genitals. The poor devils have to go back to their barracks like that. A fate worse than death, if you ask me." Gustavo was silent for a moment, then he asked, "Do you want to know anything else, *Francés?*"

"No, thank you."

"Right. Then I'll go back. *Salud.*"

I turned to Julio. "How do you get your conventional weapons—rifles, pistols, machine guns, and so on?"

"At first our pals in exile at Miami or in Guatemala sent us those in small aircraft that parachuted arms, ammunition, and food. But air supplies have stopped for the past year. It seems that to avoid trouble the Yankees have asked our friends to be more cautious. So we've had to change our tactics. Now we get our weapons direct from the Communists. A militiaman killed or taken prisoner means an extra rifle for us. At the moment we have U.S. carbines, Czech submachine guns, hunting rifles, and heaps of revolvers of all calibers. The carbine is easily the best—you can knock off a man with it at 300 yards."

"What is your primary task, would you say?"

"To let everyone know that we're always around. We never attack the same post twice."

"And what are the chief precautions you take?"

"First of all, we keep on the move. We make it a rule never to stay in the same place more than three or four days. In spite of our complete confidence in Jorge we'll be leaving him tomorrow or the day after. He won't see us again.

"Next, we have to keep the enemy under constant observation. You haven't seen all my men; several are on guard on the crests, watching the enemy's every move, so we always know what to expect. This is important, because we make a point of never accepting battle. Ten days ago we were attacked while on a night march. We at once fell flat on our faces to avoid the enemy fire and watched where it came from. But we didn't fire back; the enemy would have been only too pleased if we had. Then we beat it fast."

"What about food supplies?"

"Difficult, but they come."

"How?"

"Forgive me if I don't answer that. It's a secret."

"Do the peasants help you?"

"Not very much. A few, like Jorge, realize that the Communists have deceived them, and they will do anything for us. We have to watch out for the others—they're quite capable of betraying us."

The day was nearly over; the sun had turned orange and was about to set behind the mountain. One of the guerrillas, a lookout, came in and reported to Julio. "Nobody's moving any more than an overfed crocodile. Even the sentries on the bridge are snoozing. I was itching to use them as targets."

"If you shoot without an order from me, I'll have you shot!"

"It was just a thought."

"*Bueno.* Tell me, did you see any tanks?"

"No."

"Trucks?"

"A few."

"How many?"

"Fourteen."

"Empty or full?"

"Eleven full and three empty."

"What make were the full ones?"

"Russian Gorkis."

"Each truck can carry thirty militia men, so that means 330 men. That's not many, after all. What about the sentries on the bridge? How often did they change the guard?"

"Every six hours, as usual."

"You didn't notice anything else?"

"Yes, a move that may interest you. You know the four soldiers who guard the bridge?"

"Sure, two at each end."

"That's right," said the lookout. "The guard is changed at ten past six in the evening. Two trucks full of soldiers arrive and stop in the middle of the bridge."

"*Caramba!*" cried Julio. "What a bunch of jerks!"

"You said it, what a bunch of jerks."

"Think we can blow that bridge?"

"Easy. At night you can get as close as you like if you keep near the banana trees on the river bank. No one can see you."

"You go tonight. Take Gustavo along. Get everything ready in advance. Tomorrow, at 6:10 P.M., two truckloads of Communists will be blown to hell."

A number of guerrillas had been quietly gathering around us. One of them pointed to me and asked Julio, "When is the *Francés* leaving?"

"Tomorrow morning."

"How do we know he won't tip the Communists off?"

"We can trust him," said Julio. "He's a friend of the *coordinador*. He won't breathe a word of this plan. Will you, *Francés*?"

I prudently answered, with a smile, "What plan? I know nothing of any plan."

"But the bridge, the sentries. . . . Didn't you hear?"

"I don't know what you're talking about."

I had a talk with Agustin, age twenty-seven, a peasant from the Sierra Maestra. At the time of Batista's fall, he owned 4 *caballerias* (132 acres) of land, all of it mortgaged. "The agrarian reform cancelled my debt at one stroke," he said.

"Then why on earth are you fighting Castro? It would be easier to understand your joining the militia."

"I suppose so. You're right. Normally, I would have allowed myself to be cut into pieces for Fidel. At first, that's the way I felt. Fidel could have asked me for anything. But slowly I came to see that he had fooled the whole bunch of us, that he had fooled all the farmers. I told myself, 'Agustin, you're a cuckold, and Fidel made you one.' "

"Fidel? What do you mean?"

"Fidel himself didn't do anything. But those bastards of the INRA tried to force me to join a cooperative. But me, I wanted to cultivate my land as I pleased, just as my father and grandfather had done.

"That house, I built it with my own hands. It was surrounded by banana trees and coconut trees, and stood in the middle of my *malanga* and sugar cane fields. There were avocados too, and two enormous mango trees. It was a white house, and there was a river flowing nearby. It made a sound like little bells as it washed over the polished white pebbles. The water was so clean that my two donkeys drank directly from it, and everybody knows how fussy a donkey is when it comes to drinking. Your donkey will eat anything. But when it comes to drinking, he is as exacting as some *muchacha* in a Santiago bar."

"What happened when you refused to join the cooperative?"

"INRA sent soldiers, who spent every night in my house. They would insult me, and not only me but my father and mother, who are dead now, as well. My parents were honest *guajiros* who never did a single bad deed in all their lives. They never watered the milk they sold in the city and never cheated on the weights they used. They were good honest people. Anyway, I won't let anyone insult my father and mother.

"And not only did they insult my dead parents, but they called me a *gusano*. Me a *gusano*, imagine that. They said that some day the people would get even with me and shoot me. Tell me, who are the people, anyway? Aren't I the people too? I am not a *latifundista*. I am a simple farmer and I want to be left alone. I finally got mad and took to the hills."

Another guerrilla walked over to us. I asked him, "And you, what made you come here?"

"They jailed the priest of my village! *No me gustó.* I didn't like it."

Nighttime was drawing near. The halo of orange light that covered the mountain and gave it its hazy outline was rapidly growing fainter. There seemed to be a leaden lid over the valley. In the tropics the sun sets with disconcerting suddenness.

"Let's get to Jorge's," said Julio. "We're having dinner with him and we mustn't keep him waiting."

It was dark when we arrived at the *bohio.* Jorge had lit a kerosene lamp which flickered. "You've seen the Sierra?" he said. "Beautiful, isn't it?"

"Never mind. It was I who showed it to him," Julio interrupted. "OK, OK!"

Dinner was the same as lunch. When we had finished our *malanga,* Julio said, "Go to bed. We're going to be busy tonight. There's no need for you to come along. You'd only be taking unnecessary risks. One of my friends will come and fetch you tomorrow morning. He'll bring you to your car and show you how to go back without being stopped by the militia."

Jorge, holding up his lamp, led us to the children's bedroom. "This is where you'll sleep," he said, and added, "You're sure you don't want a pistol?"

"*No, gracias.*"

"It would be safer. Anyway, we'll try and watch over you." He put out his tanned hand. "*Adios, hermano, y buena suerte.* So long, brother, and good luck to you." I thanked him for all he had done for me. As he walked away he added, "*A sus órdenes.* At your orders."

I sat down at the window and rested my elbows on the wooden crossbar. The weather was fine. A slight wind blowing from the fields in the valley brought up whiffs of air that carried the smell of the damp earth, tobacco, and hay. Everything was so calm and still, it was hard to imagine that not far off men would perhaps soon be dying. I peered into the dark. Little by little my eyes got used to it and I could make out the outline of the palm trees.

I was about to crawl under the mosquito netting that covered my bed when firing broke out: the cracking of automatic weapons. The hollow and muffled sound reached me faintly. They must have been fighting in the hills.

Jorge woke me up at daybreak. "*He! Francés,* wake up. There's coffee ready in the kitchen."

The sun was streaming in through the window, filling the room with light. I jumped out of bed and went to look out the window. Everything seemed quiet.

I joined Jorge in the kitchen. "*Salud, Francés,* did you have a good night?"

"Fine."

"The mosquitoes didn't bother you?"

"No, they didn't."

"And the shooting?"

"I heard it before falling asleep. Tell me, what happened?"

"There was a lot of fighting near the bridge. Gustavo and Juanito were spotted just as they were trying to plant their dynamite. It seems the guards had been reinforced. Julio and his men tried to free our two friends near the bridge. They fought all night long. The fighting even came close to here. At one point I almost went to wake you up and get you the hell out of the house. You know, in such cases it is better not to fall into the hands of the militia. They'll shoot you right off."

"Any dead?"

"There must be lots among the militia."

"And among the others?"

"Gustavo. And Juanito, he is up there in the cave, dying." Jorge brought me my coffee piping hot. "Drink that down," he said, "then go wash in the river. We'll soon be pulling out of here."

"How did you hear about the fighting?"

"Julio sent one of the men on watch to tell me to accompany you. He'll stay up there till you've gone, and then he'll leave with his men."

"Where will they go?"

"Somewhere else. It's getting dangerous here. The Communists are sure to come back in numbers."

"And you, what are you going to do?"

"I'm going back to Santiago with you. There I'll go and hide with some friends."

We left a few minutes later. We went up the path that climbed toward the road. Jorge had taken a pistol. Before we got to my car, a man with an automatic rifle suddenly appeared from behind the aloe trees. "Halt. Is that you, Jorge?"

"*Salud.*"

"Where are you going with the *Francés?*"

"I'm taking him back."

"*Buena suerte.*"

"*Adios.*"

We reached Santiago toward the end of the afternoon. The city lay at our feet, crescent-shaped. The sky was very clear and the fields along the road were green. Mauve flowers hung from the banana trees. They shivered in the sea breeze.

Jorge, who hadn't spoken for a while, said, "Juanito must be dead by now. He wasn't a bad guy. Gustavo wasn't a bad guy either."

CHAPTER 27

So here I was back in Havana, a little shaken up by the bus ride. Day was just breaking. My suitcase in my hand, I was leaving the parking lot and walking towards the taxi line when a woman's voice called me from the street. "Victor!" An old car pulled up to the curb. Maria, the *coordinador*'s secretary, was at the wheel. "Get in," she said.

We drove around the *Plaza Civica* and down toward the sea. I asked Maria, "Were you waiting for me or were you just going by?"

"I was waiting. The *coordinador* has quite a story for you to cover."

"All right, except if it's a question of personally taking part in one of your fights."

"Don't worry. All the *coordinador* is asking you to do is not to leave Cuba before the end of the week."

"Why not?"

"You'll see. In the meantime it's better not to return to the Presidente. A room has been reserved for you at the Roosevelt. The hotel is at the corner of Calle Amistad and Calle San Miguel. It is a simple sort of hotel, but before the week is over, you'll be glad to have moved there." Maria stopped in front of a cab stand. "It's better for me not to bring you all the way to the hotel. See you later."

I thought a lot about it, but couldn't figure out what she was getting at. What was going to happen at the Roosevelt Hotel at the end of the week? This was a commercial district with lots of small jeweler's shops, haberdashers, cafés, and department stores. There had been some sabotage here, but nothing very spectacular.

After having moved into my new hotel I went for a walk around town. On the Prado I ran into a procession of about two hundred women led by some Negro musicians. These women were employees of the Corona cigar factories. The Negro musicians were playing the *pachanga* then in fashion—some had tom-toms hung around their necks, some played trumpets or maracas. The women moved with rhythm, swinging their hips, throwing up one leg, then the other. Their eyes sparkled and they were singing out at regular intervals, "*Paredón! Paredón! Paredón!*" summoning up the image of the firing squad and the execution post. A robust brown-skinned woman of fifty called to me, "Come and join the protest march."

"What are you protesting about?"

She threw up her arms, made some circles and arabesques above her head. She laughed, displaying her dirty teeth. "We are demonstrating against the counterrevolutionaries and the *blandos,* and for the Revolution."

"The *blandos?* The soft?"

"Too many people are soft in Cuba. All the softies should be done away with as counterrevolutionaries. We should be tougher and send everybody who is keeping Fidel from accomplishing his Revolution to the firing squad. At Corona we have set up a Revolutionary Watch Committee to obey Fidel's orders."

"What did Fidel say?"

"He said we had to be constantly on the alert: in the street, in

the shops, at home. We have to find the counterrevolutionaries.
As soon as I hear a counterrevolutionary word, I run to the police
and say, 'This is what this counterrevolutionary bastard said!'

"Fidel has told us to set up Revolutionary Watch Committees.
Take me, for example. I live in an apartment building near here.
We've organized a Committee. My daughter, a member of the
militia, is secretary of the Committee. She's only fifteen, but I can
tell you she's smart. She knows everything about all the people in
the apartment house. She keeps an eye on them. It's easy, we live
on the ground floor. My daughter makes a note of everyone who
comes in and goes out. Every day, she sends in her report to the
police. She warned me, 'Mother, if some day I see that you are
no longer 100 per cent revolutionary, I'll report you.' I congratulated her."

Josefa—that was her name—kept dancing and moving forward
while telling me all this. I almost had to run to keep up with her.
She ended up giving me quite a description of life at the cigar
factory.

The head office of the Corona firm, as well as its main factory, is
on the Prado, near the Capitolio, which is a faithful replica of the
Capitol in Washington. The work of cleaning and rolling the
tobacco leaves is performed by women sitting at long narrow tables
and working all together in a large room. The working day is ten
hours, the work is monotonous, and the workers are always in-
haling tobacco. Under these conditions, they are threatened with
nervous depression, and in order to distract them, an elderly man
reads to them. Before the Revolution, when the factory was still
privately owned, he used to read love stories. The women told him
each week what they wanted to hear. Now he is no longer allowed
to read just anything. Every morning he finds a pile of "educational" writings, selected by the Watch Committee, waiting for
him on his desk. The day before he had finished a book by Lenin.
"A book of 400 pages," Josefa pointed out.

That afternoon, he had finished reading Fidel Castro's most re-
cent speeches. On several occasions, he had been taken to task by
the foreman for not using the correct declamatory tone of voice.
She shouted at him, "Show more fire! Put some life into it. You
don't convey Fidel's fury."

At six o'clock, when the day's work was over, the workers were about to leave when the supervisor, who was also in charge of the Watch Committee, said, "We can't part just like this, without having accomplished some small revolutionary act. *Vamos a manifestar contra los blandos y los contra-revolucionarios!*"

"*Vamos a manifestar!* Let's go demonstrate!" repeated all the cigar rollers.

The parade was soon formed and the ubiquitous Negro musicians appeared out of nowhere. In Cuba, whenever people decide to form a parade, for whatever reason, a number of musicians will suddenly appear to take the lead, playing what tunes they feel like. They struck up the new Cuban hit: "*Mamá no quiere que yo juegue a la pelota*, Mama won't let me play pelota."

The cigar rollers all took up the chorus, but their leader, whom Josefa pointed out to me, had interrupted them, calling them fools and shouting, "This isn't carnival! We are accomplishing a revolutionary action! Comrade musicians, pick another tune. Don't you know some good patriotic songs?"

The good-natured Negro musicians struck up a rumba the only words of which, endlessly repeated, were, "*Yanqui no! Cuba si! Yanqui no!*"

After a hundred yards the leader took the whistle hanging around her neck and blew it imperatively. The cigar rollers stopped and the musicians put their instruments down on the road. "Now you play that magnificent revolutionary pachanga our genial and beloved Fidel himself sang over the radio the other day."

"Which one?" a musician asked.

"You know! '*Paredón.*' The pachanga, '*Paredón.*'"

I found Anita waiting for me in the lobby of the Roosevelt Hotel, sitting in an easy chair like a good little girl. I liked her grey shirt with its shoulder straps, but not her green pants with big patch pockets. At her belt she was wearing a small pistol in a black holster. An automatic rifle was lying across her knees. I jokingly said, "I see you're off to war."

Her face darkened. "Don't make fun of me. I phoned you several times last week and was told you had left town. Where did you go?"

"To Oriente Province."

"Did you like it?"

"I certainly did. Not at all like Havana!"

I invited her to dinner. We walked toward the top of Calle Amistad. Anita walked next to me, carrying her automatic rifle much as a British officer of the Indian Army would have carried his stick in earlier days. I was annoyed at going out with a girl who was playing soldier.

It was a hot and heavy tropical afternoon. We went into a snack bar that was much like a subway station and sat down somewhere at the back, on canary yellow plastic stools.

There were only American and Chinese dishes on the menu. We ordered hamburgers and French fried potatoes. They weren't very good. "You don't seem very pleased," said Anita.

"I prefer Cuban cooking. At least it has some taste."

"Say we were in Paris now. Where would you be taking me?"

"To some little place."

"What would you have ordered?"

"A good steak and a bottle of Beaujolais."

"What's that?"

"Wine."

"You drink a lot of wine in France."

"I guess."

"I'm told most French people are alcoholics."

"Who told you that?"

"I read it in *Revolución*."

Nearby, four girl soldiers in uniform were talking with animation about Lumumba. "Lumumba," said Anita, "was a great man. What a shame that he was murdered. Have you ever been to the Congo?"

"Yes, I have."

"When was that?"

"Just before independence. I stayed only two days."

I recalled an anecdote. When I was passing through Brazzaville, President Fulbert Yulu had talked to me about Kasavubu. "He's a decent fellow. Unfortunately, he's not very much on the ball. Naturally, since he's a Flemish nationalist!"

Anita eyed me suspiciously. "Flemish nationalist? Is that an insult?"

I tried to explain President Yulu's joke to her. She didn't seem to get it.

"I hope you're not trying to insult the memory of Lumumba. Here in Cuba we honor him. All the papers wrote about him. An avenue, a school, and a factory have been named after him. In France, what did you do to remember him by?"

We went back to the hotel, and my soldier friend took her seat facing the door, as before. I sat down next to her. Outside, the sky was overcast, the good weather had come to an end. "The good days are over," said Anita, "soon now the rain will start."

The storm broke. The porter went to shut doors and windows. Anita got up and walked silently over to the window. She seemed fascinated by the glittering of the asphalt under the rain.

"What's the matter, Anita," I asked.

"Nothing."

"Do tell me. There is something wrong."

"I'm afraid, afraid of everything. I'm afraid of being alone and dying."

"You won't die."

She spoke softly, looking out at the rain. "Yes. I'm afraid of dying. That's the way I feel whenever I think about myself. I imagine myself dead. Not dead on my bed. Dead in the street, or on a beach, or in a field. Dead with a lot of small holes in my chest and in my head. Dead, with a lot of blood everywhere. You think I'm crazy, don't you?"

"No, you're not the crazy one. It's the whole country that's gone crazy. Cuba has gone crazy. Ever since I came here I've felt as if I were at the movies watching a horror film. Times goes by, the rhythm gets faster and faster, and things become more and more horrible."

I told her about the cigar makers' demonstration. I said the woman who had led the parade was mistaken. Carnival time was not over. In Cuba, every day was carnival. "But it's not an ordinary kind of carnival. In Rio or in New Orleans carnival is a celebration. People dance for joy there. But the women of Havana who twist and writhe to the tune of *'Paredón! Paredón!'* remind me of African sorcerers and their curses. They sing hatred. I feel like shutting my ears to their *'Paredón! Paredón!'*

"This morning I witnessed another curious scene at the INIT office. The setting was quite austere, notwithstanding the revolutionary posters and the casual attitude of the *barbudos* who stood guard. A line of visitors was waiting in front of the girl soldier on duty. One of the visitors carried a transistor radio that played dance tunes. Suddenly the sweet music stopped and was followed by the '*Yanqui no! Cuba sí! Yanqui no!*' rumba.

"Hearing this, the girl soldier got up as if moved by a spring, hung up the telephone, lifted her arms above her head and joined in, yelling like a wild animal, '*Yanqui no! Cuba si! Yanqui no!*' And all the others joined in: '*Yanqui no! Cuba si! Yanqui no!*'

"All the people in the INIT hall seemed to have gone berserk. Visitors, receptionists, and *barbudos* all joined the dance, elbows against the body, swinging their hips to the rhythm of the rumba. It lasted a couple of minutes.

"Then the dancers stopped with the music. The visitors returned to their place in line, the *barbudos* to theirs at the door, and the soldier girl sat down at her desk."

Anita had her black eyes on me while I told the story. She burst out laughing when I had finished. "We're always dancing in Cuba," she said. "Any time or place will do to sing and kick around. We even dance walking behind a funeral." Her face froze. Fresh tears appeared at the corners of her eyes and slowly slipped down, leaving a shiny trail on her brown cheeks.

"Why are you crying, Anita?"

"I don't know."

"What's wrong? Did my story shock you?"

"No, it's something else."

"Tell me?"

"No."

"Tell me—maybe I can do something."

"I'm afraid. I'm afraid. I've told you already. What can you do about it?"

"Nothing. I'm leaving Cuba tomorrow."

Anita hung her head. "I shouldn't say in front of a foreigner that I'm afraid. You'll write about it and then people will think that all Cuban women soldiers are afraid. They'll poke fun at us."

"Nobody will make fun of you, nor of your comrades. A girl of twenty isn't meant to wear a uniform, stand guard, and fight a war. The meaning of her life lies elsewhere." The rain had stopped. The porter opened the windows and the door. Anita murmured, "I'm ashamed. I'm ashamed of myself and of everything. I'm sad and I'm disgusted." She was trembling. "I've got to go now," she said. "I came to ask for a favor. When you're back in Paris, will you find me a pen-pal? A boy who'll write me regularly?"

I promised I would. Her face lit up. But she was still worried. "You're sure he'll want to write?"

"I'll see to it."

"Do you think he'll write in Spanish or in French? I don't know French."

"I'll try and find a student of Spanish."

"That'll be better. But never mind if he doesn't know Spanish. I'll buy a textbook and learn French. Tell him not to use difficult words at first."

"I'll tell him."

"And tell him I don't want to hear about war and revolutions. Tell him to write about girls and boys—simple boys and girls without any special stories."

"I'll tell him."

"Maybe he'll become my *novio.* Who knows? I wouldn't mind becoming engaged to a Frenchman. I'll start my letters with '*Querido,*' and end them, '*Te quiero.*' I ought to learn to say it in French so that he'll understand. Good-by now."

CHAPTER 28

"Fire, fire! *El Encanto*'s on fire." These shouts reached my ears shortly after Anita left. There were people running in all directions.

El Encanto was fifty yards away from my hotel, right across from my window, the largest, grandest, most luxurious of Havana's department stores, which Fidel had nationalized as soon as he gained power. Since then it had become a kind of symbol of the Revolution. Its two thousand employees had the reputation of being fanatical Castrists, and its Revolutionary Watch Committee never missed an opportunity to demonstrate its enthusiasm. The employees wholeheartedly joined the militia, and organized an around-the-clock guard over all exits. In the course of his speeches, Fidel had referred to the store again and again as an example of the success of the Revolution. "If all businesses were like *El Encanto*," he said on television one evening, "we would have no more problems in Cuba. There would not be a single counterrevolutionary left, and socialism would be triumphant once and for all."

Once before, while I was on my way to Santiago, an MRP group had attempted to set fire to the department store. But the alarm had been given soon enough for the flames to be brought under control. The next day, thirty of *El Encanto*'s two thousand loyal revolutionaries had been arrested and charged with "criminal sabotage and counterrevolutionary activity."

I ran toward the store, which was between Galiano, San Miguel, and San Rafael streets. I arrived at the same time as the first fire engine and some fifty idlers. Black smoke was pouring out of a fourth floor window.

The firemen set up their ladder, broke through the windows with their axes, and brought their hose into action. Suddenly, the whole façade was shaken by a loud explosion. I saw the ninety-foot wall toppling toward me. I leapt backwards instinctively and ran out of the way. A fraction of a second later the whole front of the building came crashing down with a deafening roar, taking the firemen on the ladder with it and burying the onlookers who had not reacted as quickly as I. The whole street was filled with a thick cloud of suffocating dust. Stones and pieces of wood and metal flew in every direction. Something hit me in the back, I lost my balance, staggered, managed to right myself, and kept on running. My fear was so acute that I didn't even feel the pain.

I went back to my hotel and up to my room where I removed my shirt. Thank God, it was nothing serious; a violet-colored bruise about four inches in diameter.

I went downstairs again. But this time I was more cautious. The Agence France Presse correspondent had his office right in San Rafael Street, in a tall building with a large roof terrace, which now became my observation post.

It was a wild sight. The flames rose as high as 150 feet. Fanned by a light wind, they occasionally licked the walls of the houses surrounding *El Encanto*. There was a series of explosions that sounded like exploding shells.

Some militiamen blocked off the streets, others saw to the evacuation of the buildings threatened by the flames. From my vantage point on the terrace I could see families leaving their houses, without hurry in spite of the danger. One man held a little boy by one hand and carried a suitcase in the other. A woman walked with him, carrying a baby in her arms, turning around repeatedly to look at a window, the window of her home, no doubt.

In San Rafael Street an enormous crowd had gathered in front of the barricades. A profound silence alternated with loud shouting. I thought I caught the strains of *"Paredón, Paredón."*

Jean Huteaux, the AFP correspondent, spent his time running up and down the two flights of stairs between his office and the terrace. Each time he appeared he had some news. "Other outrages have been committed at *Marianao Vedado*. . . . It appears that eight people have been killed and twenty injured."

The glow from the blaze lit up the whole district and made the moonlight seem dim. A few yards away from *El Encanto*, the neon sign of a shoe store continued to blink.

I looked at my watch. Time to think about writing my article for Paris. I went back to my hotel room, sat down at the table in front of the wide open windows, and got down to work. It was like having a ringside seat. The flames were dancing only a few dozen yards away. It was so hot I had to take off my shirt. My back hurt me a good deal.

By midnight I had finished my article and went out to the post office to cable it. The militia now blocked the entrance to the hotel. I spoke to an NCO. "I'm a journalist. I've got to send my article off to Paris right away."

"Where's the article?" I showed him my eight pages, which he seized and stuffed into his trouser pocket. "You'll get it back tomorrow."

"But why?"

"The boss has to read it first."

"But I'm in a hurry. The paper's waiting for it."

"Too bad."

I insisted. He got angry and ordered me back to the hotel. I protested. A militiaman came at me, hit me in the stomach with his rifle butt and sent me rolling to the other end of the hall. When I got up, the porter, who had been casually looking on, called to me, "You're wanted on the phone."

Feeling a little groggy, I picked up the receiver at the reception desk, without thinking. It was Maria, the *coordinador's* secretary. Her calm voice came as a strange contrast to the hysterical shouts of the crowd, the wailing of ambulance sirens and the crashing of falling timber. "I hope you're satisfied," she said, "with the show and the seat of honor we arranged for you. Good luck. *Adios!*"

She hung up. I was in a real spot now, imagining that the porter and the NCO had overheard her rash words. I tried to tell myself that I was dreaming and that in a short while, when my last night in Cuba finally ended, I would forget all about this horrible nightmare. But my smarting back and a dull pain in my kidneys were there to bring me back to reality and prove to me that I was wide awake and that the nightmarish situation was only too real.

29

The departure hall at Havana airport has glass walls. On one side you can see the waiting room, on the other the runway. The DC-6 that was to take me away from Cuba was on the runway. A clock struck noon. Its twelve notes seemed endless to me. We had been summoned at eight o'clock in the morning, and were still awaiting the pleasure of the authorities. They had not yet arrived, although we were supposed to have taken off at nine thirty.

There were a hundred passengers or so. Four foreigners were easily recognizable: one chubby Englishman, two immaculate Germans, and one silent Japanese. My other companions were obviously Cuban. They were serious and absorbed, like people expecting trouble. They looked as if they were leaving their country for good and were afraid of being found out. Perhaps they were also worried that the police officials would have something against them. It was Victor Hugo who said, "If I were accused of having stolen the towers of Notre Dame, I would begin by running away."

Seated in club chairs lined up as in a theatre, they watched the table at the back where—God knows when—the *Immigración* officials would hold court. No attempt was made at conversation. The atmosphere was cold and uneasy. Even the many children remained quiet, stiffened into a state of reserve unusual for their age.

I tried to exchange a few words with my neighbor. He responded politely with three or four '*si*'s.' Then he took a newspaper from the briefcase he was holding on his knees and ostensibly lost himself in reading the sports page. I resigned myself to imitating him and unfolded the *Revolución* I had bought when I arrived at the airport. Four lines in big print took up the middle of the first page. They were about the fire that had destroyed the department store, and they demanded the death penalty for "the instigators of the sabotage and their accomplices."

On the other side of our enclosure, men and women were pushing their faces against the glass partition. These were the passengers' relatives. They too were waiting in silence and obviously in a state of anxiety.

The children were getting restless. They didn't understand this interminable waiting. Like the grownups, they had noticed the luncheon being carried aboard the plane. A mulatto who was having some trouble controlling the five young children standing around her chair said to them, "Look there! We are soon going to eat."

Another woman accompanied by three little boys left her seat to go and chat with the militiaman on guard at the door. She was asking permission to buy some sandwiches and orangeade. She said, "The refreshment stand isn't far, I can see it over there. I won't be out of your sight." The sentry shook his head in refusal. The woman insisted. "It's not for me, but for the little ones. They're hungry." With the end of his machine gun the militiaman waved her back to her chair.

At twenty past one, five gentlemen of the *Immigración* arrived, wearing police uniforms. They crossed the hall without hurrying and took their seats behind the table. An airline employee handed them a handful of papers filled in in violet ink: the passenger list.

One of the officials called out: "Antonio G." A man with a small moustache and wavy hair got up. The first official asked for his passport. He gave it a glance and passed it on to his colleague, who did the same, and so on down the line to the last official. "Why are you going abroad?" asked the first.

"I have family business to attend to," replied the traveler.

"When are you planning to return?" asked the second.

"Next week."

"Who are you going to meet?" asked the third.

"My parents."

"And if you don't come back?" asked the fourth.

"I'll come back."

"You know," said the fifth, "that if you don't come back within thirty days you will be considered a traitor. Your property will be confiscated and you will never be allowed to return."

"I'll come back."

Then the cycle began again. Each official in turn, starting with the first, asked his question:

"Who paid for your trip?"

"My father-in-law."

"What does he do?"

"He's a businessman."

"Why is he living abroad?"

"He has been living in New York for twelve years."

"So you're going to New York?"

"Yes, I am."

"Why are you going via Kingston? It is not the shortest way."

"There was no room on the direct flights to New York."

"Do you know that it is forbidden to take money out of the country?"

"Yes, I do."

"How much have you got on you?"

"Nothing."

"Have you any jewelry?"

"No."

"A watch?"

"Yes."

"Hand it over; you can't take it out with you." Antonio G. unfastened the watch from his wrist and put it on the table. He was not given a receipt.

"We are through with you," said the first. "On to customs." A militiaman made a sign to Antonio to follow him. They left by the door that opened out onto the airfield.

"Achilles B." The second passenger underwent the same questioning, as did all those behind him. The officials asked the same questions in the same order. Most of the passengers were forced to give up some object or other. It apparently is forbidden for Cubans to travel with an electric razor, a camera, a typewriter, a tape recorder, a portable radio, a watch, jewelry, etc. The list is endless.

My turn came around four o'clock. I was the first of the foreigners and was entitled to a different set of questions:

"What did you do in Cuba?"

"Reporting."

"Whom did you see?"

"Officials," I answered carefully.

"Who?"

I cited a few of the known leaders at random: Fidel, Che Guevara, Jiménez.

They asked to see my notes. I secretly rejoiced at the thought that they had already left Cuba in a way worthy of Agatha Christie. I innocently replied, "What notes?"

"Those you took during your stay."

"I didn't take any notes."

"You didn't take any notes?"

"No, I didn't."

"But how do you intend to remember what you have seen?"

"I don't need notes for that. Everything is noted down in my mind." And I added, touching my forehead, "I have the memory of an elephant."

The officials were taken aback. "You never forget anything?" they asked, amazed.

"No, never."

"You must have a prodigious memory."

"That's right," I said, without any false modesty.

"Let's have a look at your briefcase and wallet." The officials emptied the contents of both on the table. They examined each paper, each object, one by one. "You have two pens," they remarked.

"True."

"Why two? One should do." I explained to them that for me a

second pen is as important as a spare tire for a car. "But," they insisted, "you don't need a pen since you don't take any notes."

"I need a pen very much."

"What for?"

"When I write an article, for example."

"*Bueno, bueno.*"

The third official was stopped by a picture. "Who is this?"

"My wife."

"*Bueno, bueno.*"

The fourth brandished an envelope containing some tourist publicity material and some picture postcards of the island. "And that?"

"Those are tourist pictures."

"Where did you get them?"

"INIT gave them to me."

"Do you have permission to take them out of Cuba?"

"I didn't know I needed it." I handed over the pictures without much regret.

"Where are you going after Kingston?" asked the fifth official.

"Home to France."

We were finally allowed to board at seven in the evening. The air hostesses hustled us along. They also were eager to be off.

Now we were in the airplane. The red signs went on: "Fasten your seat belts." The motor started. Next to me sat a young mulatto woman with feverish eyes, very erect, hands crossed over her knees.

The DC-6 raced down the runway, took off, started climbing. My neighbor turned to me and said gravely, "Now I'm not afraid any more. It's over." She repeated two or three times, "It's over," then suddenly burst into shrill laughter, shouting, "I'm not afraid any more. It's over! Over! Over!"

A kind of dizziness overcame me as we got further and further away from Cuba, that island of paradise darkened again and again by the shadow of hell. I thought of Cuba as of an immense arena scorched by the sun and by passion, where a tragedy is being endlessly repeated. But the Cuban revolution is not Shakespeare. It is a tragedy in the Spanish manner, akin to bullfighting. Grimacing death rises up amidst the cheers and songs of an infernal saraband danced by seven million men and women in the throes of insanity.

Epilogue

When I came back to Europe, I found that I had a good many enemies. I was attacked for not having hidden my disappointment. It was considered a sin to show that Castro's coming to power did not entail the oncoming of a better world; it was sinful to describe the sufferings of the people broken by the leaders of the 26th of July Movement, to speak of the writers, teachers and students who had been imprisoned because their opinions did not coincide with those of the Communist newspaper *Hoy*.

I was told I had no right to pay attention to the sundry details of daily life, since the Cuban Revolution is part of Human History on the March—in capitals—and due to change the face of the American hemisphere. I was informed that I should have observed events from a towering altitude, at least that of the planet Sirius. I had forgotten that dialetical materialism will not let itself be bothered by the realities of day-to-day existence. That men and women are rotting away in the cells of Pine Island, that others are put against the wall of the *Morro* does not matter; all this is being done in the name of History and Revolution.

In fact, it was when I returned to the old world that I understood the hypocrisy of using words taken directly from a ready-made vocabulary, to be used in a specific, dishonest context. When Castro resorts to shooting and torture, his apologists tell us that he is merely eliminating obstacles to his reforms, and invoke the precedent set by Batista.

Since World War I, a real sect of pseudo-idealist fanatics has arisen not only in Europe but on both sides of the Atlantic. What this sect preaches in the guise of intellectualism is not real Revolution, but a sort of social upheaval intended for snobs who have known neither hunger nor fear. Like all artificial religions, it is forever seeking a god, forgetting that human divinity cannot but be ephemeral. One after the other, Lenin, Trotsky, Stalin, Tito, Khrushchev, Mao Tse-tung, Soekarno, and Nkrumah have been set up as deities. Whatever they say or do, however scandalous or demented their actions, they have been admired as geniuses. These men are no longer judged as ordinary mortals: what in others would be criminal in them becomes exemplary.

It is hard to believe how far the high priests of Castrism went in sanctifying their idol. To call him a Communist or compare his actions to those of Communists was paramount to blasphemy.

It took an international crisis that brought the world to the brink of thermonuclear war to make these apostles of totalitarianism add some water to their wine. It became difficult for Jean-Paul Sartre and his brethren to continue denying that Cuba was a Soviet satellite when Khrushchev himself proclaimed it.

Suddenly, in the summer of 1962, we learned that the adventure of the *barbudos* had transformed the largest and most beautiful of the islands of the Carribean into a Soviet bridgehead. The U.S.S.R. had defied the Monroe Doctrine and the basic security of the U.S.A. and transformed Cuba into a giant logistical base sheltering some 20,000 Russian troops under the orders of four Russian generals headed by General Slazenko. Even more serious was installation of launching pads for medium-range missiles 100 miles off the Florida coast, and aimed at the U.S.A., as well as the bombers, jets, submarines, etc.

The American Government suddenly became aware of the seriousness of the Cuban cancer, sounded the alarm, and ordered the blockade of Cuba. President Kennedy drafted a note worded as an ultimatum demanding the dismantling of the Soviet military installations. From October 22 to 28, the whole world waited with bated breath and expected the worst. To the general surprise, Khrushchev gave in and agreed to withdraw the forty-two medium-range missiles and the IL-28 bombers.

Now the Cuban problem has lost some of its urgency. The curtain has set on the island's tragedy, and the victims of Castrism are alone with their executioners.

The other day I received a letter from W., the Latin American economist now on a mission to Cuba.

> Here I am about to return home, and I am filled with despair. There is no one left to be concerned and worried by the fate of the unfortunate Cubans. . . . The sugar crop has not been up to standard. And since sugar is the source of Cuba's wealth, the amount of food imports will have to be lower than that of last year.

You can imagine what a disaster this means! Certain regions receive hardly any food supplies. The coming years will be lean years. Not for the foreigners whose number is constantly on the increase—they will always eat their fill, for they pay with guns. But I sincerely pity the *quajiros* to whom the Revolution made such great promises, and who will have to go hungry!

Anita, the little militia-girl, has also sent me a long letter, a sort of diary full of sadness:

I am writing from the Ministry. I have hung my machine gun on the hatrack behind me, so that I don't have to look at it. . . . It is very hot outside, the summer is rapidly coming on. Through the window, I see a gang of children playing war against the Yankees.

A woman is sitting on a chair just in front of me. She is wearing a pale dress, her hair is covered by a printed cotton scarf. She comes every day, hoping for news from her husband Felipe. I don't know where Felipe is. She says he was summoned to headquarters a couple of months ago, and she hasn't heard from him since. She says that they are trying to kill him. I should like to help her, at least do *something* for her, but I really don't understand much of her story. If Felipe were in jail, we'd know about it. I'd like to know whether the stories that are being whispered about people disappearing are true. Do you think it really possible for our Revolutionary G-2 to act like Batista's criminals? Is it? What do you think?

I don't believe in very much any more. I'm just letting myself go. Maybe you were right when you said that war wasn't meant for women and girls. For a long while now I've been feeling things just weren't going right. It is true a girl was made to love a man, and not a revolution. I would have done better to look for a *novio* rather than enroll in the militia. I would not be feeling so lonely right now, among all these people who speak only about war, death, hatred, and the *paredón*.

Caro amigo, I so much want to feel like a little girl in a plain dress, not in a uniform, and without a machine gun.

I am scared. I am scared and bored. . . . Have you thought about that pen pal you were supposed to find for me? Have you found him or are you still looking? Please, hurry up! I want to hear words different from those I hear from morning till night—words like those I found in the books you gave me to read. In one of those books, a boy and a girl are talking. He calls her by pet names, and she speaks to him about the stars, the sea, the trees, and the sun. It is true that this was in time of peace. It's only in peace time that one can use crazy words like that, gentle words without any complications and with no end. . . . The boy kisses the girl and the girl kisses the boy. It's only in peace time that this can happen, kissing someone just because you feel like kissing him. Me too, I kiss you, as if the war were far off, as if I had a flowered dress, as if I weren't afraid. . . .